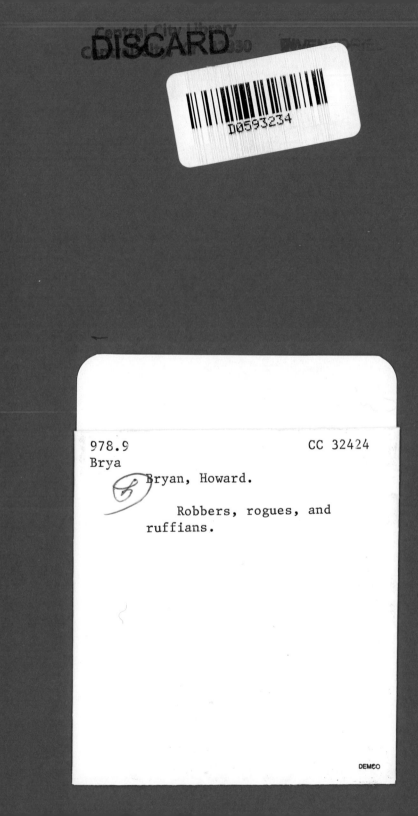

ROBBERS, ROGUES

AND

RUFFIANS

ROBBERS, ROGUES
⊰AND⊱ RUFFIANS

True Tales of the Wild West
in New Mexico

Howard Bryan

Foreword by
Tony Hillerman

22.⁹⁵

Clear Light Publishers
Santa Fe

Library of Congress Catalog Card Number: 91–72481

Library of Congress Cataloging in Publication Data
Bryan, Howard.
Robbers, Rogues, and Ruffians: True Tales of the
Wild West / Howard Bryan : Foreword by
Tony Hillerman.
     p. cm .
     Includes bibliographical references and index.
     ISBN 0–940666–04–9 (cloth) : $22.95
  1. Frontier and pioneer life – New Mexico – Anecdotes.
  2. Outlaws – New Mexico – History –Anecdotes.
  3. New Mexico – History –1848 –Anecdotes. I. Title.
     F801.B89 1991
     978.9'05 – dc20

ISBN 0 – 940666 – 04 – 9

Printed in the U.S.A. by R.R. Donnelley & Sons Company

FIRST EDITION

FRONT COVER: *Roundup on the VV Ranch in Lincoln County, circa 1889.
Pete Burleson, friend of Clay Allison, shown with quirt.*
(Courtesy Museum of New Mexico, negative 5324)

Clear Light Publishers, 823 Don Diego, Santa Fe, N.M. 87501

Dedicated to the memory of
J.R. "Chief" Galusha
1879 – 1961
A pioneer New Mexico lawman
and good friend who launched
me on my career as a writer
of western lore.

Contents

List of Illustrations

Foreword

For many of us the fascination with the history of the Old West lies in its lawlessness. We wonder how we would have fared out there beyond the reach of orderly civilization. Would we have carried a pistol? Joined the vigilantes? Tried to impose our own sense of justice on the place we inhabited? In a system in which it was often hard to tell the good guys from the bad ones, would we have been a bandito ourselves? We wonder what it was really like.

In his *Robbers, Rogues, and Ruffians* Howard Bryan gives us some answers to exactly such questions. We meet the murderous innkeeper Charles Kennedy; "Kid Swingle," who managed to rob two stagecoaches in a single caper; Milton J. Yarberry, the first constable of New Town Albuquerque, who was so trigger-happy he had little need for a jail; and assorted others. Taken together they form a picture far different than the tidier one popular culture gives us.

You won't find much of the "Code of the West" dreamed up by Owen Wister in *The Virginian*. Yarberry, for example, shot his final victim in the back, and the man wasn't even armed. Another of the ruffians you'll meet herein would ask his intended victim for a chew of tobacco, shoot him when he reached for his pocket, and then claim he thought the fellow was going for his gun. Nor do you find those mythical gunslingers of the movies who rarely missed what they shot at, never ran out of ammunition, rode tireless horses, and did their dastardly deeds with flawlessly efficient advanced planning. In *Robbers, Rogues, and Ruffians*, Bryan brings us bad men who were, alas, merely human, and sometimes barely that.

Bryan is the author of previous works on our corner of the southern Rockies and is now more or less retired from his career as a newsman for the *Albuquerque Tribune*. For thirty-seven years he wrote "Off the Beaten Path"— an aptly named column dealing with odds and ends of New Mexico's past. He is my nominee as the fellow hardest to beat at the game of swapping anecdotes. The last time I saw him I came away with two memorable bits of data. One concerned how the notorious killer Clay Allison reacted when a ham-handed Cheyenne dentist broke off one of Allison's teeth. (Allison extracted two from the dentist.) The other was a faux pas committed by a judge brand new to the Albuquerque court. When a local defense attorney noted for ferocity in appearance as well as conduct approached the bench with a man she was representing, the judge asked the defendant: "What's she charged with?"

These anecdotes tell you something of the quality of Howard Bryan's memory — that he values the whimsical as much as the serious. The book you hold in your hand is filled with better ones. Good reading.

Tony Hillerman

Introduction

Attempts to assemble authentic accounts of outlaws and desperadoes of the Old West might be compared to attempts to
assemble a complicated jigsaw puzzle in which half the pieces are
missing. Bad men of the western frontier were not in the habit of
detailing their lives and unlawful careers in autobiographies,
diaries, or letters, leaving posterity to piece together their stories
from widely scattered and often unreliable sources; often there are
wide gaps in the stories of their lives that are now impossible to fill.

Few of them were known by the names given them at birth,
some using as many as four or five aliases, so what on the surface
might appear to be three or four different outlaws might in truth
be only one. As one pioneer lawman once told me, "Those guys
changed their names more often than they changed their socks."

During the period covered in this book, the latter part of the
19th century, there also were some confusing name changes
involving New Mexico towns, railroads, newspapers, and so forth.
As examples, the town of Eddy became the town of Carlsbad, the
Atchison, Topeka and Santa Fe Railroad became the Atchison,
Topeka and Santa Fe Railway, the Atlantic and Pacific Railroad
became the Santa Fe Pacific Railroad, and the *Cimarron News*
became the *Cimarron News and Press.*

In an effort to portray as authentically as possible the "Wild
West" figures in this book, I have drawn their stories principally
from 19th-century newspaper articles that gave contemporary and
running accounts of their activities. While these newspaper articles were not always entirely accurate, and sometimes exaggerated,

they usually are more reliable than the dimming memories of latter-day pioneers recalling events of the past.

Nevertheless, I have included reminiscences of some New Mexico pioneers who were involved, either intimately or casually, with some of the figures in this book. These pioneers include lawmen J.R. Galusha, Robert W. "Bob" Lewis, and Fred Lambert; and cattle ranchers Montague Stevens, Henry Brock, John "Salty John" Cox, and George Crocker. All references to interviews in this book, unless otherwise noted, are interviews conducted years ago by the author, mostly during the 1950s. These long-gone pioneers knew the answers to many of the questions I encountered in writing this book, but at the times I interviewed them, I did not know the questions.

Not included in this book is the story of New Mexico's most famous desperado, Henry McCarty, alias William H. Bonney, alias Billy the Kid. So many volumes have been written about him over the years that I feel I can add nothing new to his story, preferring instead to concentrate on some of the lesser-known robbers, rogues, and ruffians whose stories have not been told, or who have been the subjects of highly inaccurate or garbled accounts.

Also missing from these pages are such common words and phrases of today as "gunfighter," "fast gun," and "top gun." They apparently were not in common use during the period covered, as I have not found them in any of the many 19th-century newspapers I have examined.

Many of the episodes in this book are based on my New Mexico history columns, "Off the Beaten Path," which appeared in the *Albuquerque Tribune* from 1953 to 1990. Early newspaper files studied in preparation for these stories are in the libraries of the University of New Mexico, the Albuquerque Publishing Company at Albuquerque, the Museum of New Mexico at Santa Fe, and in my own private collection.

Howard Bryan

Cimarron's historic St. James Hotel, pictured here in about 1880 was the scene of many shootings during Cimarron's wild west period. It is still in operation today. (Courtesy St. James Hotel)

The Inn of Death

Veiled in mystery and legend is the bizarre story of Charles Kennedy and his New Mexico wayside inn, where many a weary traveler went to an eternal sleep. Various accounts of the story, including those left by eyewitnesses, do not agree on all the details; and the recollections of eyewitnesses vary in some aspects from the few and sketchy newspaper accounts at the time.

Kennedy, described as a large and sinister-appearing man with rough features and a grizzly beard, was said to have been a Rocky Mountain hunter and trapper who gave up his life as a wandering mountain man to settle in Taos, on New Mexico's northern frontier. Here he took as his wife, or mistress, a young Hispanic woman (some said she was a Ute Indian woman), and a son was soon born to them.

In 1868, after several years residence in the Taos Valley, Kennedy moved his family twenty miles east over the Sangre de Cristo Mountains and established a small ranch at a road junction at the eastern foot of the range, overlooking the broad and largely uninhabited Moreno Valley. Here he built a log cabin of several rooms with a stone fireplace and chimney, a structure that was to serve him both as a home for himself and his family and as an inn and tavern for travelers.

The spot Kennedy selected for his house was an isolated one at the mouth of Fernandez Canyon. Here the primitive mountain road from Taos, after winding east over the range through Palo Flechado Pass, merged with the long and lonely wagon road that extended from the new gold mining community of Elizabethtown

(in a high mountain valley eighteen miles to the north) nearly one hundred miles south through the verdant Moreno and Mora valleys to Mora and Las Vegas. The log house, set against a hillside and almost concealed by pines, presented a foreboding appearance to the wayfarer who wanted to break a lonely journey to obtain food, drink, and lodging for the night.

As hosts, the Kennedys left much to be desired. Guests felt strangely uncomfortable in the presence of the sullen proprietor, and noticed that his wife appeared to be his virtual slave. She appeared fearful of her husband, seldom spoke to anybody, and was not permitted to leave the house alone.

It was not long after Kennedy opened his rustic inn that lone travelers began to vanish on the roads between Elizabethtown, Taos, and Mora. Some of them could be traced as far as Kennedy's home, but no farther.

The story of the vanishing travelers was recalled years later by Joe Kinsinger, one of the original 1868 founders of Elizabethtown, or E'town, as it was generally called, who in 1885 was living in Socorro in south central New Mexico. His recollections originally were published in the *Socorro Bullion* in 1885, and the article was reprinted in the *Southwest Sentinel,* in the New Mexico mining town of Silver City, on November 24, 1885.

The article, which referred to Kennedy as "the hero of the criminal history of New Mexico," said the hostelry had just commenced to do a fair business in 1868 when a young physician left E'town for Santa Fe, by way of Taos, promising to write his friends in the mining town as soon as he arrived in the territorial capital. He did not arrive in Santa Fe, however, and was never heard from again.

Soon afterwards, the Kinsinger account continued, a Taos

merchant named Edwards, carrying $1,400 in his pocket, stopped for the night at the Kennedy inn. He was found dead the next day a few hundred yards from the inn. An examination of the body revealed that he had been robbed, for there was only a trifling sum of money left in his pocket. Kennedy claimed that Indians had attacked his ranch and killed the merchant, pointing to bullet holes in the side of his log quarters to substantiate his story.

The authorities were suspicious of Kennedy but were unable to disprove his story. The suspicions against Kennedy grew as other travelers disappeared in the vicinity, but still no evidence could be found linking him with the disappearances.

Kinsinger said a man named Coleman hired a wagon from him in E'town one day and started south toward Mora on business. The newspaper article continued:

> *The weather was exceedingly cold, and as night approached, with many misgivings and faltering heart, Coleman entered Kennedy's ranch with the intention of staying all night. After eating a well-cooked meal, and while seated near the fire, conversing with Kennedy, the latter, without any provocation and in the most unexpected manner commenced a deadly assault upon the unarmed traveler, who, however, by some fortunate interposition of providence, managed to escape from the den, and reached Elizabethtown, some eighteen miles distant, on foot. A posse of citizens and officers immediately proceeded to the ranch, and arrested Kennedy, who was brought in and tried before the alcalde, but let off without penalty.*

Time was running out for Kennedy, however. The mounting

suspicions directed against him were confirmed, to the satisfaction of the citizens of Elizabethtown, when Mrs. Kennedy appeared unexpectedly in an E'town saloon and sobbed out hysterically a story that shocked all those who gathered around her. She said her husband, in a fit of rage, had just killed, or threatened to kill, their child, and that she had managed to escape from the house and flee on foot the eighteen miles north to the mining town. During the time she had lived with him at the inn, she said, Kennedy had murdered a number of travelers who had stopped there to spend the night, taking their money and valuables and burying their bodies in and about the house.

Kinsinger, in his recollections, said a group of Elizabethtown citizens accompanied the woman back to the homestead. The 1885 newspaper account continued:

> Directed by her, the posse disinterred a large number of bodies beneath the dirt floor of the house, and many others were found outside in various places, as well as the half-burnt bodies of others, which he had attempted to cremate. She said the infamous wretch, after completing a murder, would bury the body, and then force her to smooth the spot over with fresh clay.

A contemporary newspaper account of the affair, however, indicated that the only evidence uncovered at this time consisted of a number of bones, found in Kennedy's garden, and made no mention of a murdered child. Kennedy was arrested and taken to Elizabethtown on a charge of murder, with a bag of bones as evidence.

The *Daily New Mexican* at Santa Fe, on October 13, 1870, said that two Elizabethtown physicians, Dr. Westerling and Dr.

Bradford, examined the bones but could not swear that they were human, although both were of the opinion that some of them, at least, were from a human body. The testimony of the physicians came during a preliminary hearing for the prisoner, conducted by Justice of the Peace McBride at Elizabethtown on October 3, 1870. The only witness against Kennedy was Joe Cortez, whose testimony was summed up by the Santa Fe newspaper on October 13:

The trial came off on the 3rd instant, when Joe Cortez testified as follows: That he was at Kennedy's house on Christmas of last year and that while there he saw Kennedy shoot an American with a pistol and gave the following particulars: A stranger came to the house afoot and stopped for the night; he was an American and had large red whiskers; witness said the stranger had gone to bed and witness was asleep when a pistol shot awakened him; that there was no light in the room, but Kennedy soon after lit a candle, and witness saw the stranger lying dead with a bullet hole through the head; witness knew that Kennedy killed the man, because there was no one in the house but Kennedy, his wife, the stranger and himself; after refusing to help Kennedy bury the dead man, witness ran away to Taos, but did not tell anyone there what had happened. The counsel for the defense attempted to invalidate Cortez's testimony, but failed.

Kennedy, bound over by the court to await grand jury action, was placed in irons and confined in a log house in the mining town, the jail being considered insecure.

On October 6, the Santa Fe newspaper article continued, a

Taos Indian arrived in Elizabethtown with the news that the skeleton of a man had just been uncovered from beneath the floor in a room of the Kennedy house. A delegation of E'town citizens, led by Justice McBride, proceeded at once to the scene.

The skeleton, they found, was that of a large man. There was a bullet hole through the skull, the bullet apparently entering through the right temple and passing out through the back of the skull. An inquest was held over the remains, and the citizens, serving as a coroner's jury, ruled that the unknown victim had come to his death at the hands of Charles Kennedy. The skeleton was taken to the mining town.

A public meeting was held in Elizabethtown that night, the Santa Fe newspaper reported, for the purpose of giving Kennedy an "impromptu trial." Twenty-five men were selected from among the crowd, and Kennedy was told to select twelve of them to serve as a jury. A trial was held, with the new evidence collected that day, but the jury was unable to reach a verdict.

Melvin W. Mills, a young lawyer who defended Kennedy at the public trial, confided later that he had managed to convince two of the jurors to "hang up" the jury and prevent it from reaching a verdict. Kennedy was returned to his place of confinement, and two guards were placed on duty to see that he did not escape.

At 11 o'clock the following night, October 7, 1870, a group of armed and masked men surprised Kennedy's guards, overpowered them, and took the shackled prisoner from his place of confinement. The *Daily New Mexican* at Santa Fe said they carried him to an old slaughterhouse about a half mile from town and hanged him from a rafter until he was dead. Mills, his lawyer, said years later that he was hanged from a pine tree, and yet other versions had him hanged in front of the courthouse, from a beef-skinning windlass in a corral, and dragged to death along the ground with a rope around his neck.

A coroner's jury, convened the next morning, ruled that Charles Kennedy "came to his death by hanging at the hands of parties unknown."

Kennedy's last words, according to the Kinsinger recollections in 1885, were that he was reconciled to death, but that he would die happier if he had succeeded in killing four more men, including Joe Stinson and John Fitzmaurice of Elizabethtown. Kinsinger said that Kennedy confessed before dying that he had killed twenty-one men during his life. Subsequent investigations revealed that he had murdered at least nine men during the time he was operating the inn, Kinsinger added, including an Indian, whom he had murdered for his pistol, and a Mexican, whom he had killed for a small sum of money.

Mills said that Kennedy had murdered fourteen men at the inn. One of his unidentified victims, it was said, was a brother of a former governor of Kansas. Mills also said, according to his recollections as published in volume three of *The Leading Facts of New Mexican History*, by Ralph Emerson Twitchell, 1917, that Kennedy's skeleton was afterwards "wired and sent east, largely owing to the peculiar character of the skull." There also is a legend that his head was taken to Cimarron, twenty-five miles east of Elizabethtown, and placed on a fence post.

In summing up the lynching of Charles Kennedy, the *Press and Telegraph*, Elizabethtown newspaper, commented at the time:

> *So ended the life of this cold-blooded assassin. No doubt, if the truth were known, the crime which was brought to light is but one of many he has perpetrated.*

7

There is a general feeling of satisfaction that he is at last beyond power of doing further harm. Still, while we have no word of pity for the murderer, we cannot commend the action of those who hung him. The time has passed when it was necessary for the people of this community to take the punishment of offenders in their own hands. We have laws that will give justice to all, and we have faithful and efficient officers to execute them, and it is time the citizens of this place should realize that vengeance is not justice — nor a midnight mob the proper guardian of public safety.

Three Cimarron Desperadoes:
Coal Oil Jimmy, Davy Crockett,
and Clay Allison

Cimarron is a Spanish word meaning wild, untamed, or unruly, and the community of Cimarron in northeast New Mexico lived up to its name in every respect. The settlement did not achieve its name because of its wild reputation, however, but because it was situated on the banks of the Cimarron River, a narrow and shallow stream carrying waters from the Sangre de Cristo Mountains, on the town's western horizon, eastward through deep and narrow Cimarron Canyon and across grassy plains to the Canadian River.

As originally settled in the late 1850s, the site was known as Maxwell's Ranch, as this was the ranch headquarters of Lucien B. Maxwell, a veteran frontiersman who through his wife's inheritance and his purchase from other heirs had become sole owner of a 1,714,765-acre (2,679-square-mile) Mexican land grant. The Maxwell Land Grant, as the vast acreage had become known, covered most of northeast New Mexico and a portion of southern Colorado.

Maxwell, a native of Kaskaskia, Illinois, had built a large home close to the south bank of the Cimarron River, where a branch of the Santa Fe Trail crossed the stream. His rambling, two-story mansion, with pitched roofs and dormer windows, contained his living quarters and accommodations for overnight guests, including dining and drinking facilities and game rooms. The home became a popular stopping place for trail travelers.

Maxwell also erected a stone gristmill, three stories high, where Ute and Jicarilla Apache Indians from the nearby hills and plains gathered periodically to receive government rations. The ranch community also included corrals, stables, and living quarters for Maxwell's farm and ranch employees.

Maxwell sold his huge land grant in 1870, and it came into the possession of an English syndicate as the Maxwell Land Grant and Railway Company. Shareholders and officers included members of the Santa Fe Ring, a powerful group of New Mexico politicians and office holders who ruthlessly controlled the political and economic destinies of the Territory.

Maxwell's departure from the scene came at the beginning of a decade of violence and lawlessness on his former domain that was seldom matched on the western frontier. Cimarron, as the grant headquarters was now known, experienced a population boom as new settlers converged on the region, establishing ranches, farms, and mines on what they considered public lands, but which the land grant company regarded as private property.

The refusal of many of the newcomers to pay rent or fees to the company for their holdings culminated in what became known as the Colfax County War, which continued for years at the cost of many lives.

In the early 1870s, cattlemen from Texas established ranches on the plains north and east of Cimarron, prospectors and miners hurried to the bustling new gold mining community of Elizabeth-town on grant land to the west, and business entrepreneurs flocked to Cimarron, focal point of the developing region, to establish hotels, saloons, gambling halls, stores, a newspaper, and other enterprises.

Among the first on the scene was Henri Lambert, a native of France, who since his arrival in the United States had served during the Civil War as field cook for Gen. Ulysses S. Grant and White House chef for President Abraham Lincoln. In 1872, the year Cimarron was designated the seat of Colfax County, Lambert bought a small rooming house and saloon in the center of Cimarron, just south across the street from the Maxwell mansion, and he developed and expanded it as the St. James Hotel. Lambert's, as the place was known locally, had the reputation of serving the best barrel whiskey in town, at twenty-five cents a drink, so it drew the largest crowds, and, correspondingly, was the scene of the most violent episodes.

Cimarron, at the time, played host to Santa Fe Trail travelers, stockmen, miners, gamblers, soldiers, and drifters, most seeking the various diversions the town had to offer. Groups of Utes and Jicarilla Apaches, in town periodically to draw rations, added to the colorful array of humanity.

The Cimarron saloons, particularly Lambert's, and Schwenk's (also referred to as Swink's) Gambling Hall down the street, served as springboards for much of the violence that rocked Cimarron in the 1870s. Since law enforcement was often lax, and in some cases practically nonexistent, shooting up the town and terrorizing citizens became a favorite pastime with some of the frequent patronizers of the bars.

By the middle of the decade, the prevalence of fatal shootings in town prompted the *Las Vegas Gazette* to remark in one issue, "Everything is quiet in Cimarron. Nobody has been killed for three days."

Among the earliest of the Cimarron desperadoes were several who left town in 1871 to embark on brief careers as stagecoach robbers in the vicinity.

Coal Oil Jimmy

The stagecoach driver pulled the horses to a halt where Clear Creek enters the Cimarron River, deep in the narrow recesses of Cimarron Canyon, and climbed down to water the thirsty animals at about 9 o'clock on the morning of October 9, 1871. The eastbound coach, carrying both passengers and mail, had left the mining community of Elizabethtown several hours before, and was due to arrive in Cimarron that afternoon.

While the driver was busily occupied watering the horses, three men with drawn revolvers stepped out from a place of concealment in the pines. Holding the driver and passengers at bay with their weapons, but making no attempt to molest them, they took the express box from the coach. Breaking it open, they robbed its contents of about $500 in cash, and disappeared quickly into the brush and trees.

The bandits wore no masks, and were readily identified as Tom Taylor, who reportedly had deserted from a U.S. Infantry regiment in Arizona some years before, and who recently had escaped from the Cimarron jail, where he was being held for murder; Frank Jones; and a young man commonly known as Coal Oil Jimmy, whose name was first given as James Buckley, his surname later given as Buckner and eventually as Burns.

"The robbers are well known hereabouts," the *Cimarron News* reported after the robbery, adding that they recently had been discharged from the employ of the Maxwell Land Grant and Railway Company at Cimarron, and since then had decided to rob and steal for a living. The newspaper added:

Some time ago they went to the Montezuma Mills, on Ute Creek, and stole several fine horses, since which time they have been in the mountains, but last week commenced their work of committing depredations on the road between here and Elizabethtown. They have stopped several persons at different times, demanding any and all money and property they had with them.

It is reported that "Coal Oil Jimmy" shot at, and it is supposed hit, a Mexican, "just to see him jump and kick."

These men are all desperadoes of the worst description, and it is high time that suitable rewards be offered and prompt action taken by our public officials to rid the country of them.

Eight days after the Clear Creek robbery, on October 17, Taylor and Coal Oil Jimmy were making news again, this time without Frank Jones, on the Santa Fe Trail about ten miles northeast of Cimarron. An eastbound stagecoach, which had left Santa Fe the day before, was stopped a few miles from the Vermejo River crossing by the pair, armed this time with double-barreled shotguns. Pointing their guns menacingly at the stage driver and passengers, they demanded that the express strongbox be taken out of the coach and placed on the road.

The *Santa Fe Weekly Post*, on October 21, told how the demand was received:

The conductor, Charlie Bryant, was in an obliging mood and at once yielded to the request, the safe being taken out. Charlie was then informed that his safety

13

depended upon the haste which he made to ascend to the conductor's seat and drive off. This, too, he complied with in a spirit of obedience and promptness which, if possessed by its members, would make an army the best disciplined in the world.

Again, no attempt was made to rob the passengers in the coach, which was fortunate for at least one of them, a Mr. Alderete from Chihuahua, Mexico, who was carrying $15,000 in bank notes and drafts on his person. The other passengers were prominent New Mexico citizens, Chief Justice Joseph G. Palen of the New Mexico Supreme Court; Col. J. Francisco Chaves, who represented the Territory of New Mexico in Congress, and Lehman Spiegelberg of the Spiegelberg Bros. mercantile firm in Santa Fe.

The express box yielded but little to the two road agents, for the overland mail had not been accepting money packages for delivery since a previous robbery. The box was found later alongside the trail, broken open and most of its contents gone. An investigation indicated that the letters taken from it had yielded the two robbers about $10.75. They had overlooked $147 in cash that was in a side pocket of the box, which was found intact when the box was reclaimed.

Officials of the Maxwell Land Grant offered a $1,000 reward for the capture of their former employees, and about thirty-five well-armed men mounted their horses and left Cimarron in pursuit of the outlaws. The posse trailed Taylor and Coal Oil Jimmy to an isolated ranch cabin occupied by Jack Booth near the Vermejo River, and learning that the two outlaws were inside eating dinner, secreted themselves around the small house.

Booth, who did not know the two outlaws, had invited them

in for supper when they arrived at his cabin a short time before the posse appeared on the scene.

Taylor, when he had finished eating, got up from the table and walked outside to stretch his limbs, unaware of the danger that lurked about him. The hidden possemen opened fire on him without warning. Taylor dashed back into the cabin unharmed. It was estimated that twenty shots had been fired at him from a distance of only twelve to fifteen paces.

The two outlaws, holding Booth in front of them as a shield, edged out the door and escaped into the darkness. The possemen held their fire, fearing that any move on their part would bring certain death to the rancher.

Taylor and Coal Oil Jimmy took their hostage miles into the hills that night before stopping to make camp. Coal Oil Jimmy wanted to kill the rancher, but his partner prevailed upon him to wait until morning. After Coal Oil Jimmy had gone to sleep, Taylor released Booth, and the rancher walked home.

Henry Wetter, acting governor of the Territory of New Mexico, issued a proclamation on October 23 promising rewards for the capture of the outlaws and asking citizens to assist in their apprehension. The proclamation, as it was published in the *Santa Fe Weekly Post* on October 28, read:

PROCLAMATION

$1,500 REWARD

WHEREAS: *On the 9th day of October, 1871, the Cimarron and Elizabethtown Mail was stopped and robbed by three men named Tom Taylor, alias "Barber," James Buckner, alias "Coal Oil Jimmy" and Frank Jones, and*

WHEREAS: *On the 17th day of October the Mail from Santa Fe was stopped and robbed while going from the Vermejo Station, by the above named Tom Taylor alias "Barber" and James Buckner alias "Coal Oil Jimmy," and* WHEREAS: *The above named desperadoes have stolen a great many head of stock, and have also threatened the lives of several of our citizens, Now, therefore, I, Henry Wetter, Acting Governor of the Territory of New Mexico, do issue this my Proclamation, earnestly requesting all good citizens in this Territory and elsewhere to assist in the apprehension and conviction of the perpetrators of these outrages. The Executive is not authorized to offer any reward, but assurance is hereby given that the following rewards will be paid by the authorities of Colfax County. For the apprehension of Tom Taylor, $600. For the apprehension of James Buckner, $600. For the apprehension of Frank Jones, $300. In testimony whereof I have hereunto set my hand and the great seal of the Territory, at Santa Fe, N.M., this 23rd day of October, A.D. 1871.*

> *H. Wetter*
> *Acting governor of New Mexico.*

Among those hoping to collect the rewards were two Ute Creek residents, Joe McCurdy and John Stewart, who were acquainted with the outlaws. They arranged to rendezvous with Taylor and Coal Oil Jimmy, the latter now referred to in the newspapers as James Burns, and at a meeting on October 31 near the village of Loma Chiquita, the two Ute Creek men offered to form an alliance with the outlaws. The outlaws took the bait.

"As Taylor and Burns had only one horse between them, and that a poor one, the party agreed to start for Collier's station, about six miles from Fort Union, and there steal a good mount," a dispatch from Cimarron to the *New Mexican* at Santa Fe said later.

The four arrived in the vicinity of Collier's Ranch on the evening of October 31, and McCurdy and Stewart suggested that they make camp there in the mountains and rest until after dark, when an attempt would be made to steal the horses. A campfire was started, and Taylor stood by the fire, warming himself, while Coal Oil Jimmy laid down to rest.

This was the moment McCurdy and Stewart had been waiting for. Without any warning, McCurdy drew his pistol and shot Taylor through the forehead, while Stewart shot Coal Oil Jimmy dead. In the morning McCurdy and Stewart obtained a wagon, and transported the two bodies to Cimarron.

The dispatch from Cimarron, published in the *New Mexican* on November 6, said in part:

> *As they laid in the wagon, the bodies presented a horrible sight — Taylor was lying on his back, booted and spurred, with one gloved hand raised and his double barreled shot gun by his side, resting in the hollow of his arm; Burns was on his side with his legs drawn up and hands clenched as if he had died in terrible agony.*

The article closed:

> *It is sincerely to be hoped that other evil disposed parties in our community will take warning from the terrible end of these two men, and seek some honest mode of gaining a livelihood.*

David "Davy" Crockett

The following article appeared in the *Herald*, a Silver City weekly newspaper, on October 7, 1876:

> *Advices from Cimarron, N.M., chronicle the death of two noted desperadoes named Crockett and Heffron. Among many other crimes they were implicated in the killing of three colored soldiers last spring at the St. James Hotel in Cimarron. They had been "running" the town for a week past, poking six-shooters and shot-guns in the faces of citizens.*
>
> *On the evening of the 3rd Sheriff Rinehart and two others started to arrest them and found them in the western part of town getting ready to leave. They were called upon to surrender. The criminals at once assumed the defensive and were immediately fired upon by the sheriff and his party, and as the outlaws started on a run for the river they were sent the contents of the other barrels of their guns after them. Crockett was found dead on the other side of the river and Heffron has since been arrested having been shot in the head.*

Only one of the desperadoes was killed, despite the opening sentence, and the fatal shooting took place not on the evening of October 3, but on the evening of September 30. While it was not generally known at the time, the victim, David "Davy" Crockett, was a grandson and namesake of the famous Tennessee frontiersman and congressman who died at the Alamo in 1836.

Crockett, described in Cimarron as "an arrogant young fellow," was born in Tennessee, the son of Robert P. and Matilda Porter Crockett. According to George Crocker, a Cimarron pioneer, he was born on February 4, 1853, and was twenty-three at the time of his death.

The family moved to Texas when Crockett was a child, eventually settling on land that Texas had given Robert's widowed mother, Elizabeth Crockett, on the Brazos River near the village of Acton in north central Texas. Robert Crockett operated a toll bridge across the Brazos River, and it was on the Texas homestead that young Davy grew to manhood.

It is not certain when David Crockett headed west for New Mexico, but by the mid-1870s he was operating a small cattle ranch on the plains east of Cimarron. Neighboring cattle ranches were owned by Robert Clay Allison and Pete Burleson, whom Crockett knew in Texas, and it was reported that he had accompanied Burleson to New Mexico, and that his mother had asked Burleson to "look after" her son.

Crockett apparently grew tired of cattle ranching, for he sold his cattle and began hanging around Cimarron with his foreman, Gus Heffron, the surname given a variety of spellings over the years, including Hefferson, Heffner, and Heifner. Crockett, tall and slender with blue eyes and brown hair, was well liked in Cimarron, and was popular at social functions. Heffron, on the other hand, was disliked, being considered a braggart and a coward. Neither man was considered particularly troublesome, until a drunken spree one night sparked Crockett to embark on a six-month career as a desperado of the worst sort.

The turning point came on the evening of March 24, 1876, at

a time when a troop of the U.S. 9th Cavalry, consisting of black enlisted men commonly referred to as "buffalo soldiers," was camped at a barn in Cimarron. The troop was stationed at Fort Union, forty miles to the south.

Crockett and Heffron, together with Henry Goodman of Cimarron, had been making the rounds of the Cimarron bars that evening and Crockett, at least, had become quite drunk. As Crockett and Heffron were preparing to leave town, they entered the bar of the St. James Hotel to buy a bottle of whiskey to take along. The two, accompanied by Goodman, bought the whiskey, and started to leave, with Crockett in the lead.

Crockett had trouble opening the door, as somebody was pulling on it from the outside. Jerking the door open, he saw a cavalry trooper attempting to enter the door from the outside. Crockett, in a rage, pulled his pistol and shot him dead. Whirling around, he opened fire on three other cavalrymen who were at a table in the bar, two of them playing cards and the third looking on. Two of these soldiers were killed, the other wounded.

Crockett and his two companions ran from the bar. Goodman darted across the street and hid behind a pile of lumber. Crockett and Heffron decided not to go for their horses, as their horses were at the barn where the cavalry troop was camped. They hurried out of town on foot, hiding out at the Dick Steel Ranch, later known as the Springer Ranch. Soldiers searched the area in vain for the man who had killed their three comrades.

Reports circulated that the three soldiers had been killed by Texas cowboys who were prejudiced against Negroes, particularly Negroes in federal uniform. In a hearing before a Cimarron justice of the peace, Crockett said he was drunk and fired at the soldiers in a fit of anger, and he was released on grounds that he had acted under the influence of alcohol. Later, in September, a District Court judge fined Crockett $50 and costs on a reduced charge of "carrying arms."

Crockett, meanwhile, had embarked on a campaign of terrorizing Cimarron and its citizens. Periodically, he and Heffron raced their horses up and down the streets, firing their guns into the air and at various objects along the way. They rode their horses into stores and saloons, firing bullets into the ceilings. They forced citizens into saloons and compelled them to buy drinks for everybody.

An unidentified citizen of Cimarron, in a lengthy letter to the Santa Fe *New Mexican*, wrote in part:

> *We have had quite a lively time in and around Cimarron for the last two weeks, caused by two men, Dave Crockett and Gus Hefron [sic], undertaking to "run the town."*
>
> *During the past two days these two men have defied arrest, threatening to kill anyone who should attempt it; have rode their horses into saloons, stores and offices, and with their double barreled shot guns cocked have compelled persons to comply with their demands no matter what they were.*
>
> *On Saturday they halted the sheriff, and with their shot guns loaded, cocked and aimed at his breast told him he only lived at their pleasure, and politely informed him that when he made any attempt to arrest them to be sure to have "the drop," or his time on earth would be short. Things went on this way until no one was safe in town....*

The sheriff, I. Rinehart, was intimidated by the two desperadoes and felt helpless to do anything about the situation. Crock-

ett, realizing that he had "buffaloed" the sheriff, began torment-
ing and taunting him, and defying him to arrest him and his
partner. He bought clothing at a Cimarron store and ordered the
storekeeper to charge it to the sheriff. On one occasion, it was
reported, he dragged the sheriff into a saloon and forced him to
drink until he passed out.

Sheriff Rinehart approached Joseph Holbrook, a rancher east
of town, and asked for his help in apprehending Crockett and
Heffron. Holbrook declined, and Crockett began taunting the
rancher. Holbrook soon grew tired of this abuse, and on September 30 (1876) he and John McCullough, the Cimarron postmaster, told Rinehart they would serve as special deputy sheriffs to
help him bring the two desperadoes to justice.

Learning that Crockett and Heffron were in the west part of
town that evening, the three secured double-barreled shotguns
and concealed themselves alongside the road the two desperadoes
would take when leaving. Holbrook hid behind a well curb near
Schwenk's barn, and Rinehart and McCullough concealed themselves behind a nearby haystack.

At about 9 o'clock, Crockett and Heffron approached the
concealed men on horseback, and Holbrook stepped out in front
of the two, pointed his shotgun at them, and ordered them to
throw up their hands. Crockett laughed, and invited him to
"shoot." Holbrook did not need a second invitation, and fired a
shotgun blast into Crockett's body. At the same moment, Rinehart
and McCullough rose up and fired at the two.

The noise "spooked" the two horses, which began running
toward the Cimarron River, the two riders still in the saddles.
Crockett's horse stopped on the opposite bank of the river, and
onlookers found that Crockett was dead in the saddle, his hands

so firmly gripped on the saddle horn that they had difficulty in breaking the grip. Heffron, slightly wounded in the head and one hand, sped on out of town.

Rinehart and his two special deputies, not realizing that they had killed Crockett, mounted their horses and left town to search the surrounding area. Heffron rode quickly to Pete Burleson's cow camp, told Burleson what had happened, and the rancher hurried to Cimarron. Taking possession of Crockett's body, he removed it to a rooming house across the street from the St. James Hotel.

Rinehart and his two companions learned of Crockett's death upon their return to Cimarron and went to the rooming house to view the remains. Burleson became so enraged when the three men entered the room without removing their hats that he had to be restrained by force.

Crockett was buried in the Cimarron cemetery. Heffron returned to town a few days later, was jailed, escaped from jail on October 31, and disappeared north into Colorado. Later, Holbrook, Rinehart, and McCullough were tried and acquitted in District Court in Taos of a murder charge brought in connection with the killing of Crockett.

Robert Crockett, it was reported, arrived in Cimarron from Texas to view his son's grave. He removed a crude wooden marker over the grave, explaining that he was shipping a more suitable stone marker to Cimarron to replace it. The stone marker never arrived, however, and in the years that followed, only a few Cimarron pioneers could point out the exact burial spot of Davy Crockett, who died much less gloriously than did his famous grandfather.

Generally credited to be a photograph of Clay Allison, at the age of 26, rancher and gunman "who never killed a man who did not need killing." (Courtesy University of Oklahoma Library, Western History Collections, Rose No. 2143.)

Clay Allison

Clay Allison, perhaps the most legendary figure of the Cimarron scene in the 1870s, was described as a perfect gentleman when sober and a raving maniac when drunk, always ready to kill anybody he thought needed killing. His erratic nature may have been due in part to a severe head injury he received as a child.

A successful cattle rancher and Confederate veteran of the Civil War, Allison became the subject of so many legends during his own lifetime that it is almost impossible to separate fact from fiction. In newspaper interviews and conversations with friends, he often spun wild yarns about himself that enhanced his reputation as a dangerous man. Enough is known about him, however, to indicate that he would have become a legend even without his own embellishments.

Born Robert Clay Allison in Wayne County, Tennessee, on September 2, 1841, the fourth of eight children of Jerry and Maria Brown Allison, he was generally known by his middle name, although New Mexico newspapers usually referred to him as R.C. Allison. His father, it is believed, was a Presbyterian circuit rider in Tennessee.

Allison grew to manhood on a Tennessee farm, and in October, 1861, soon after the outbreak of the Civil War, he enlisted as a private in the Tennessee Light Artillery. According to his military record, he was twenty-one years of age at the time, stood five feet nine inches tall, and was light complected with blue eyes and dark hair. The military record conflicts with later accounts that estimated his height as six feet two inches.

Allison was given a medical discharge the following January as "unfit for duty," a military surgeon noting that he was incapable of performing the duties of a soldier because of a blow received many years before that apparently caused a depression of the skull, since which time emotional or physical excitement produced epileptic and maniacal convulsions and suicidal tendencies.

In September, 1862, Allison reenlisted, this time as a member of the 9th Tennessee Cavalry, and apparently served with this unit until the end of the war. In later years, Allison boasted that he had served as a scout and spy for Gen. Nathan Bedford Forrest, and that he was captured and sentenced to be shot, but had escaped from federal authorities on the eve of his scheduled execution by swimming to shore from Johnson Island, Ohio, in Lake Erie's Sandusky Bay, where he had been held with other Confederate prisoners. Military records cast some doubt on these boasts, but Allison, it was said, remained a "Yankee-hater" for the rest of his life.

Shortly after the close of the war, Allison left the Tennessee farm and headed west for Texas, accompanied by two of his brothers, Monroe and John Allison; a sister, Mary; and her husband, Lewis G. Coleman. They settled on the Brazos River in Texas.

Legend says that Allison killed a ferryman named Colbert in a knife duel at a river crossing during the trek west, and that he later fought a knife duel with a man named Johnson in an open grave they had dug, with the understanding that the loser would remain in the grave and be covered over by the winner.

Once settled in Texas, Allison went to work as a cowhand for several prominent cattlemen, including Charles Goodnight and Oliver Loving, and it is believed that he first visited New Mexico while helping to drive Goodnight-Loving cattle north to Colorado through the eastern part of New Mexico in the late 1860s. By

1870, he had established his own cattle ranching operation at or near the junction of the Vermejo and Canadian rivers on the Maxwell Land Grant east of Cimarron. It was shortly after his arrival in New Mexico that he accidentally shot himself in the instep of his right foot, causing him to limp for the remainder of his life, sometimes using his rifle as a crutch or cane to help steady his steps.

There are unverified stories that Allison, as well as young Davy Crockett, took part in the 1870 lynching at Elizabethtown of Charles Kennedy, the murderous innkeeper, although contemporary newspaper accounts of the lynching do not mention either of the two.

It was early in 1874 that Allison began achieving his reputation in New Mexico as a man handy with a gun. This came about when he rid the region of John "Chunk" Colbert, a desperado of the worst sort who had killed a number of men and was always threatening to kill others.

Colbert spent much of his time hanging around the Red River stage station, about thirty miles northeast of Cimarron, where a branch of the Santa Fe Trail crossed the narrow Canadian River, referred to as the Red River at the time. The tiny settlement was centered around the Clifton House, a three-story hotel with fine dining facilities that had been erected by rancher Tom Stockton and leased to the Barlow and Sanderson Stage Company as one of its principal stations.

The Red River station was a popular gathering place for area ranchers, due to the fine hotel and a quarter-mile racetrack, where the ranchers brought their fastest horses to compete in matched races. Colbert owned one of the fastest horses in the region, which he took to various racing meets.

During a visit to Cimarron on July 23, 1872, Colbert picked a fight with and killed unarmed Charles Morris, a Cimarron resident who worked as an "enforcer," or hired gun, for the Maxwell Land Grant Company. It was believed that Morris was married to Colbert's ex-wife at the time. Colbert and Morris met and began arguing in a Cimarron saloon, Colbert threatened to kill Morris, and told him to go home and get his gun. As Morris was leaving the saloon, he turned and grabbed Colbert, telling him that he would fight him without a gun. Colbert drew his pistol and shot Morris in the head, killing him instantly.

Colbert was back in the news nearly eighteen months later. On December 30, 1873, the *Daily New Mexican* reported that George Walter was murdered on the night of December 27 at the San Francisco Ranch, fourteen miles east of Trinidad, Colorado, "by a man from Red River known as Chunk." The article said that citizens of the region had gone to the ranch for some horse races, that much whiskey was consumed, that Walter called Chunk a liar, and that Chunk had a friend hold Walter against a wall "while Chunk fired six shots at him, five taking effect." Some other accounts gave the victim's name as Walton Waller.

Colbert fled the scene, followed by a posse that trailed him south over Raton Pass to the Red River station. Newspapers said the pursuers arrived at Red River at night, entered Clifton House, asked for Colbert, and were told that he was upstairs in bed. Proceeding to the room in which Colbert supposedly was sleeping, they opened the door, and seeing a man rise up from the bed, shot him. It wasn't Colbert, but another hotel guest.

Colbert, who was sleeping in another house about forty yards away, learned of the posse's arrival and got up and left, telling a friend he was heading for Texas. He returned to Red River a few days later, however, where he made the mistake of taking on Clay Allison. Details of the fatal encounter were published in the *Daily*

New Mexican on January 13, 1874:

> The man "Chunk," whose attempted arrest at Red
> River was chronicled some days since, was killed on
> Wednesday last (January 7, 1874) under the following
> circumstances, as we take them from the Cimarron News:
>
> It seems that when Chunk left for Texas after murdering
> Walter he reconsidered the matter and determined to come
> back and declare himself "chief" and try to maintain his
> reputation as such. After having been back a day or two he
> thought it time to begin to wear his laurels and on the morning
> in question he began his operations by going on a general
> drunk with promiscuous shooting accompaniments.
>
> A few exercises, such as shooting the eyes out of pictures
> on the walls of the Red River saloon, opening champagne
> bottles with pistol balls, only made him thirst for fresh
> glory which he tried to obtain by shooting at one man and
> hitting another by the name of Cooper. He only succeeded,
> however, in shooting Cooper in the hand, inflicting a
> painful but not dangerous wound.
>
> During the day there had been a horse race, and Chunk
> made himself quite conspicuous and generally disagree-
> able. He threatened to kill several persons in and about the
> Red River house, against whom he had taken a dislike.
>
> Finally his attention was drawn to Mr. Allison, a
> stockman from the Canadian, who was present and with
> whom, we are informed, he had had some previous
> difficulty. The latter, however, divining his intentions,
> kept his eye on Chunk, and when at the supper table
> Chunk drew his pistol and laid it in his lap full cocked, he

also kept his arms where they would be handy.

The sequel showed that he was not mistaken, for Chunk, when "he thought he had the drop," reached out with his left hand for a cup of coffee and cautiously raised the muzzle of his pistol to the edge of the table and fired it at Allison.

But Allison, who discovered the movement in time, drew his own pistol, anticipating Chunk's second shot, and caught Chunk just above the right eye, effectually preventing him from making any further use of the pistols of this world, and sending him where, if he had a pistol, it would hardly stay loaded.

Chunk was a desperate and dangerous character and Mr. Allison ran a narrow risk of his own life and only saved it by his coolness and courage.

The shooting took place in a small chili parlor across the road from Clifton House. It was reported that the muzzle of Colbert's gun hit the edge of the table when he lifted it from his lap, causing the bullet to miss its mark. It was believed that Colbert may have been a relative of the ferryman named Colbert, whom Allison reportedly had killed some years before.

According to one version of the shooting, Allison and Colbert stirred their coffees with the barrels of their six-shooters while facing one another across the table, after which Allison placed his gun on the table. It also was said that Allison, following the shooting, picked up a dinner bell and rode his horse up and down the street, ringing the bell and announcing that a fight scheduled between him and Colbert that night had been called off "due to an accident to one of the contestants." Colbert was buried behind Clifton House.

Charles Cooper, the man Colbert had accidentally shot in the hand, reportedly was an Englishman who had served as a judge at a matched race between an Allison horse and a Colbert horse, which was declared a tie; he was seated at the end of the table when Allison killed Colbert. Allison and Cooper left Red River at about the same time, and Cooper disappeared mysteriously, prompting authorities later to accuse Allison of murdering Cooper, even though no evidence was found that Cooper was dead.

Allison, the gentleman cattle rancher, began to glory in his increasing reputation as a dangerous man, and proceeded to make the most of it, particularly when drunk. After drinking bouts in Cimarron and other communities, he would sometimes race his horse up and down the street while giving what onlookers described as "war whoops," but which may have been "rebel yells." On at least one such occasion, it was said, he war-whooped his way through a town wearing nothing but his boots.

Entering the Red Brick Saloon in Cimarron one Christmas Eve, and finding a boisterous crowd inside, he forced the customers at gunpoint to calm down and hold Christmas Eve religious services with appropriate music and prayers.

It may have been a latent religious nature that caused him to become an admirer of the Rev. Franklin J. Tolby, a Methodist circuit rider who served both Cimarron and the mining town of Elizabethtown. Tolby, who lived in Cimarron with his wife and two daughters, was an outspoken critic of the New Mexico political machine known as the Santa Fe Ring, and the Maxwell Land Grant Company, which the Ring dominated. He expressed his views from the pulpit, and in letters published anonymously in the *New York Sun*, and aroused further antagonism by pushing to set aside a portion of the private land grant as a reservation for

Ute and Jicarilla Apache Indians.

On September 14, 1875, the thirty-three-year-old preacher, while returning home on horseback from a visit to Elizabethtown, was shot to death by an unknown assailant in Cimarron Canyon about twenty miles east of Cimarron. Robbery was ruled out as a motive, as his horse and other belongings were found near his body, and it was generally agreed that Tolby was the victim of a political assassination.

Taking the lead in investigating the murder was Tolby's assistant, Oscar P. McMains, a Congregational minister who worked as a printer for the *Cimarron News and Press.* His investigations led him to believe that the prime suspect was Cruz Vega, a Cimarron laborer and newly elected constable, who on the day Tolby was murdered, and that day only, had been hired as a substitute carrier to haul the mail between Elizabethtown and Cimarron. This would have placed him in Cimarron Canyon at about the time Tolby was killed.

McMains, wanting to question Vega in private, persuaded one of Vega's employers, William Low (or Lowe) to steer Vega to an isolated spot where pressure might be brought on him to confess, noting that a $500 reward had been offered for the apprehension and conviction of the person or persons responsible for Tolby's death. Low agreed to hire Vega to stand night watch on a cornfield on Ponil Creek, about two miles northeast of Cimarron, to guard it against animal predators.

On the night of October 30, while Vega was at a campfire at the cornfield, he was approached by McMains and a group of masked and drunken cowboys. They dragged him to a nearby telegraph pole, looped the end of a rope around his neck, and threatened to hang him from the pole if he did not tell what he knew about

Tolby's murder. After being hoisted off the ground once, and let back down, Vega told his captors that he did not kill Tolby, but saw the shooting, and identified the killer as Manuel Cardenas of Taos.

The cowboys decided that Vega was an accomplice to the murder, shot him to death, and rode off, leaving his body at the foot of the pole.

Angered by the shooting of Vega was Francisco "Pancho" Griego, a tough gunman and "enforcer" for the Maxwell Land Grant Company, who was believed to be an uncle, or other relative, of the victim. Griego told friends in Cimarron that Clay Allison was one of the leaders of the cowboy lynch mob, and threatened to kill him.

On the evening of November 1, Allison arrived in Cimarron from his ranch with a wagon load of beef for the Indian agency. He stopped at the residence of Florencio Donaghue, the mail contractor, where he ate supper and put his team up for the night. After supper, he and Donaghue began walking toward the St. James Hotel and were accosted on the street by Pancho Griego and several of his friends.

Griego told Allison he wanted to talk to him, and invited him to accompany him to his home. Allison refused. After more words, Allison, Griego, and Donaghue began walking toward the hotel.

Allison was well aware of Griego's reputation as a dangerous man. On the previous May 30, for instance, while dealing monte at the St. James Hotel, Griego had attacked three U.S. 6th Cavalry soldiers following a dispute, shooting two of them fatally and slashing a third, who survived, with a knife. His escape from indictment or punishment for the crime was attributed to the influence of the Santa Fe Ring.

Entering the barroom of the St. James, Allison and Griego

began drinking at the bar, while several other customers sat at tables, drinking and smoking cigars. Griego motioned Allison to the southeast corner of the room, saying, "I want to talk to you." As they reached the corner, three shots were fired in quick succession, and the patrons all darted out of the room into the street.

Henri Lambert, the proprietor, who was in the kitchen when the shots were fired, entered the barroom, and seeing that it was empty, extinguished the lamps and retired. While sweeping out the room in the morning, he found the lifeless body of Griego behind a chair in the southeast corner of the room, with bullet holes in his right temple, right breast, and abdomen.

Allison, successful in his claim of self-defense, said that Griego was reaching for his gun when shot, at the same time trying to distract attention away from his gun hand by fanning himself with his hat with his other hand. The ruse did not work, Allison noting that it was not normal for a man to fan himself on a cold winter night.

"Francisco Griego was well known in Santa Fe, where his mother resides," the *New Mexican* said in reporting his death. "He has killed a great many men, and was considered a dangerous man."

Manuel Cardenas, the man Vega had identified as Tolby's killer, was apprehended at Elizabethtown and taken before a justice of the peace for a hearing. Eleven years before, in September, 1864, Cardenas had been convicted of murder in Taos and sentenced to be hanged, but the sentence was commuted to life imprisonment, and he was either later released or escaped from custody, according to conflicting accounts.

During a hearing before Dallas Cummings, Elizabethtown justice of the peace, on November 5, 1875, Cardenas signed a sworn statement in which he said that the late Cruz Vega had been paid $500 by four prominent Cimarron citizens to kill the Rev.

Franklin J. Tolby. He identified the four citizens as Dr. Robert W. Longwill, a physician and probate judge; Melvin W. Mills, an attorney recently elected to the New Mexico Legislature; Florencio Donaghue, the mail contractor, and the late Francisco "Pancho" Griego. All four had close ties to the Santa Fe Ring.

Cardenas said that all four men contributed to the fund, and that Donaghue, as "treasurer" for the group, paid the money to Vega, his substitute mail carrier. He said Dr. Longwill offered him (Cardenas) the $500 to kill Tolby, but that he told him he would not do it under any circumstances.

"Pancho (Griego) told me they had paid the mail carrier to kill Tolby," Cardenas said in his statement. "Pancho told me that Tolby had been killed. He told me that I was a damned fool, that I might have had $500 in my pocket as well as not. He said if you betray me or the other man we will kill you."

A transcript of the hearing, published on December 5, 1875, in the *Herald* at Silver City, noted that R.C. Allison was present and testified at the hearing.

Cardenas, held for action by the grand jury, was escorted to Cimarron and placed in jail. By this time, the community was in such a state of upheaval by the recent developments that a detachment of twenty soldiers from Fort Union was sent to the town to help preserve law and order, arriving on November 8.

On November 10, during a hearing in Cimarron, Cardenas recanted his earlier sworn statements that the four Cimarron residents had paid Vega to kill Tolby, claiming that he had been pressured into accusing the four. As he was being led back to the stone jail that night, a shot was fired from a group of men in the darkness, and Cardenas fell dead just outside the jail with a bullet in his head. The killer was never identified, although there was a general belief that he was Clay Allison, who once said, "I'm not good at shooting at a mark, except when the mark is a bad man."

The Silver City newspaper, on November 28, 1875, published an account of some of the recent developments in Cimarron:

> *The* Cimarron News and Press *gives much space to the recent developments in regard to the assassination of the Rev. F.J. Tolby on the 14th of September last, in Colfax County, and of the killing of Cruz Vega and Manuel Cardinas [sic], two of his accredited murderers. It is charged that these two men were simply employed to execute the fell purpose of enemies of Tolby and that they were paid $500 for the job.*
>
> *One of them, F. Donoghue, has had a preliminary hearing before two justices of the peace, and held to answer, in the sum of $20,000, the action of the grand jury. Mr. M.W. Mills was discharged for the want of sufficient testimony to justify commitment. Dr. R.H. Longwill, present probate judge of the county, also charged with subornation of murder, skipped out upon ascertaining that he was one of the accused party, and although hotly pursued and overtaken by Capt. R.C. Allison, James and Pete Burleson escaped, it is charged, through the action of U.S. authorities at Fort Union.*

Newspapers reported that Cimarron was in a near state of anarchy, that groups of armed men roamed the streets "bent on violence," and that some of the citizens, fearing for their lives, had left town.

Articles and editorials in the *Cimarron News and Press*, slanted in favor of the political machine and land grant management, soon drew the wrath of Allison and his cowboy friends. On the night of January 26, 1876, they broke into the newspaper offices, smashed the press, and carried parts of it and drawers of type to the Cimarron River bridge and dumped them into the river.

Finding unfinished pages for the next edition in the office, printed on one side but blank on the other, Allison reportedly scrawled "Clay Allison Edition" on the blank sides and hawked them on the streets in the morning for twenty-five cents each.

The *Republican Review* at Albuquerque, in telling on January 29 of the destruction of the Cimarron weekly paper, added:

> *But Cimarron is an interesting place to run a paper. The Editor is criticized so severely and paid so poorly that the two exactly balance each other; besides, sudden death watches over him by day and guards him by night, and thus he is prevented from running into sinful excess. He has a pleasant calling.*

Will Dawson, editor of the Cimarron weekly, soon had it back in operation again, reportedly with the help of $200 that an apologetic Allison handed over to Mrs. William R. Morley, wife of one of the owners, saying, "I don't fight women. Go buy yourself another press."

The Cimarron residents accused of plotting the murder of Tolby were exonerated on grounds of insufficient evidence, but Oscar P. McMains was indicted on a murder charge brought in connection with the shooting of Cruz Vega. After much delay, he stood trial in the village of Mora, south of Cimarron, and on August 23, 1877, the jury returned a meaningless verdict finding him "guilty in the fifth degree" and recommending a $300 fine. Defense attorneys immediately noted that the verdict did not say what McMains was guilty of in the fifth degree, and a new trial was granted, but it never materialized.

The Santa Fe Ring, meanwhile, appeared determined to prosecute Allison on some pretext or another, accusing him of murdering the missing Charles Cooper, and of being an accomplice, with Davy Crockett apparently, in the killing of the three black soldiers at the St. James Hotel. Nothing came of these charges.

A more serious charge was lodged against Allison late in 1876, this time as the result of a dance hall shooting in the community of Las Animas, in the southeast part of Colorado.

On the night of December 21, 1876, Clay Allison and his brother, John, were "whooping it up" in a Las Animas dance hall when Charles Faber, the town constable, approached them and ordered them to hand over their pistols. They refused, and a heated argument ensued.

Faber left the dance hall, and returned a few minutes later carrying a double-barreled shotgun. Without warning, it was said, he fired a blast that dropped John to the floor. Clay drew his pistol and shot the constable, who, as he fell to the floor dying, fired a second blast that hit John again.

Clay, believing that his brother was fatally wounded, dragged the dead constable's body over to him and said, "John, here's the man that shot you. Look at the damned son of a bitch—I killed him."

John Allison recovered, and Clay was jailed on a manslaughter charge. A grand jury decided later that Clay had shot in self-defense, and he was released.

Clay Allison moved from New Mexico in the late 1870s, and in 1880 was ranching on the Washita River in the Texas Panhandle, near the town of Mobeetie. Early in 1881, he married Dora McCullough, whom he had met while ranching in New Mexico, and they eventually established a home at Pecos, Texas, with a cattle ranch on the east bank of the Pecos River, about fifty miles northwest of town, and just south of the New Mexico border.

During business trips around the country, Allison's tough reputation followed him wherever he went, and new stories were added to the growing legend. While passing through Dodge City, Kansas, according to one story, when he was told by local lawmen that he must remove his weapons, he replied, "Gentlemen, when these weapons go off, they will go off smoking."

One of the best-known stories about Allison was published in the *Optic*, at Las Vegas, New Mexico, on June 26, 1886:

> *Clay Allison, the cow man who has just left this city for Lincoln County, is known as a holy terror when he is aroused, and although increasing years and different conditions have made him less vindictive, he still has a decided fondness for getting even with his enemies, and is pretty likely to do so as a general rule.*
>
> *Clay was up in Cheyenne a few days ago with his "bunch of steers," about fifteen hundred in number, which he sold at a good profit, and as he was suffering with toothache while there he went to a dentist to get relief. The dentist, who was "on the make," sized up the man as a cow man with plenty of cash and was determined to make some money out of him; so instead of applying a little creosote to Clay's aching tooth he got him in his dental chair and proceeded to bore a hole in one of the cow man's best teeth for the purpose of filling it, which it didn't in the least need.*

He was a clumsy quack and he inadvertently broke about half the tooth off. Clay got mad and left and went to another dentist who repaired the damage at the expense of twenty-five dollars and told the victim that he had been treated by an arrant quack who evidently wanted only to make some money out of him.

This fired the blood of Mr. Allison, who fairly thirsted for revenge, and he got it too. He proceeded to the quack's office, seized a pair of forceps, threw him down upon the floor and in spite of the yells of the victim inserted the instrument in his mouth and drew out one of his best molars. Not content with this he grabbed for another and caught one of the front teeth together with a large piece of the upper lip and he was tugging away at it when the agonized shrieks and yells of the poor devil, upon whose chest Allison was pressing his knee, drew a crowd that ended the matter. This story is said to be absolutely true and Clay admitted it.

Clay Allison met his death in a freak accident one year later. While driving a loaded wagon toward his ranch on July 3, 1887, the wagon apparently hit a thick clump of grass, or a chuck hole, the jolt catapulting him headfirst against a wagon wheel. Survivors included his wife; a two-year-old daughter, Patti; and an as yet unborn daughter, Clay Pearl Allison.

He lies buried at Pecos, Texas, the epitaph on his tombstone reading, "He never killed a man that did not need killing."

The Trial of "Dutch Joe" Hubert

A large crowd of spectators gathered in the small courthouse at Mesilla on the afternoon of June 27, 1877, after word got around that Joseph "Dutch Joe" Hubert, who was standing separate trials on four indictments charging him with robbing and delaying the U.S. mails in connection with two stagecoach robberies, had dismissed his attorney and elected to defend himself against one of the indictments. The spectators anticipated an interesting and entertaining afternoon, for the middle-aged, loquacious Dutch Joe, who regarded himself as an honorable man, was as furious and outraged as any honorable man would be who was being sent to prison on the testimony of jailed horse thieves.

Hubert already was certain of a prison sentence because the U.S. District Court jury had found him guilty of two of the four indictments, but had delayed sentencing until after he was tried on the remaining two. His attorney, John Ryan, had defended him at the first two trials that began on June 19, and after two convictions Hubert decided he might do better defending himself.

The principal witnesses for the prosecution were two of southern New Mexico's most notorious horse thieves, George W. "Buffalo Bill" Spawn and Nicolas Provencia, who agreed to testify against the defendant in exchange for their release from the Mesilla jail, where they were being held on charges of stealing government horses and mules. In two previous trials, they had told the jury that Dutch Joe had boasted to them in jail of his achievements in holding up and robbing the two stagecoaches, and now they were back in court prepared to give additional testimony that could add more years to the prison sentence he faced.

The indictments against Hubert linked him with the holdups and robberies of two stagecoaches on the road between Silver City, a thriving new mining town in southwest New Mexico, and Mesilla, seat of Dona Ana County, on the east bank of the Rio Grande about one hundred miles to the southeast. Both robberies had occurred at almost the same spot in Cooke's Canyon, midway between the two towns, a narrow mountain passage on the old Butterfield Trail that was popular with the Apaches as an ambush site.

The first of the two stagecoach robberies in which Dutch Joe was accused of having a hand occurred early on the morning of January 12, 1876. The *Herald*, a weekly newspaper published at Silver City, took a rather facetious view of the affair, reporting on Sunday, January 16:

> *The mail coach, which left this place for the East Tuesday evening, was taken in by three road agents in Cook's canyon [sic] about three a.m. the following morning and robbed of all the treasure it contained.*
>
> *Two passengers, Messrs. Thomas F. Conway (lawyer) and John S. Chisum (cattle king) also suffered by the depletion of their pockets to the last nickle, and had the robbers caused them to slip their wind they never could have crossed the river Styx, for the reason that the legal tender would have been wanting to pay Charon the ferriage fee. Their watches were taken and everything else of value except a photograph of Don Thomas' sweetheart, which we presume they rejected on account of the squint in the left eye.*
>
> *The robbers after completing the job ordered the coach and its inmates to the right about and travel in the*

direction whence they came, which they did with about the same alacrity as a weaver's shuttle, whilst the highwaymen went east.

The stage, after traveling a mile and a half or perhaps a mile and a half an inch stopped, when Loyd's map of the world was produced and spread upon the ground with a view of ascertaining in which hemisphere they were, but before satisfying themselves upon that point the wheels of the western bound coach were heard thundering on the way. The map was re-rolled and shoved into the front boot just as the coming coach drew up, and the conductor enquired, "What's up?" and upon being informed of the robbery announced having met the trio of robbers traveling leisurely on the road.

The loss to the stage company and passengers is large, and rumor has it, amounting to $30,000 in greenbacks, bullion and drafts.

It was learned later that John Chisum, the Pecos Valley cattle king, had $1,000 in currency on his person at the time of the robbery, but had shoved most of the money into his bootleg before the robbers reached him and had handed over only a small amount.

Civil authorities made no serious effort to pursue the robbers, for sheriffs and other law enforcement officers had to pay their own expenses while on the trail of fugitives. Captain Charles Beyer, the commanding officer at Fort Bayard, a few miles east of Silver City, sent nine enlisted men and an experienced civilian tracker to the robbery scene with orders to attempt to pick up the trail of the outlaws and apprehend them if possible, but their search was in vain.

The following reward notice was published in the *Herald* on January 23, 1876:

The reward notice, although providing an incentive for pursuit of the robbers, brought no results.

Sixteen months later, another stagecoach was held up and robbed in Cooke's Canyon. This robbery occurred at approximately the same spot as the first, a mile west of Fort Cummings, a temporarily abandoned military post that had been erected in 1863 at the mouth of the canyon. The *Herald*, on May 12, 1877, told briefly of the robbery:

> *Coach coming west was stopped by two masked men last night in Cook's Canon [sic], one mile this side of Fort Cummings, and passengers robbed — mail not molested. John B. Morrill, F.B. Knox, Miss Maggie Wilson and Joe Kaier were aboard. Robbers captured $1.50 from John and a revolver. Morrill told them they ought to have known better than to strike such a poor crowd. They were after paymaster. The gentlemen hid their watches.*

Three weeks later, the *Herald* published this dispatch from Mesilla, dated May 28:

> EDS. HERALD — *Deputy Sheriff Armijo captured "Dutch Joe" at Santa Barbara, near Fort Thorn, who is doubtless one of the party who robbed the coach some two years ago in Cook's Canon [sic]; also on May 9th near Cummings. Mariano Barela, Sheriff*

The *Herald* noted in the same issue that Joseph Hubert was once a resident of Silver City and worked at Robert Swan's meat market.

The *Daily New Mexican* at Santa Fe, on June 9, provided additional details on Hubert's movements and capture. After the first coach robbery, the article said, Hubert struck out for Chihuahua, Mexico, where he sold about $5,000 worth of silver bullion at greatly reduced rates. He spent the money freely, and went to El Paso, Texas, where one of his crime partners, Roscoe Burrell, died.

Later, the article said, Hubert was arrested in El Paso for killing another of his partners, Fredrico Lopez, while another partner, Enrique Rodriguez, had joined some revolutionary forces in Mexico. Hubert placed about $500 in the hands of El Paso attorneys and friends, "and left jail suddenly without the knowledge of authorities."

Mariano Barela, sheriff of Dona Ana County, learned that Hubert was prowling around the Mesilla area, and sent Deputy Sheriff Jacinto Armijo and a force out to capture him. The sheriff's posse caught up with him about twenty-five miles north of Mesilla, near the village of Santa Barbara, close to the abandoned ruins of Fort Thorn, and demanded and received his surrender. The article gave this description of the prisoner:

He is about five feet seven to nine inches high, rather dark hair and complexion, very little thin beard, a separation between his front teeth of about one-eighth of an inch, the muscles from cheek bones on each side of his nose down towards the chin distinctly noticed particularly when he talks; he speaks with a slight lisping Dutch accent. He says he will get even with persons at El Paso that got his money, etc.

Jailed in Mesilla, Hubert shared a cell with two acquaintances, the horse thieves Spawn and Provencia, who soon found an opportunity to gain their freedom. They told Sheriff Barela, who also was the contractor for the mail transported on the coaches that had been robbed, that Dutch Joe had boasted to them that he had robbed both the coaches that had been held up in Cooke's Canyon. Barela took this information to U.S. Attorney Thomas B. Catron, who agreed to drop charges against Spawn and

Provencia in exchange for their testimony.

Hubert was taken before U.S. Commissioner J.S. Crouch, who after listening to Spawn and Provencia at a preliminary hearing, bound Hubert over to the federal grand jury, which quickly returned four indictments charging him with robbing and delaying the U.S. mails and attempted mail robbery. Hubert pleaded not guilty to all four indictments, and the first of his four trials was set for June 19.

Judge Warren Bristol presided at the opening trials on June 19 and 20 during which Hubert was convicted of robbing and delaying the U.S. mails in connection with the first stagecoach robbery. Prosecuting for the government was Thomas B. Catron, and Hubert's defense attorney was John Ryan.

Spawn and Provencia were the principal witnesses at both trials. Questioned by Catron, they said Dutch Joe had told them that he held up the coach with the assistance of Roscoe Burrell and a man named Henry, and that the robbery had netted a large quantity of silver and a gold watch, the latter taken from one of the passengers. They said Dutch Joe also told them that the silver was buried near the scene of the robbery, that he and one of his companions had returned for it four or five days later, and had taken it to Santa Theresa, a ranch on the Rio Grande near the Mexican border, where they had left it for about a month before taking it to Chihuahua, Mexico, where it was coined.

Judge Bristol, at the close of the second trial, announced that he would pass sentence after Hubert was tried on the remaining two indictments brought in connection with the second coach robbery. It was then that Hubert fired his attorney and announced that he would defend himself.

Hubert's third trial on June 27, when he defended himself

against an indictment charging him with attempted mail robbery, turned out to be what the *Mesilla Valley Independent* called "the sensation of the week." The Mesilla weekly newspaper published a lengthy synopsis of the trial, which was picked up and republished by the *Herald* at Silver City on July 7, 1877.

The article said several amusing incidents occurred while the jury was being empaneled:

> *One juror was asked if he knew the accused, when Joe promptly responded, "He knows nothing but good of me, then." When asked if he had any objection to the jury, he said, "Yes, I want to get all the ugly men off." After the jury had been sworn one of the jury complained of being ill and asked to be excused. The Court stated that he could not be excused except by consent of both parties. The U.S. Attorney said he had no objection to excusing the juror, and Joe exclaimed, "Let him go, I don't want to be tried by a sick jury."*

Sam Eckstine, the stagecoach driver, was the first government witness. He testified that he knew one of the masked robbers was Hubert because he recognized his voice and the robber had used the expression, "pshaw, pshaw, pshaw," one of Hubert's favorite expressions.

Hubert cross-examined Eckstine at some length about the voice recognition, then, losing patience, dismissed him with these words:

"Pshaw, pshaw, pshaw, there's been too much pshaw, pshaw, pshaw in this case. I don't think Sam would appear against me if he could help it. Let him go. Sam, you're dismissed."

Spawn and Provencia then testified that Hubert had told them in jail that he had held up the second coach in company with

Robert Martin, that he had taken a pistol from one of the passengers, J.B. Morrill, and had sold it to a Mexican in the village of Santa Barbara north of Mesilla. The newspaper article continued:

> *Joe cross-examined Provencia at some length. He asked*
> *him if he, the witness, had not proposed to defendant to*
> *organize a band to rob coaches in Arizona after they got*
> *out of jail, to which the witness replied that Joe had made*
> *the proposition to him and he had acquiesced in it.*

At the close of the brief trial, U.S. Attorney Catron delivered his closing arguments to the jury, after which Dutch Joe rose and addressed the jury, speaking slowly at first, then gathering verbal momentum as he launched into a long tirade against his accusers. Occasionally he would pause in his long harangue to inquire of the court reporter, "Have you got that down?"

The crowd in the courtroom enjoyed it immensely, and Hubert, making the most of his day in court, enjoyed being in the spotlight. The newspapers published his remarks to the jury:

"Gentlemen: You must allow me a little as I am an uneducated man. I ask you to pay particular attention so you will not mistake me.

"I am accused of robbing the coach in Cooke's Canyon. Sam Eckstine, the German, he knews me very well. Oh, yes! He knew me not at the time the coach was robbed, because he thought I was dead with the smallpox in El Paso. He did not see me for one year and three months, but now he finds I am alive, and he says he recognized my voice that night.

"He did not recognize my voice. He was driving the coach and the wind was blowing, and the man who made the coach stand spoke Spanish and appeared to be drunk, and the other man held a gun and made the passengers get out and they was robbed, but the passengers was robbed of one dollar and a half, and a pistol was lost. He don't say I stole the pistol, but he says he knew my voice over a year afterwards, but didn't know it then when all this was done.

"Then Nicolas Provencia come into court and says I told him all about it two or three weeks ago and that I told him I sold the pistol in Santa Barbara. If I sold it there to a Mexican there are gentlemen in this town who would give a thousand dollars to get it as evidence against me. It's all a lie. This thief has been here six or seven times in jail, and he's hired for a few dollars to testify a lie against me. He can stand in front of you and swear lies all day, and his face has no shame.

"Americans is pretty smart. I mean Irishmen, Dutchmen, and Americans. Some Mexicans are, too. They come and make up lies to testify against me.

"There's Bob Spawn, that big lummux of an American, he testifies against me so that he can get clean out of jail.

"That man sitting over there (Sheriff Barela) he is the contractor for the mail line. Why don't he have a man hired, with a shotgun, to kill any thieving son of a bitch that tries to rob the coach. He carries $20,000 in gold or silver on the coach and to make it safe he wants to make an example of a stage robber. It is more honest to make an example of a thief by shooting him than to enter the jail and hire horse thieves to testify against an honorable man.

"Since I have been in jail I have been chained hand and foot. I am no desperado, and in jail are thieves and murderers who have no chains and who can come here to swear against me.

"This gentleman is the sheriff and owns the mail line, and he wants to send me to the penitentiary, and I expect you will send me there. I am not a bad man. I tell the truth and you can believe it or not as you like. I never stole anything, and if two thieves send me to the penitentiary, I am better off there in heart than they are here in New Mexico.

"They say Martin was with me. Why didn't they arrest him? They didn't want him very bad. When the coach was robbed, Martin and I were hunting for horses that Nicolas Provencia stole.

"So these thieves help one another. I am now all alone. I don't want anybody to help me out of here. There are gentlemen who would help me if they knew the truth.

"You all know Nicolas Provencia. If you don't know him, I advise you to make his acquaintance. When he was sworn before that gentleman (U.S. Commissioner J.S. Crouch), he knew nothing. When a man is sworn and knows nothing, it looks strange when he knows a great deal afterwards.

"Spawn sleeps with Nick, he is his bosom friend, and as soon as these two thieves get through appearing against me they will be set free from jail and have a horse and rifle given to them, so that they can go into Arizona and steal Apache horses. That's their business.

"Sam Eckstine didn't recognize my voice on the night when the coach was robbed and the mules was moving and the wind blowing, but sixteen months afterwards he recognized my voice. I believe he lied, before God and Heaven.

"I know Nick Provencia. I have followed his track from one end of the river to the other. He is a damned thief. He wanted to rob the government mules from Fort Selden, and came to me to help him, but the mules was put in a high corral, so we couldn't get them, so for spite he stole three grey horses and a mule."

Hubert was interrupted at this point by Judge Bristol, who informed him that while great latitude would be allowed him, such a line of argument was improper and would not be permitted. Hubert continued:

"I beg you honor's parden and ask to be excused if I say anything improper.

"Gentlemens, I have but few words to say. Good men will believe a good man. If a man has a bad name, they won't believe him, but I can look you in the face and say I have not a bad heart, and nobody has said I have a bad name. You all know what I am accused of and what is the evidence against me.

"Gentlemens, the smartest man that ever lived in the United States, and that was Daniel Webster, says in a speech he made in Louisiana, that I read in a book, that a man should not be held guilty unless he is proved guilty by good evidence, and that if the evidence is not good the man should not be sent to the penitentiary. A thief's evidence should not send a man to the penitentiary.

"I leave my case to God and you. If you don't think them thieves swore to the truth, you can't find me guilty. The Dutchman (Eckstine) knows nothing. The big American (Spawn) was a soldier ten years and don't know A B C. He makes his living by stealing and robbing. Nick is nothing but a common thief, and you can't take his evidence, and so I leave this case with you and God."

The jury, after a brief deliberation, returned a verdict finding Joseph "Dutch Joe" Hubert guilty as charged. In another quick session, he was tried and convicted of delaying the mails.

Asked by Judge Bristol if he had anything to say before sentence was pronounced, Hubert replied:

"I wish your honor to make it as light as possible. I am a man of middle age, and a long term would let me out an old man with no means of making a living. I ask your honor to be as lenient as you can."

Judge Bristol then sentenced him to confinement at hard labor in the Missouri State Penitentiary for a period of thirteen years and ordered him to pay a fine of $200. (The Territory of New Mexico had yet to build a penitentiary.)

The *Herald* at Silver City, commenting editorially on Dutch Joe's prison sentence, said:

> *We do not mourn, as Rachel for her first-born, because of Joe's departure, but rather rejoice that he is going to a place where his acquisitive disposition will not interfere with the welfare of others and where the chastening rigor of prison discipline may learn him to respect the law of* meum et tuum.

Nicolas Provencia and George "Buffalo Bill" Spawn, having won their release from the Mesilla jail, quickly returned to their old ways, just as Dutch Joe had predicted.

Provencia was soon identified as a member of a notorious gang of rustlers, led by Jesse Evans and Frank Baker, which preyed on government horses and mules and became involved in the bloody Lincoln County War of 1878.

Before the end of the year, Spawn had been tried and convicted in U.S. District Court in Mesilla on charges of stealing government mules from the Mescalero Apache Agency in Lincoln County and sentenced to five years in the Missouri State Penitentiary.

Marino Leyba:
The Sandia Mountain Desperado

The fact that the thirty-year-old government worker had been missing for nearly two months was first reported in the *Albuquerque Daily Journal* on November 29, 1880:

> *Several letters and telegrams have just been received by citizens of Albuquerque, making inquiry as to the whereabouts, or any information that may lead to the discovery of the whereabouts of Col. Charles Potter, who has been missing since about the 11th of October last.*
>
> *Col. Potter, it will be remembered by many readers of the* Journal, *was in Albuquerque during the sitting of District Court, and occupied rooms at the home of Col. Branford. He represented himself as being connected with the United States Geological Survey, and was down here for the purpose of writing up the mineral resources of this part of the country, for publication in the forthcoming census report. After remaining here for several days, he left, on horseback, on the 11th of October, for Santa Fe, intending to go via Tijeras Canyon and the New Placers. He was dressed in a fustian suit of clothes, and rode a very fine sorrel horse, with one white hind foot. Nothing has been heard from him after leaving here, and his fate is shrouded in the darkest mystery.*

The *Journal* described Potter as being five feet ten inches tall, with a rather spare build, brown hair, a light mustache and small goatee, bluish-grey eyes, weighing about 165 pounds, and dressed in a corduroy suit with dog-head buttons.

Additional information on the background and movements of the missing man was published in Albuquerque and Santa Fe newspapers in the days that followed, including the fact that Potter was a member of a prominent Rhode Island family and a stepson of Rhode Island Governor Charles C. Van Zandt. He had been given the honorary title of colonel due to his political appointments to the personal staffs of his stepfather and a previous Rhode Island governor. He maintained a fashionable home at Newport, Rhode Island, where his wife of eight years anxiously awaited word from him.

While traveling alone through western states in 1880, Potter had paused in Leadville, Colorado, to visit a relative of his stepfather, Ferdinand S. Van Zandt, who was involved in banking and mining, and while there he met S.F. Emmons, a geologist with the U.S. Geological Survey. Emmons offered Potter the job of visiting mining districts in New Mexico to gather mineral production statistics for the forthcoming 1880 U.S. Census. Potter accepted the offer.

During the course of his survey work in New Mexico, Potter arrived in Albuquerque early in October, and spent a week or two at the home of Edward Branford. On or about October 13, he saddled his horse and departed for Santa Fe, not by the most direct route to the north, but by a route that first led east through Tijeras Canyon in the Sandia Mountains, which form Albuquerque's eastern skyline, and then north to Santa Fe through the New Placers mining district, centered around the bustling new mining town of Golden.

December passed with no clue as to the fate of the missing man, and the deepening mystery brought Ferdinand Van Zandt to Albuquerque from Colorado to conduct his own investigations. Following the route Potter had taken from Albuquerque, he traced him as far as the village of Tijeras, in the Sandia Mountains about fifteen miles to the east, where he learned that Potter was last seen riding north from that village on the road leading to Santa Fe by way of the New Placers.

Beginning January 3, 1881, this reward notice began appearing in the *Albuquerque Journal*:

$1,000 REWARD!

One Thousand Dollars Reward is hereby offered for information regarding the whereabouts, if alive, of

COL. CHARLES POTTER.

In case of his death a reward of $200 will be paid for information leading to the recovery of his body.

Col. Potter was last seen on October 14, 1880, leaving Tijeras, Bernalillo County, N.M., on the road leading via San Antonio to the New Placers.

Col. Potter was a tall, spare man, dressed in a corduroy suit, light in color, and was mounted on a fine sorrel mare 15½ hands high, with one hind foot white.

Any information to be addressed to F.S. VAN ZANDT, *care of Gen. Edward Hatch, U.S.A., Santa Fe, N.M., or to* MAJOR HARRY R. WHITING, *Albuquerque, N.M.*

The reward notice brought no response.

During the last week in January, Bernalillo County Sheriff Perfecto Armijo of Albuquerque learned that an open-faced gold watch and chain, answering the description of one carried by

Potter, had been left in pawn at the Albuquerque loan office of J.K. Basye. Sheriff Armijo and Van Zandt went to the loan office to examine the watch, only to discover that the case and chain had been melted down by Basye a few days before, and only the works remained. From an examination of the works, however, Van Zandt was able to identify the watch as the one carried by Potter when he disappeared.

The watch, it was learned, had been left there in pawn the previous November 3 by Pantaleon Miera of Algodones, a village about twenty miles north of Albuquerque. Miera was believed to be a member of a gang of robbers that had been operating out of Algodones for some years.

Miera was considered the prime suspect in the disappearance of Potter, but it was too late to question him. Miera and a companion, Santos Benavides, arrested December 28 on a charge of horse stealing, had been taken that same night by an armed mob from their place of confinement in the constable's home at Bernalillo, a few miles south of Algodones, and hanged from a cottonwood tree.

Sheriff Armijo left immediately for Bernalillo, about eighteen miles north of Albuquerque, to see if he could find any trace of Potter's sorrel mare, believing it might have been left in the vicinity by Miera. He did not find the horse, but his trip was not in vain, for he received information indicating that a man loitering around Isleta Pueblo, a centuries-old Indian town about fourteen miles south of Albuquerque, knew something about Potter's fate. Armijo sent two of his deputies to Isleta Pueblo to arrest the man.

Arrested at Isleta on January 29 was Escalastico Perea, who readily confirmed suspicions that Potter had been murdered.

Perea claimed that he had been a witness to the murder, but denied having taken any part in it. He said Potter had been killed by a small group of robbers led by Marino Leyba, sometimes referred to as "The Sandia Mountain Desperado" for his practice of bullying and terrorizing villagers and travelers along the eastern slopes of the Sandia Mountains. In addition to Leyba and himself, Perea said, the robber gang consisted of the late Pantaleon Miera, Miguel Barrera of Tejon, and a man identified only as California Joe of La Madera, Tejon and La Madera being tiny settlements north of Tijeras.

Perea told the sheriff that Leyba and two of his companions had met Potter near Tijeras on October 14, that Potter had asked them some questions about the road north to Santa Fe, and after giving him some directions, had hurried ahead by a shortcut to prepare an ambush for him in a lonely part of the road. As the *Albuquerque Journal* reported on January 31:

> *Here they waited till their victim approached, when they closed in on him, one in front and one on each side. One of the assassins fired a shot at Col. Potter, which took effect, but did not kill him; another shot was fired which struck Potter's horse, badly wounding the animal. Col. Potter drew his revolver and, although disabled by his first wound, fought bravely and desperately, one of his shots taking effect in the arm of the villain Leibor [sic]. This struggle could not last long, as the fiendish assassins were on all sides of the brave man, who soon fell from his horse, pierced to the heart by the bullet of one demon whose aim had been only too deadly. He met his fate bravely, never speaking after he was attacked.*

> *Potter's horse proved to be so badly wounded after the murderers got possession of it that they considered it of no value, and taking it a short distance shot it.*

Perea led Sheriff Armijo and a posse to the murder scene, which proved to be near the Chimal Spring about a dozen miles north of Tijeras at the southern edge of the New Placers district. Potter's decomposed remains were found in a dry stream bed, and were identified by bits of his clothing. Before returning to Albuquerque with the remains, Sheriff Armijo rounded up Barrera and California Joe at their nearby homes and took them along. Perea said that Barrera had led Potter off on a false trail, and that California Joe had furnished the weapons used to kill Potter but had remained home and took no active part in the killing.

Perea, Barrera, and California Joe were placed in the Bernalillo County jail just east of the Old Albuquerque Plaza on the night of January 31, 1881, upon the return of the sheriff from the murder scene, but their stay in jail was a short one. The *Albuquerque Journal*, the following day, reported:

> *This morning dawned clear, bright and beautiful over the city of Albuquerque, and as the sun came up from behind the peaks of the Sandias and shed its bright rays over the roofs of the flat-topped adobe buildings, they fell on three human forms, stark and stiff, dangling from a wooden beam in front of the county jail. They were those of the three prisoners brought in last evening by Sheriff Armijo and placed in jail to await trial for the murder of Col. Charles Potter, of which they had confessed themselves guilty.*

The three victims, before taken out of jail and lynched by a mob of citizens, had implicated yet another man, Faustino Gutierrez, in the conspiracy to waylay and murder Potter for his valuables. The *Journal,* on February 1, reported that Gutierrez was believed to be lurking near the village of Chilili, south of Tijeras, and that a posse had just left Albuquerque "to capture and bring him in." Captured at Chilili and lodged in the county jail at Albuquerque, Gutierrez contended that he had nothing to do with the murder, and knew nothing about it except what Marino Leyba had told him.

Gutierrez remained in jail three weeks, and was then subjected to the same fate as Perea, Barrera, and California Joe. The *Journal* revealed his fate on February 25:

> *Seven men in all are supposed to have been engaged in the murder of Col. Charles Potter last October, and it is known to readers of the* Journal *that two of them were hanged at Bernalillo and three in this city about one month ago. Marino Leiba [*sic*], the leader, is still at large, but Faustino, another of the gang of desperadoes, was arrested about three weeks ago and lodged in jail in this city. This morning his lifeless body was found hanging in front of the jail, with a little piece of paper tacked to his clothing, which told the story of his fate, and read as follows: "Hanged by the 601 — assassin of Col. Potter."*

The *Journal,* the same day, expressed doubt that Marino Leyba, leader of the gang, would ever be brought to justice:

*Only one more of the band remains at large, and it is
feared that he will succeed in escaping into Old Mexico.
Whether he is ever captured or not there is but little
probability that he will ever trouble this part of the country again; and thus, at last, one of the most desperate bands
of robbers and cut-throats that ever preyed upon any community is effectually broken up.*

*   *   *

Although speculation was rife that Marino Leyba had escaped
south into Mexico, Sheriff Perfecto Armijo was not convinced.
He turned his attention to Leyba's home base, the small town of
Puerto de Luna on the Pecos River more than one hundred miles
east of Albuquerque, where it was learned the outlaw had a family.

Sheriff Armijo sent one of his deputies on a secret mission to
the Pecos River town in an effort to locate the wanted man. The
deputy sheriff was accompanied by a deputy U.S. marshal. Upon
their arrival at Puerto de Luna they contacted the town constable,
Lorenzo Sanchez, told him they had a warrant for the arrest of
Leyba, and asked his assistance in locating and capturing him.

Constable Sanchez, who was well acquainted with Leyba and
his usual haunts, agreed to assist the two officers from Albuquerque, but Leyba, who was hiding out at home, saw them before
they saw him. The *Las Vegas Daily Optic*, publishing the details
weeks later, reported on March 18, 1881:

*Leiba [sic] was on the alert, fearing that he would be
pursued, and gave unmistakable evidence of his guilt by
escaping from the vicinity on a stolen mare. He cut across
the country to White Oaks, being familiar with every foot*

61

of the ground, and here attempted to steal a fresh horse, but his nefarious plans were nipped in the bud by the near approach of his pursuers, whom, he well knew, were barking low on a warm trail.

Escaping his pursuers at White Oaks, a mining town about one hundred miles southwest of Puerto de Luna, Leyba headed toward home again, pausing at Vallejos, ten miles south of Puerto de Luna, to steal a horse owned by Pablo Analla. He was next seen on March 14, stealing another horse at the Donaciano Serrano Ranch near Puerto de Luna, and Serrano rode quickly into town to inform Constable Sanchez of the matter.

Sanchez quickly rounded up a posse of local citizens to go after the fugitive, and volunteers were easy to find, as Leyba had achieved the unpopular reputation of the town bully. Riding beside Sanchez at the head of the posse was John G. Clancey, a retired Vermont sea captain who had established a large sheep ranch on Alamo Gordo Creek south of town, and for whom Leyba had once worked as a sheep herder. Others in the posse included Pablo Analla and Donaciano Serrano, from whom Leyba had stolen horses; Robert Mingus, Hugo Zuber, Louis Le Testu, Juan Silva, G.M. Wilson, W.H. Burnett, Ignacio Lucero, Bernardo Romero, and Refugio Chavez.

Picking up Leyba's trail, the posse tracked him to a point twelve miles beyond the Serrano Ranch. There, in high grass about two hundred yards from a ranch house, the possemen spotted Leyba lying on the ground, the horse he had stolen from Serrano standing close by. Startled by the approach of the horsemen, Leyba roused himself quickly, removed his boots so that he would leave no tracks, and disappeared into the high grass. The posse recovered the stolen horse, and searched the area in small squads, but could find no trace of the elusive outlaw.

After resting at a sheep camp that night, the posse resumed the search in the morning, splitting up into squads again to inspect the various sheep camps in the vicinity. Picking up a fresh trail at one sheep camp, nine members of the posse under Constable Sanchez followed it southeast toward Alamo Gordo Creek.

As the posse neared the creek, one of the members, G.M. Wilson, spotted Leyba crouching in the grass with a Winchester rifle in his hands. Wilson shouted to his companions, warning them to scatter as Leyba was preparing to shoot, and at that moment Leyba did shoot, the bullet grazing Louis Le Testu's stirrup. The only casualty of Leyba's shot was Leyba himself, however, for in his haste he had inserted a .45-caliber shell into the .44-caliber rifle, and when the shell exploded, it knocked the block from the rifle, wounding him in the left forearm.

Weaponless, Leyba threw up his hands and surrendered, after asking and receiving assurances that he would be protected from any lynch mob. His captors took him to the Mingus Ranch and treated his arm wound, at the same time finding and removing a butcher knife Leyba had hidden in his sleeve. The prisoner was taken to Puerto de Luna, and then escorted on north to Las Vegas, seat of San Miguel County, where he was placed in the county jail on the evening of March 17.

The *Las Vegas Optic,* reporting the capture and jailing of Leyba, said:

> *On the way to this place the prisoner talked very little but positively denied having committed the murder. However, it can be proven that in conversation with some*

sheep herders he stated that he fired the shot that killed Col.
Potter. Others were implicated but he was the chap who
did the work.

The same article also gave a description of the notorious outlaw:

He is a tall, cruel looking scoundrel, is only 23 years of
age and has a slight impediment in his speech. He has a
wife, a boy four years old, and a mother residing in Puerto
de Luna, and has long been known as a notorious thief
and murderer.

Sheriff Armijo, who went to Las Vegas from Albuquerque upon learning the news of Leyba's capture, furnished this description to the *Albuquerque Journal*:

Sheriff Armijo says Leiba [sic] is about 22 years old, and
has ways and actions like an overgrown boy. He is very
stout, and is a bold, reckless character. Leiba, it is said,
killed a man at Whitewater, a few weeks ago, and at the time
of his capture was trying to escape from this fresh crime.

The *Optic*, on March 19, published an interview with the visiting sheriff in which he expressed the belief that Leyba would meet the same fate as his accomplices:

Sheriff Perfecto Armijo, of Bernalillo County, whose
name casts a chill to the heart of every criminal in New
Mexico, arrived last night from Albuquerque and was

interviewed by The Optic *at the St. Nicholas (Hotel)*
this morning:

"I am told you are here for Marino Leiba [sic], the
Potter murderer," said the reporter.

"Yes, he is wanted very much at Albuquerque. About
three thousand people are anxious to interview him. He
has always been a desperate character and is known to our
people as a man who delights in murder. He has been
mixed up in several killing affairs and, as I said before, he
is wanted badly."

"Do you anticipate that he will be lynched when you
take him back?"

"From the fate of his accomplices, I can look for no other
move. I actually believe that Leiba has trouble in store
for him."

The Bernalillo County sheriff returned to Albuquerque without the prisoner, however, the reason for which was explained in
the *Albuquerque Journal* on March 21.

To bring Leiba [sic] to this county for trial he must be
indicted for murder; and this will be hard to do, as all the
witnesses who could testify against him were hung re-
cently. The case is rather complicated, and we do not see
how it can be unravelled.

Judge L. Bradford Prince ruled that Leyba could not be taken
to Albuquerque until a Bernalillo County grand jury indictment
was returned against him. No such indictment was ever returned
against Leyba for the Potter murder, however, for, as Sheriff

Armijo pointed out, all those who could testify against him had been lynched.

Meanwhile, lesser charges were piling up against Leyba in San Miguel County, and he remained in jail pending trials. The *Optic*, on March 21, reported:

> *He (Leyba) was indicted by our grand jury, for shoot-ing with intent to kill at Pat Garrett while the latter was escorting prisoners through Puerto de Luna.*

A week later, on Monday, March 28, the *Optic* reported:

> *The mother of Marino Leyba, the Potter murderer now confined in the Las Vegas jail, died Sunday morning at her home in Puerto de Luna.*

On June 16, the *Optic* reported:

> *Complaint is brought to this office that Leyba, one of the murderers of Col. Charles Potter, now in the Las Vegas jail, is allowed the privilege of the city without wearing shackles, but of course is under the escort of a guard.*

It was not until August that Leyba was brought to trial on the indictment charging him with shooting at Lincoln County Sheriff Pat Garrett with intent to kill. This episode had occurred at Puerto de Luna on December 10, 1880, at a time when the fate of the missing Col. Potter was yet unknown.

Garrett, at the time, had paused at Alexander Grzelachowski's store in Puerto de Luna while en route to Las Vegas with two prisoners, John Joshua Webb, a convicted murderer, and George Davis, charged with stealing mules, who had been captured by Garrett and a posse following their escape from the Las Vegas jail.

Garrett was eating crackers in the store, according to trial testimony, when Leyba entered the store and approached him.

"No *cabron* (goat) like Pat Garrett can take me," Leyba told the lawman.

"I don't want anything with you," Garrett answered. "I have no warrant to arrest you."

Leyba walked out on the porch, cursing the lawman, and Garrett followed him outside. Leyba continued his abuse of Garrett, who pushed him off the porch with the words, "Go away from here."

The shove sent Leyba sprawling to the ground, and he jumped to his feet, drew his revolver, and fired two quick shots at Garrett, both missing the six-foot-four-inch target. Garrett returned the fire, wounding Leyba in the left shoulder, and Leyba fled the scene, Garrett's friend Barney Mason shooting at him without effect as he ran down the road.

The jury found Leyba guilty as charged, and he was fined $80.

In October, 1881, the grand jury in Las Vegas returned indictments charging Leyba with stealing several horses immediately preceding his capture, and resisting an officer, Constable Lorenzo Sanchez of Puerto de Luna. He was tried and convicted of these charges in March, 1882, and Judge L. Bradford Prince imposed prison sentences totaling seven years.

Leyba was taken to the federal prison at Leavenworth, Kansas, as New Mexico did not yet have a territorial prison, and he remained there until March, 1886, when he was returned to New Mexico to complete his sentence at the new territorial prison that had been erected the year before in Santa Fe.

Leyba earned points in the New Mexico prison by warning the warden that another prisoner had stolen a butcher knife and intended to kill him. New Mexico Governor Edmund G. Ross pardoned Leyba on July 21, 1886, after Pablo Analla, from whom Leyba had stolen one of the horses, told the governor that he was "mistaken and misinformed" as to the real facts of the crime and that there were mitigating circumstances connected with the taking of his horse.

Leyba walked out of the Santa Fe prison a free man, but New Mexico had not heard the last of him.

* * *

Joseph Lackey, a well-to-do immigrant from Ireland, and Julian Tessier, a native of Switzerland, were partners in the 1880s in one of the largest sheep ranches in the broad Estancia Valley of central New Mexico. The elderly men, both quiet and mild mannered, lived alone in a cabin in a secluded spot on the grassy plains near Buffalo Spring, about forty miles east of Albuquerque. Their 20,000 head of sheep provided large clips of wool that the partners transported periodically north to Las Vegas, returning home each time with large sums of money.

On the afternoon of March 4, 1887, shortly after Lackey had returned home from a wool selling trip to Las Vegas, sheep and cattle men on neighboring ranches noticed a dense column of smoke rising into the sky from the direction of the Lackey cabin. There seemed to be no great cause for alarm, however, and as Lackey was expected at the home of some friends that night, they waited for him to bring word of any problem.

A group of the ranchers, growing apprehensive the next morning after Lackey had failed to put in an appearance, saddled their horses and rode to Lackey's cabin. They discovered that it had been burned to the ground, and nearby they found the body of Tessier, with bullet holes in his head, chest, and hips. Later, the body of Lackey, partially consumed by fire, was pulled from the ashes of the cabin.

The *Albuquerque Morning Democrat*, on March 9, told of some of the testimony presented to a coroner's jury.

> *A neighboring ranchman testified before the coroner's jury that six shots were heard in the direction of the cabin, at three o'clock on Friday afternoon, and that soon afterward four Mexicans were seen riding away from the place. Tessier was found a distance from the house with three bullet wounds, evidently fired from behind as he fled from the assassin. His hands were covered with wet meal, as if he had been mixing corn bread in the cabin when Lackey was killed and rushing out to escape from the murderers was shot in the back. The irons from Lackey's trunk were found in a disarranged condition in another part, where they were saved from burning by a log which fell on top of them, showing that the trunk had been rifled and pointing with unerring directness to the motive of robbery which moved the desperadoes to the terrible crime.*

The *Albuquerque Daily Citizen* also expressed the belief that robbery was the motive for the crime:

> *Those who are familiar with Mr. Lackey's circum-*

stances say that he was known to have constantly on his person, or in his cabin, a considerable sum of money, and certain circumstances which were laid before the coroner's jury lead to the belief that murder was committed for the purpose of robbery, a belief that is emphasized by the fact that so far as is known, neither of the murdered men had an enemy in the country, and they were especially friendly with their cowmen neighbors.

Both newspapers indicated that the coroner's jury had been given some significant facts about the crime that were to be kept secret, possibly the identities of some of the men seen riding away from the murder scene. The *Democrat*, on March 16, revealed that the identity of at least one of the suspects was known:

A gentleman from Las Vegas yesterday said that he had met Mr. Lackey at Las Vegas, where he sold a quantity of wool, three or four days before he was murdered at Buffalo Springs. He also said the murdered man formed the acquaintance of three Mexicans, one of whom is known, and that these three men are known to have followed Mr. Lackey to Buffalo Springs. The Mexicans were present when Mr. Lackey sold his wool, and knew that he received a considerable sum of money.

Two of the three suspects were arrested March 19 at Las Vegas. The arrests were reported March 21 in the *Las Vegas Optic*, which said:

Porfirio Trujillo, a worthless vagabond, and Ricardo Valdez, who has been driving Mike O'Keefe's coal wagon,

were arrested on the night before last by Sheriff Frank
Chavez, of Santa Fe, ostensibly on the charge of stealing
horses, but, in reality, for the murder of Messrs. Lackey
and Tesure [sic], at Antelope Springs, some days ago. The
fiendish fellows are now confined in the county jail here,
and are undoubtedly guilty of the horrible crime with
which they are charged.

The Las Vegas newspaper revealed that two Estancia Valley ranchers, Johnny Carroll and a Mr. Metcalfe, had picked up the trail of three horsemen shortly after the bodies of Lackey and Tessier had been found and had followed the trail north toward Las Vegas. Some soft snow on the ground had made it easy for the ranchers to follow the hoof prints for a distance of about thirty miles, but on the second night out the snow froze so hard that the prints could no longer be seen and the trail was lost.

The two ranchers continued on to Las Vegas, where they continued their search through saloons, gambling dens, and dance halls. They believed they knew the identities of the men they were looking for, and soon found two of them, both disguised, acting suspiciously and frequenting out-of-the-way places.

Carroll and Metcalfe sent for Santa Fe County Sheriff Frank Chavez, who hurried to Las Vegas to make the arrests, since the murders had occurred in his jurisdiction. The *Optic* said that one of the suspects was arrested in the J. Rosenwald and Co. store, and the other in the Masonic Cemetery. A search of the two prisoners revealed that Valdez had about $300 in cash on his person, while Trujillo had about $80 in cash and a new revolver.

The identity of the prime suspect in the murder case, however, was revealed in the same March 21 issue of the *Optic* in a letter to the editor signed "Traveler," written from the Santa Fe mining camp at Old Placers near Cerrillos on March 17:

> *A great deal of excitement prevails here over recent and most fiendish murders. A fellow named Mariano Leiba [sic] is suspected, he having made divers threats against the lives of our best citizens. It is thought that his capture will soon be effected. Citizens whose lives are in jeopardy are armed to the teeth and do not propose to be caught napping. With the exception of the presence in this vicinity of this desperado, the camp is peaceable and quiet, very few disturbances ever occurring.*

Marino Leyba, it was revealed in the newspapers later, following his release from prison had taken up abode in the Sandia Mountain village of San Antonio, not far from where Col. Potter had been murdered, and had been living up to his reputation as "The Sandia Mountain Desperado."

Albuquerque newspapers, in the spring of 1887, occasionally made note of Leyba's troublemaking, but, oddly enough, failed to connect him with the sensational Potter murder of seven years before. The *Albuquerque Morning Democrat*, for instance, published this brief item on March 27:

> *A Mexican named Merino [sic] Leyba tried to do the cowboy act at Golden the other day, and for a time he made things lively on the street with his pop, but some of the boys got after him and he took refuge in the hills. Sheriff Chavez went out to arrest him.*

Sheriff Chavez was convinced that Leyba had murdered Lackey and Tessier, and a $1,200 reward was offered for his capture. The sheriff sent deputies into the mining districts south of Santa Fe to search for Leyba, and on the morning of March 29, 1887, two of them encountered him on the road a few miles southwest of the mining town of Golden. The *New Mexican* at Santa Fe gave details of the encounter the next day:

> *Joaquin Montoya and Carlos Jacome, deputy sheriffs whom Sheriff Chavez had commissioned to "lay for" Mariano [sic] in and about Golden, were riding through the timber seven miles west of town at 9 o'clock yesterday morning, when Jacome spied their man coming down a mountain trail on horseback some 300 yards across the gulch and ahead of them. Jacome, who knew Mariano well, was commissioned by Montoya to ride ahead, ascertain positively if it was Mariano, and if so to engage him in conversation. Mariano had some months previously proposed to Jacome to go [to] Mexico and organize a banditti for operating on the border, and when the two men met and the usual* como le va, amigo *was passed, Jacome began discussing the proposition to go to the frontier, when Montoya came in sight, Mariano turned quickly to Jacome and said: "What are you doing here?" At the same instant he sprang from his horse and stood with his two hands across his stomach in such a position that his right hand rested on his six-shooter. He wore a belt, but had no scabbard, and the weapon was pushed through the belt and held in place immediately in front of him, after the most approved frontier style.*

He eyed Montoya suspiciously, and when the latter rode
up and extended his hand, Mariano grasped his revolver
with his right hand and proffered his left to greet Montoya.
Said the latter: "Don't draw your gun; give me your right
hand; we shall not harm you, but you must consider
yourself our prisoner."

At this Mariano uttered a vile oath, drew his six-
shooter, and each of the three men fired at the same
instant. Mariano fell forward between the two horses
dead. Only the three shots were fired. Mariano's bullet
grazed the left side of Montoya's head, and cut a three-inch
hole in his broad hat brim.

Ironically, Leyba met his death only a short distance from the spot
where Col. Charles Potter's body had been found six years before.

The two deputies obtained a wagon, placed Leyba's body in the
bed, and headed north for Santa Fe, pausing in Golden and other
mining communities along the way so that curious spectators
could view the remains of the once feared outlaw. In Santa Fe,
where the body was placed on a table in the jail, an estimated
2,000 persons went to the jail to view the remains.

The *Albuquerque Democrat*, on April 1, said:

The bandit Marino Leyba was buried in the Santa Fe
potter's field, after an inquest exonerating the officers who
killed him.

Some of Leyba's friends, contending that he had been shot to
death needlessly while shaking hands with one of the two deputies, eventually managed to have a murder indictment brought

against Joaquin Montoya. On June 15, 1889, Montoya stood trial in Albuquerque, and the jury promptly acquitted him. Montoya contracted pneumonia while in Albuquerque for the trial, and was taken home to Santa Fe, where he died eight days later at the age of thirty.

"He was a splendid specimen of physical manhood," the *New Mexican* said, "and malignant indeed must have been the disease that did its work in so short a time."

As late as the 1950s, an antique wooden cross, about three feet high and held upright by rocks, stood alongside the two-lane highway south of Golden, marking the spot where Marino Leyba met his death in 1887.

The Gus Mentzer Affair

RATON, June 26 – No town of New Mexico has had such excitement and frightful casualties for a long time, as Raton had yesterday afternoon. Gus Mensel, a gambler, is hanging at this time in front of the bank building. Hugh Eddleston, John Jackson and Justice Moulton are dead and Deputy Sheriff Granger is fatally wounded and C.L. Latimer slightly so.

Thus began an article in the *Santa Fe Daily Democrat* on June 27, 1882, describing a hectic and bloody afternoon in Raton the day before that was to prompt citizens of the northeastern New Mexico community to rise up and order all undesirables out of town.

Raton was only two years old in that early summer of 1882, and like most new railroad towns on the western frontier, it already had attracted more than its share of saloonkeepers, gamblers, thieves, confidence men, and drifters. The townsite, only a few years before, had been merely a camping place known as Willow Springs on the Mountain Branch of the Santa Fe Trail, a rest haven for travelers at the southern foot of Raton Pass, a high, winding, pine-covered passage through the mountains straddling the New Mexico-Colorado border.

Raton sprang into existence in the summer of 1880 when the Atchison, Topeka and Santa Fe Railroad, after building into New Mexico through Raton Pass, selected the site for the erection of a division headquarters, depot, and machine shop. This provided the nucleus for a business district that was quickly filled with

76

saloons, gambling halls, and brothels. The honky-tonk places were frowned upon but tolerated by most citizens of Raton, for they had spawned but little trouble during the first two years of the town's existence. Occasionally, when the citizens believed that things were getting out of hand, they would take the law into their own hands and make an example of some wrongdoer.

One such example was a drifter who gave his name as James J. Devine, and who was thought to be the J.J. Devine who had served in Company D of the Seventh Maine Volunteers, where he had been known as "the regimental thief." While living in Arizona, he had used the name James Johnson in Tucson and James Curran in Tombstone.

On Friday night, April 15, 1881, Devine cut up and pounded an unidentified old man, also a stranger in town, without any apparent provocation. The old man died of his wounds. The next night, Devine struck George Gartang on the head with a piece of wood and started to run away, but was overtaken by officers and hauled to jail. The *News and Press* at Cimarron, on April 28, 1881, told of the trouble Devine had caused in Raton that Saturday:

> *During the course of the evening it was found that he had been up to his meanness all day long, had beat up two innocent and quiet men, had run two or three Mexican families out of their houses and tried to commit a rape on a Mexican woman over 60 years old. Putting the whole thing together the people were thoroughly aroused.*

At about 9 o'clock that Saturday night, a large group of masked men appeared at the jail, covered the guard with their guns, led Devine from his cell with a rope around his neck and escorted him to a pine tree about a mile west of town. Sunday morning he was found hanging from a limb of the tree, a sight that attracted hundreds of men, women, and children to the spot and excited the curiosity of passengers aboard a Santa Fe train.

It was the Gus Mentzer affair, however, more than a year later, that caused outraged Raton citizens to take even more drastic action to rid the town of troublemakers.

New Mexico newspapers, in describing the tragic series of events that occurred on the afternoon and evening of June 25, 1882, used a variety of spellings in referring to the twenty-four-year-old gambler who caused the trouble, identifying him variously as Gus Mentzer, Mensel, Menser, Mensull, and Metzger. A variety of spellings also was used for the names of some of the victims and leading participants.

Conflicting accounts of Gus Mentzer's background also were published at the time. One version, published in the *Santa Fe Daily Democrat* on June 28, 1882, said that Mentzer, before arriving in Raton, had been known as the "Billy the Kid of Kansas," where he had been associated with the outlaws Dave Rudabaugh and Dutch Henry. "Their headquarters were at Salina," the article said, "and their deeds of crime were as numerous as their deeds of virtue were few."

The three men moved on to Great Bend, Kansas, the article said, adding:

> *There, their reputation as desperadoes was soon established and for a long time they were the terror of the town. They frequently would ride into saloons and shoot all the lights out, break all the glass and bar fixtures and wind up by making the frightened bar-keepers "Set 'em up."*

More probable is the story that Mentzer had arrived in Raton from Texas during the winter of 1881 to 1882 with a partner, William Burbridge, and had gone into the saloon business. The two had been partners in a saloon in Texas, and were forced to leave when Mentzer killed a man in a duel. The unidentified victim, it was said, had challenged Burbridge to a gun duel, and Burbridge had refused to accept the challenge. Mentzer, wanting to settle the quarrel and uphold the honor of his partner, offered to fight the duel for him. After a few drinks, Mentzer met the challenger in the street. They stepped off twenty paces, and Mentzer proved to be the better marksman.

This episode apparently marked the beginning of some ill feeling between the partners, Mentzer believing that Burbridge was not as grateful as he might have been for his fighting the duel for him.

Upon their arrival in Raton, the two partners opened and operated the Bank Exchange Saloon on what later was to become the 100 block of South First Street. Hot-tempered and a heavy drinker, the youthful Mentzer, who became known as "The Kid" in Raton, soon was causing much trouble at the gambling tables in the saloon, and continued to do so despite repeated warnings from his partner. Finally, Burbridge lost his patience with Mentzer, dissolved the partnership, and threw him out of the saloon.

Mentzer did not stay put, however. Late in the afternoon of June 25, 1882, he walked back into the Bank Exchange Saloon and demanded that Burbridge reinstate him as a partner, reminding him of the duel he had fought for him in Texas. Burbridge refused to renew the partnership, and Mentzer challenged him to step out into the street and settle their differences with pistols at twenty paces. Burbridge refused the challenge, and Mentzer decided to start the duel right then and there.

Customers ducked under tables as the two ex-partners fired away at one another, the bullets smashing into bottles, glasses, the water system at the bar, and the skylight overhead, but not causing bodily harm to anyone present. Mentzer fled from the saloon, followed by a crowd of angry citizens who had volunteered their services to Deputy Sheriff Pete Dolman, who was in the saloon and saw the shooting.

Mentzer soon was spotted hiding among some packing cases at the railroad depot, and the crowd gave chase but lost him just as the evening train pulled in. A search of the train failed to reveal him, and it was believed that he had escaped under cover of growing darkness into the woods across the tracks.

The crowd adjourned to the Jackson Saloon, where Deputy Dolman, a partner in the saloon with John Jackson, his name also given as S.H. Jackson, bought the drinks. After an hour of drinking in the Jackson Saloon, the crowd moved over to the Bank Exchange to survey the extensive damage. The group in the Bank Exchange soon was enlarged by others who began arriving for the opening of a show at the Music Hall over the saloon.

Suddenly, to the astonishment of all in the saloon, Mentzer entered the door, walked calmly to the bar, and ordered a drink. Recovering from their surprise, the men in the saloon surged forward toward Mentzer, and one of them, C.L. Latimer (or Lattimore) opened fire on him. Mentzer retaliated with a shot that put Latimer out of action, but which did not prove fatal.

Mentzer ran out the door and down the street, heading for the railroad depot again, the crowd in pursuit. He made his way to a switch engine in the railroad yards, which had been left there momentarily by an engineer, and which was all steamed up and ready to go.

Mentzer ran behind the locomotive and waited, gun in hand, for the first man to round the front of the engine. That man was Hugh Eddleston, who saw Mentzer and shouted "There he is" seconds before Mentzer shot him dead with a bullet through the throat.

As the crowd paused to examine the fallen Eddleston, Mentzer climbed up into the cab of the steamed-up switch engine and pulled the throttle, hoping to ride to safety. The engine failed to move, however, as the engineer had left the mechanism in a neutral position.

As Mentzer was working the throttle frantically in an effort to get the engine moving, another of his pursuers, saloon owner John Jackson, climbed up in the cab after him. Mentzer stuck his pistol into Jackson's stomach and fired, and his second victim fell dead from the cab.

Mentzer's gun was now empty, and the crowd of pursuers had little trouble entering the cab and overpowering him. He was taken to the Moulton House Hotel and placed in the custody of a deputy sheriff named Granger, although some accounts gave his surname as Bergen or Jones.

The deputy was just starting to place some shackles on Mentzer's legs when he was approached by Harvey Moulton, a Raton justice of the peace who was a partner in the Moulton House with the late Hugh Eddleston. Moulton demanded that the deputy turn Mentzer over to him at once for a quick hanging, and the deputy refused.

Justice Moulton started for the prisoner, and Granger, sworn to protect the prisoner, shot Moulton, who lived just long enough to get off one shot that was to prove fatal to the deputy sheriff.

Mentzer, now left unguarded, slipped off a shoe, removed a shackle that had been fastened to one leg, stepped over the body of Moulton and the prone figure of Granger, and ran out the hotel

Lynched by angry citizens, Gus Mentzer, a young gambler, hangs from a sign post in front of the Raton Bank following a wild afternoon and evening during which four other Raton citizens were killed. (Courtesy Andrew Gregg)

door. The crowd outside, seeing the escaping prisoner, gave chase once more.

Mentzer darted into the Williams Butcher Shop, where the surprised butcher took one look at him and exclaimed, "Why Gus — we've been looking for you all evening."

The crowd surged into the butcher shop, and the butcher turned Mentzer over to them, handing them a rope at the same time. A noose was placed around Mentzer's neck, and he was led out into the street, cursing and fighting.

The citizens paused in front of the Raton Bank on First Street under the bank sign, which was about ten feet above the wooden sidewalk, and which was held in place against the building on one side and by a tall post on the other. The rope was thrown up over the bank sign, and Mentzer was swung into the air, but only for a moment. The sign, poorly supported, came crashing down, and Mentzer with it.

The mob then boosted a boy to the top of the signpost, and he fastened one end of the rope to the top. Mentzer was then pulled by his neck to the top of the post, where he died after a brief struggle.

Mentzer was left hanging to the signpost all night, during which time somebody climbed up and took $300 out of his pocket. When he was cut down the next day, a deck of playing cards was found in one of his pockets, and the cards were distributed around as souvenirs.

Two Mexican citizens, given one dollar to dig a grave and bury Mentzer in a wooden box, got tired of digging a hole big enough for the box, buried the gambler without the box, took the box home, and made a cupboard out of it, the newspapers reported.

The *Las Vegas Optic*, on June 29, told of the aftermath:

RATON, N.M., *June 29 – The funeral of Edelson [sic] and Moulton took place at 3 o'clock yesterday afternoon and was attended by fully one thousand people. The procession was led by the Raton band.*

Raton is rid of gamblers and gambling dens, and it will be of houses of prostitution from the first of July on; but, oh! what a price she paid for their riddance.

At the open air indignation meeting a committee was appointed to draw up resolutions concerning gambling, prostitutes and etc., and they are ironclad and will be supported by the people.

A Raton citizens' committee, appointed to take steps "to prevent further disturbances," issued a report signed by committee members J.K. Para, J.R. Givens, Cosby Duncan, M.A. McMartin, E. Parsons, A.H. Jones, J. Osfield, Jr., John Jelfs, and D.F. Reed, which read:

Whereas, our growing and prosperous little city of late has been the scene of great bloodshed which resulted in the deaths of several of our most prominent citizens, and,

Whereas, the law-abiding citizens of Raton now being aroused to full realization of the necessity for immediate action and with a determination to protect the lives and property of our citizens and uphold the hitherto untarnished name of our city, therefore be it

Resolved that hereafter no public gambling of any sort whatsoever shall be allowed in any saloon or other place of business in this town.

Resolved that hereafter no public dance hall shall be

permitted to exist anywhere within the limits of the town.

Resolved that our mutual protection demands that we should be organized, for in union there is strength, and concert of action is needed to forever sever from our midst the destroying elements of peace and happiness. And be it further

Resolved that in order to take the first proper step in this matter and show that we are determined and mean just what we say, all professional gamblers, footpads, thieves, cappers, dance hall men, bunk men and all those who have no visible means of support are hereby notified and publicly warned to leave this town within 48 hours from 12 o'clock noon the first day of July, 1882, under penalty of incurring the just wrath of an indignant and outraged people.

The notice was published in full in the *Raton Comet*.

Years later, it was said, a sister of Gus Mentzer arrived in Raton, had the remains of her late brother exhumed from an unmarked grave, and shipped them out on an eastbound train for reburial.

Photograph of Joel Fowler, "the human exterminator," taken in Socorro by Joseph E. Smith, pioneer Socorro photographer, and a member of the Vigilantes who lynched Fowler in 1884. (Author's collection)

Joel Fowler:
"The Human Exterminator"

Toward the end of his short and violent career in the early 1880s, Joel A. Fowler was referred to as "the human exterminator" in New Mexico newspapers, some claiming that he had killed as many as twenty-six men, not including an unknown number of victims in Texas. Some said he was mean and ill-tempered only when drunk, others that he was mean and ill-tempered all the time, drunk or sober.

Montague Stevens, an Englishman who knew Fowler when both were ranching in Socorro County in the early 1880s, recalled seventy years later (at the age of ninety-four) that his former neighbor had an unsavory reputation as a deceitful killer.

"When Fowler had a bone to pick with a man, he would sometimes corner him in a crowded saloon, ask for a chaw of tobacco, then shoot him when the man obligingly reached for his hip pocket," Stevens said in a 1953 interview. "Then he would turn to the bystanders and ask, 'You saw him reach for a gun, didn't you?' and all would agree that they did, not daring to argue with him."

Another of Fowler's favorite tricks, Stevens said, was to follow and murder some of those who bought steers from his ranch, take the steers back to the ranch, and sell them again to another unsuspecting buyer. Stories also were told that Fowler sometimes murdered his hired hands on pay day to avoid giving them their wages.

Although much that was said and written about Fowler undoubtedly was greatly exaggerated, contemporary news accounts of his escapades prove that he was a dangerous man, and one to be avoided if at all possible. Those who knew him described him as a short, slender man, with brown hair and brown eyes, making up in bravado what he lacked in physical stature.

A Santa Fe newspaper reported in 1884 that Fowler was born in Indiana in 1849, which seems to be the case, although an Albuquerque newspaper said that the Santa Fe paper "was gulled in the most unusual way," claiming that Fowler actually was born and reared in Mississippi. There is some evidence that Fowler's father was an Indiana lawyer, and that both his parents were respectable, well-educated citizens.

As a young man, in the 1870s, Fowler traveled to Fort Worth, Texas, to live with his father's brother, a prominent political leader who served as a senator in the Texas Legislature. While there, it was reported, Fowler met and married a young woman, shot her lover when he found the two together, and embarked on the outlaw trail in Texas as a rustler and stagecoach robber.

While little is known about his early life in Indiana (or Mississippi) and Texas, most of his activities in New Mexico are fairly well documented, beginning with his appearance in Las Vegas in the summer of 1879. Fowler apparently arrived in Las Vegas at about the same time the Atchison, Topeka and Santa Fe Railroad reached the community to create a new and boisterous business district in the vicinity of the new depot. Fowler operated a dance hall and variety theater on Sixth Street, near the railroad tracks, and married one of his dance hall girls, referred to only as Josie, whom a Santa Fe newspaper later described as "his equal in grit and general cussedness."

After about a six-month stay in Las Vegas, Joel and Josie moved on down the new railroad line to Santa Fe, where he operated the Texas Saloon, on San Francisco Street just off the main plaza, and the nearby Theatre Comique, the only variety theater in Santa Fe at the time.

Fowler created a noisy but harmless disturbance in front of his saloon on the morning of February 27, 1880, the details of which were published the following day in the *Daily New Mexican* at Santa Fe:

> *Joe Fowler is the proprietor of the Texas Saloon, and is also, which is a wonderful fact, a drinking man. Joe is not by profession a "bad man from Bitter Creek," on the contrary, when his deeds are not inspired by whiskey, a pleasanter or a squarer man cannot be found.*
>
> *But as all men are mortal, Joe got drunk Thursday night, and staid [sic] in that condition until Friday morning, when he took his stand upon San Francisco Street, near the plaza, and with a breech-loading shotgun, and a full supply of cartridges, bid defiance to all.*
>
> *The time was between seven and eight, and when Fowler first made his appearance upon the street, it was crowded with people. However, this was soon changed, for when Fowler pointed his gun down the street, without seeming to care whether he hit a lamp post or an Apache, the just before busy street became as deserted as a graveyard, and as far as the eye could reach not a person was in sight.*
>
> *Having thus cleared the neighborhood, Fowler began to load and discharge his weapon with extreme precision and rapidity, at one time aiming at the sun, at another at the new tank at the depot, occasionally varying the performance by putting the muzzle of the gun in his mouth and letting off a whoop which was heard by Manzanares and there mistaken for a locomotive whistle.*
>
> *Finally, after Fowler had held his position for about*

half an hour, a hundred or so of the boldest spirits in town held a council in Keyser's Saloon, and after hastily adopting resolutions of respect to the memory of those who might fall in the attack, boldly advanced upon the enemy.

In the meantime, a Mexican passed along the street on the side on which the man and the shot-gun were, and just as Fowler finished a wild and blood-curdling invocation to the pictured bills upon the wall of the Theatre Comique and discharged the gun as a sort of "Amen," he was leaped upon by the pedestrian and borne to the ground, where he lay panting and quoting all the maledictions from Shakespeare he could remember until the army came rushing down and secured him.

He was immediately taken to jail, that is, as immediately as was possible under the circumstance. He struggled desperately, and when the jail was reached, he was carried in bodily while the procession followed behind bearing as trophies his coat, hat, pants, boots and suspenders.

Then he was put into a cell, and jailer Silva sat upon him and sang a lullaby to quiet his nerves.

The *New Mexican,* along with many other New Mexico newspapers, often published Fowler's given name as Joe, rather than Joel. The "Manzanares" referred to in the article was a small railroad village about fifteen miles south of Santa Fe.

After about six months in Santa Fe, Fowler and his wife pulled up stakes and headed south for White Oaks, a new and bustling gold and silver mining town in Lincoln County, where they opened another saloon. Fowler figured prominently in a violent episode, although not of his making, that rocked the mining town soon after his arrival.

On May 31, 1880, a small group of prospectors camped at a spring just outside White Oaks, and during the afternoon two of them, Joseph Askew and Virgil Cullom, rode into town to have their horses shod. They made the rounds of the saloons while waiting for the blacksmith to complete his work, and by the time their horses were ready they were roaring drunk.

Mounting their horses, they galloped through the center of town, firing their pistols indiscriminately at stores, houses, and signboards, some of the shots passing dangerously close to women and children. Armed citizens came running from all directions, formed a line of battle in the center of a street, and the town constable called on the two horsemen to surrender.

Askew and Cullom wheeled their horses around and fired several shots at the citizen army. The citizens answered with a volley of from thirty to forty shots, and Askew fell from his horse with a bullet wound in his right arm. Cullom rode quickly to his camp, informed his comrades that Askew had been "killed," and asked them to follow him as he was going to return to where Askew had fallen "and die by his side."

The *Las Vegas Optic*, in publishing an account of the affray a few days later, said in part:

> *The constable, in the interim, had ordered Joe Fowler and Dave Riverhouse to follow and bring them back to town. Fowler and Riverhouse found Askew on the ground with his arm lying beneath him across his back. They got down and straightened his arm in place, put his hat under his head and went in pursuit of Cullom.*
>
> *They met him on the return, when Fowler, at a short*

turn around the hill on the road, met Cullom with pistol dropped on him, jumped down behind his horse with Winchester across saddle, drew on him and demanded his surrender three times as quickly as he could, and fired, the ball passing through Cullom's right lung.

Cullom still had his pistol drawn, Fowler told him to drop his gun or he would have to hurt him. This he did reluctantly and slowly when Fowler told him he was his prisoner and had to return with him to town.

Cullom's friends told him that he was not able; that he was shot. Fowler told him he could ride his horse and he would walk, when he noticed him turn pale in the face and fainted from internal hemorrhage. Cullom died at 6 o'clock the next morning.

Meanwhile, when the street fighting was just getting under way, William H. Hudgens ran into Fowler's saloon and asked the bartender, William Calhoun, to give him a gun. Calhoun handed Hudgens a gun, saying that it was not his, but that he could use it.

At that moment, Alex Colvin stepped in the door, told Hudgens that the gun was his, and took it from him, saying, "Nobody is going to use my gun." The bartender told Colvin that the gun was not his, and Colvin admitted that this was true, but said that it belonged to his partner and that no one was to use it.

Hudgens asked Colvin to go out and help arrest the two men who were shooting up the town, and Colvin replied that he would not. Hudgens became angry and told Colvin that he was no better than the men who were shooting at women and children. Both left the saloon.

A short while later, the wounded Askew was brought into town and placed in a tent, where a crowd gathered around him. Hudgens was in the tent when a Texan, I.T. "West" McCray, entered the tent and called him aside.

"That young man (Colvin) you were talking to is my brother, and you insulted him," McCray said, "and when you insult him, you insult me."

Hudgens replied that he meant what he said to Colvin, because he felt that it was every man's duty to stop the shooting in the streets.

McCray asked Hudgens if he wanted to fight him, and Hudgens, supposing that he was challenging him to a fist fight, began to unbuckle his pistol belt.

"I will shoot you — twenty steps," McCray said, pulling his pistol and firing at Hudgens.

Hudgens, seeing McCray reaching for his gun, quickly drew his own weapon, fired at McCray, jumped to one side and continued firing, hitting McCray in the body five times. McCray fired five shots at Hudgens, two of them after he had fallen to the ground, and all of them missing their mark. He died as he fired his last shot.

Hudgens asked Colvin if the dead man was his brother, and Colvin replied that he was not, although they had been passing as brothers. He told Hudgens that if he had taken McCray alive he could have collected a $1,600 reward, as he was wanted for the killing of a U.S. marshal in the Cherokee Nation, Indian territory.

A jury acquitted Hudgens on grounds of justifiable homicide. Askew, who recovered, was from Texas, and his deceased companion, Cullom, from Tennessee. Newspapers made no mention of any charges being brought against Fowler in connection with his killing of Cullom.

* * *

Joel Fowler apparently prospered in the saloon business, for in 1881 he was firmly established as the owner of a cattle ranch in Socorro County, more than one hundred miles northwest of White Oaks. Called the Alamo Ranch, it was at Bear Spring, about thirty-five miles west of Socorro, the county seat, and north of where the cattle shipping town of Magdalena soon was to be established.

Periodically, Fowler would leave his ranch to embark on drunken sprees in Socorro, terrorizing saloon customers by shooting at their feet, or making them stand on their heads in corners. These drunken escapades even took him as far as Silver City, more than one hundred miles to the south. The *Silver City Enterprise* reported in 1883 that Fowler "is a dare-devil fellow, and the only man that bluffed John Gilmo while marshal of this city."

Complaining that he was losing stock from his range, and often accusing his neighbors of appropriating cattle that belonged to him, Fowler did not hesitate to take to the trail of cattle rustlers, or in some instances, if Montague Stevens's recollections were accurate, cattle buyers. One of his forays against cattle rustlers, during the second week of December in 1881, was the subject of some rather sketchy and sometimes contradictory articles in several New Mexico newspapers at the time.

Three rustlers, identified as Jim Greathouse, Jim Finley, and "a fellow named Forrest," stole forty head of cattle from Fowler's ranch and drove them south to the mining town of Georgetown, near Silver City, where they were sold. Fowler and his chief herder, identified in the newspapers as Jim Ike (possibly Ake), followed the trail of the rustlers south, and encountered the three, who were heading back north, at an adobe building that formerly had served as stagecoach station, at or near the abandoned Ojo

Caliente Indian Agency. The three drew their guns when approached, but Fowler allayed their suspicions by telling them that he had just murdered a man in Socorro and wanted their help in moving his cattle out of the region.

All five started north together, one newspaper account said, and while pausing for lunch at a natural landmark known as Point of Rocks at the north edge of the San Mateo Mountains, Greathouse drew his gun on Fowler, and said, "I know your racket, but it won't work." Fowler, who was holding a double-barreled shotgun, quickly blasted both Greathouse and Forrest to death, and Ike killed Finley.

Of the three alleged rustlers, Greathouse, known as "Whiskey Jim" for his career of selling whiskey to Indians, was the most notorious. Until a year before, Greathouse, in partnership with Fred Kuch, had been operating a ranch with store and way station about forty miles north of White Oaks, on the road to Las Vegas, where he was accused of harboring and working hand-in-glove with various outlaws, including Billy the Kid. A White Oaks posse, led by William Hudgens, burned the ranch buildings to the ground on November 28, 1880, one day after the posse had fought a gun battle at the ranch with the Kid and four of his outlaw companions, during which Jimmy Carlyle, a popular White Oaks blacksmith, was killed.

Fowler and Ike, leaving their three victims on the ground where they had fallen, rode on north to a Gallinas Mountains ranch and sawmill owned by Dr. C.F. Blackington, one of Fowler's neighbors. Believing that the three rustlers were employed by Blackington, as they had been seen hanging around his place, Fowler accused his neighbor of complicity in the cattle theft and forced him and a companion, a man named West, to accompany him and his chief herder to Socorro.

At dusk, as the five were riding through a mountain canyon just west of Socorro, Blackington suddenly put spurs to this horse, the fleetest in the group, and disappeared into the mountains. Fowler and Ike, after a short and vain pursuit, continued on into Socorro with West and delivered him to jail. Fowler obtained warrants charging both Blackington and West with complicity in cattle rustling.

The next day, Blackington straggled into Socorro on foot, saying that he had ridden his horse until it had dropped dead, and had then walked fourteen miles to town through a winter storm, causing him to suffer "lung fever." He filed counter-charges against Fowler, accusing him of unlawfully depriving him of his liberty. During a brief hearing in Socorro, all parties apparently settled their differences amicably, and it was reported that Fowler and Blackington were seen on the streets arm in arm. Five men from Socorro held an inquest over the bodies of the three rustlers at Point of Rocks, apparently ruling that their deaths constituted justifiable homicide.

In the months that followed, rumors surfaced periodically that Fowler had been killed by rustlers, or other enemies, but they proved to be just rumors. The details of one such attempt on Fowler's life were published in the *Albuquerque Daily Democrat* on September 19, 1883:

> *Monday morning (September 15) at Alamo Ranch in the Gallinas Mountains, a cattleman named Joe Fowler started on a cattle hunt with several men. After leaving the ranch he found that one of the men, called Pony, was a brother of the man named Forrest whom he had killed the*

year before. He discharged Pony, who returned to Socorro, and with a desperado named Butcher Knife Bill, returned to the Alamo Ranch with the intention to kill Fowler.

As Fowler was returning from the hunt, he saw Pony and Bill at the house. They drew their revolvers, Bill firing at Fowler. Fowler drew a shotgun and killed Bill instantly. Pony ran behind the house, firing at Fowler five times. He then ran into the house.

A man named McGee, coming up and hearing of the trouble, went to the door of the house and called to Pony to come out of the house. Receiving no reply, he broke the door and looked in, when Pony shot him through the head, killing him instantly.

Fowler then asked Pony to come out and fight it out with him. Pony refused to do so, and Fowler set fire to the house to drive him out, when Pony shot himself through the head.

The three men were buried on the spot. Butcher Knife Bill was a gambler and a bad man. Pony was from Fort Griffin, Texas. The man McGee was a good, peaceful man and respected highly.

Fowler came to Socorro and had a hearing before Judge Beall. A man named Turk, who had some trouble with Fowler some time ago, met Fowler this morning and renewed the quarrel with him, when Fowler beat him over the head with a six-shooter, badly injuring Turk.

Other newspaper accounts of the fight at the Alamo Ranch agreed in the principal details, with added information that the house Fowler burned was known as the Stone House and was occupied by McGee, that Butcher Knife Bill's name was William Childes, and that with the deaths of Butcher Knife Bill and Pony Forrest, it made six men Fowler had killed in the previous two years.

"The statement that Pony shot himself is regarded as doubtful, to say the least," some newspapers reported.

Joel Fowler was in high spirits when he and his wife arrived in Socorro from the ranch on the afternoon of November 6, 1883. He had just sold his ranch to J.D. Reed of Fort Worth, Texas, for $52,500, and after depositing the proceeds in a Socorro bank, he went to the office of the *Socorro Sun* and placed a notice in the newspaper that he had sold his ranch, was leaving for Texas, and that all those holding claims against him should present them to the bank.

Fowler then decided that it was his night to howl, and howl he did. While his wife remained at the two-story Grand Central Hotel, he began making the rounds of the Socorro saloons, drinking heavily at each stop, and, with a six-shooter in each hand, firing bullets at the feet of customers, including a clergyman and a justice of the peace, and forcing others to stand on their heads.

The *Socorro Sun* reported the next day that by morning Fowler "was in a state of crazy intoxication," adding:

> *About daylight, he reached the Grand Central Hotel and carried things with a high hand. With two pistols in his hands, he terrorized those who happened to be there. Mr. Dorman came in and was forced to dance, was slapped in the face several times and finally struck on the head with a revolver. This lasted until about 6 o'clock.*

At about this time, several men in the hotel bar grabbed Fowler and began wresting the guns out of his hands. Fowler, in a fit of rage, drew a dirk and plunged it to the hilt into the breast of one of them, James E. Cale, a visiting clothing salesman, who fell to the floor mortally wounded. Cale was carried to a hotel room, and four men overpowered Fowler and took him to jail. Cale died hours later after signing this affidavit:

> *J.E. Cale, being duly sworn, disposes and says: That he is 36 years old, and was born at Jerico, Vermont; was at the Grand Central Hotel on the night of the 6th of November; Joel A. Fowler was with me; I was holding him off from a stockman when he struck me with a Spanish dagger; I had no trouble with Fowler; I was taking a gun from Fowler; he was drunk and swinging around; was afraid Fowler would shoot somebody else.*

Cale, who previously had sold some clothing to Fowler and who considered him a friend, was buried in the church cemetery at Socorro.

Fowler quickly was indicted on a charge of first-degree murder. With money in the bank, he hired two prominent lawyers, Thomas B. Catron of Santa Fe and Neill B. Field of Socorro, to defend him, Catron reportedly receiving $5,000 for his services.

On December 8, 1883, a month after Cale's death, a District Court jury in Socorro found Fowler guilty of first-degree murder, and Judge Joseph Bell pronounced the death sentence, ordering that Fowler be hanged and setting the execution date for January 4, 1884. Fowler's attorneys lost a bid for a new trial and filed notice that they would appeal the case to the New Mexico Territorial Supreme Court, thus setting aside the early execution date.

Fowler remained in jail pending action by the higher court, which due to scheduling technicalities would not be able to consider the appeal for at least one year.

*   *   *

Pete Simpson, sheriff of Socorro County, had serious doubts that his prisoner could be confined safely in the Socorro County jail for the year it would take before the Supreme Court could consider his case. On one hand, the sheriff feared that Fowler would engineer a jailbreak, possibly with the help of some of his cowboy friends; and on the other, he feared that the Socorro Vigilantes would storm the jail and lynch the prisoner.

In January, Simpson made his concerns known to Governor Lionel A. Sheldon in Santa Fe, and the governor ordered members of the Socorro Militia to guard the jail. A short while later, the governor rescinded his order, saying the Territory could not afford to keep paying the militia guards, and offering instead to confine Fowler in a Santa Fe jail if Socorro County would bear the expenses. The offer was declined.

Fowler, chained to a large rock in a basement jail cell, had serious worries of his own. He complained that he had spent $13,000 in legal expenses for his defense, and would not spend a cent more. His discomfort increased when his wife visited him in jail and told him what she and a new boyfriend were going to do with the rest of his money when he was gone.

Reports circulated that Fowler had confessed to four murders in Socorro County of which the authorities had been unaware, that eighteen graves of unknown victims were found on his cattle ranges, and that unscrupulous politicians had hired him to kill their enemies. A jail guard said he overheard Fowler and another prisoner named Barnes talking about their days as stagecoach robbers in Texas, adding that he heard Barnes taunt Fowler about his killing of a man in Texas for twenty-five cents.

Of greatest concern to Fowler was his fear of mob action against him by the Socorro Vigilantes, a secretive organization of about two hundred Socorro citizens that had in the past three years dragged five prisoners from the jail and hanged them. He offered his guards large sums of money to smuggle him a gun, and when this failed, he sent word to some of his former friends in Texas, asking them to come to his rescue.

The Socorro Vigilantes, known officially as the Socorro Committee of Safety, had been organized in January, 1881, to administer "speedy and severe punishment" to all those who violated "the peace and good order" of the community. The punishment included hanging for the most serious crimes, flogging for less serious crimes, and an escort out of town for troublesome transients. The vigilante membership consisted entirely of non-Hispanic latecomers to the old community that was populated principally by Spanish-speaking Hispanic settlers.

The founder and leader of the Committee of Safety was Col. Ethan W. Eaton, a prominent Socorro citizen who had mining and cattle interests in the vicinity, and who had served as an officer with the New Mexico Volunteers during the Civil War and Indian campaigns in New Mexico during the 1860s. Born in 1827 in Montgomery County, New York, Eaton had worked as a store clerk, factory worker, and canal boat operator in his native state before joining the California gold rush in 1849 and traveling overland only as far as New Mexico, where he decided to settle.

The Socorro Vigilantes carried out their first hanging during the early morning hours of March 9, 1881. Their victim was Tom

Gordon, described in a Socorro newspaper as a "gunman, gambler and frequenter of low places." On the evening of November 11, 1880, Gordon had entered the Monarch Saloon in Socorro and shot to death J.C. Thomas, the town marshal, who unlike most western marshals attempted to protect himself by running behind the bar and hiding behind the bartender.

The deceased town marshal was unpopular among the Hispanic residents of Socorro, having been accused of firing a shotgun blast at a political procession and wounding five "Mexicans," as New Mexico Hispanics were called at the time. Friends of Gordon hurried him a few miles south to the village of Luis Lopez, where an Hispanic justice of the peace found him not guilty of murder, following a brief hearing during which no prosecution witnesses were called.

Gordon left Socorro soon after the killing, and when seen back in town early in March, 1881, officers and citizens gave chase. Gordon climbed into a boxcar of a northbound freight train just as it was leaving the depot, and a short while later his pursuers boarded a northbound passenger train, catching up with the freight train at La Joya, about twenty miles north of Socorro, where it had paused on a siding. The Socorro citizens concealed themselves on the freight train and rode it north to Albuquerque, where they apprehended Gordon as he emerged from the boxcar.

Gordon was escorted the seventy-five miles back to Socorro that afternoon, March 8, and placed in jail, but his stay there was a short one, as the Vigilantes took him from the jail shortly after midnight and hanged him from a nearby corral gatepost.

Hanged from the same gatepost three weeks later, on the night of March 30, 1881, was Onofre Baca, a young member of a prominent and influential Hispanic family of Socorro, who with his two brothers, or possibly cousins, Antonio and Abran Baca, was accused of shooting to death A.M. Conklin, editor of the *Socorro Sun*, on the previous Christmas Eve.

Conklin, who was born in Ohio and reared in Indiana, had established a newspaper known as the *Advance* in Albuquerque early in 1880. In June of that year, he loaded his equipment on a flatboat on the Rio Grande and floated it downstream to Socorro to found the *Socorro Sun*. The thirty-nine-year-old editor was shot down on the evening of December 24, 1880, as he and his wife emerged from a Protestant chapel following a Christmas Eve program. The shooting followed a slight altercation in the chapel between Conklin and the three Bacas when Conklin angrily shoved Antonio Baca's booted feet to the floor when he ignored a request to remove them from the bench in front of him.

The three Bacas left the chapel, and waited outside in the darkness until the program was over and people were leaving. Shots rang out, and Conklin fell dying into the arms of the Rev. Thomas Harwood. The three Bacas were seen riding off on horseback. A justice of the peace ruled the next day that Conklin had died of a pistol shot "from the hands of one of the Bacas."

The killing of a prominent non-Hispanic ("American") citizen by members of a prominent Hispanic ("Mexican") family threatened ethnic warfare in the community and led to the formation of the Socorro Committee of Safety when Hispanic county officials hesitated to take action against the Bacas. An "American" mob converged on the home of Antonio Baca on December 28 and demanded his surrender, threatening to dynamite the house, then captured him when he was discovered leaving the house disguised in female clothing.

Confined temporarily in the one-story Park Hotel, the prisoner produced a pistol and became involved in a shoot-out with a guard, Jack Ketchum, in which Baca was killed and Ketchum wounded. Onofre and Abran Baca left town, heading south for El Paso, Texas, and rewards were offered for their apprehension.

Hoping to collect the reward money was Sgt. James M. Gillett of the Texas Rangers, who learned that Abran Baca was hiding out at the home of his uncle, José Baca, in Ysleta, Texas, on the outskirts of El Paso. He arrested him and another young man, whom he believed was Onofre, and took them to Socorro. Abran was jailed to await trial, but the other man was not Onofre, and was released.

In March, Sgt. Gillett learned that Onofre Baca was clerking in a store in Zaragoza, Mexico, a few miles south of the Rio Grande, which formed the international border, and about fifteen miles southeast of El Paso. In a highly unorthodox manner, and in violation of international law, Gillett and another Texas Ranger, George Loyd, rode horseback across the river into Mexico, kidnaped Baca from his place of employment, and raced with him back to the border, chased by a posse of armed Mexican citizens. Splashing across the Rio Grande, just ahead of their pursuers, the rangers reached Texas soil with their prisoner.

Gillett took Onofre aboard a northbound train and started for Santa Fe, where he was ordered to deliver him, but when the train stopped at Socorro on the night of March 30, a large group of Socorro Vigilantes boarded the train, forcibly relieved Gillett of his prisoner, and took him to jail.

The next morning, Onofre Baca was found hanging from the gatepost. Later that year, Abran Baca stood jury trial on the murder charge, was found not guilty, but was ordered by the Vigilantes to leave Socorro forever.

The Vigilantes, or as the Hispanics called them, *Los Colgadores*, The Hangers, carried out a double lynching during the early morning hours of October 7, 1881. The newspapers identified the two victims as "Frenchy" Elmoreau and "Butch" Clark, accused of being among four men who had held up and robbed the Browne and Manzanares store at Lamy, near Santa Fe, on September 23, escaping with cash and a large amount of merchandise and driving off with the store manager's wagon and team of horses.

The two, arrested in Socorro on the morning of October 6, were taken to jail. The Vigilantes took the two from the jail during the night, stood them on an adobe wall in what was becoming known as "Death Alley" just off the main plaza, placed nooses around their necks, fastened the ropes to an overhanging branch of a cottonwood tree, and pushed them off the wall. When found by citizens at sunrise, they were hanging from the tree limb, still chained together, with a sign on their backs reading, "This is the way Socorro treats horse thieves and foot pads."

One other victim, identified as "Juan Alari, a Mexican gambler who confessed to raping a nine-year-old white girl," was hanged by the Vigilantes in Death Alley.

*   *   *

Joel Fowler, languishing in his jail cell, was certain that the Socorro Vigilantes had selected him to be their sixth hanging victim, and were only waiting for an opportunity to make their move. His uncle in Fort Worth, State Sen. Fowler, warned Col. Eaton that he was holding him responsible for his nephew's safety. A group of cowboys and rustlers, led by "Texas Ed" Rousseau, arrived in town to see what they could do for their friend.

The Vigilantes believed their opportunity had come on the

night of January 22, 1884. Sheriff Pete Simpson, who had sworn to protect his prisoner, had left town to deliver two captured train robbers to Silver City. At midnight, a small militia guard at the jail was relieved. What happened next was revealed in New Mexico newspapers the following day:

> SOCORRO, *January 23 – Between the hours of 12 last night and 1 this morning, about 200 men surrounded the jail and demanded of the guards the surrender of Fowler. The guards making no resistance, the citizens proceeded to force the door leading to Fowler's cell.*
>
> *This was accomplished in a very few moments, and Fowler was taken out, crying murder at the top of his voice. He was taken to a tree about 200 yards west of the jail and hung. The citizens quietly dispersed to their respective homes.*
>
> *Owing to the extreme secrecy observed by everyone, we are unable to obtain further details.*

A few additional details of the lynching were published the same day in the *Las Vegas Optic*:

> *Fowler loudly called on Heaven to protect him, when some wag in the crowd called out: "It's a cold night for angels, Joel. Better call on someone nearer town."*
>
> *He then protested that law-abiding citizens should protect him. The same voice replied: "You are in the hands of law-abiding citizens, Mr. Fowler, and they will see that you get your just deserts."*

Montague Stevens, who witnessed the hanging, said that Fowler was taken to a cottonwood tree in Death Alley, a noose was placed around his neck, and the rope looped up over the limb of the tree. The lynchers then attempted to pull Fowler into the air, Stevens said, and when it was noticed that his toes were still touching the ground, some of the men threw their weight against his legs, completing the strangulation.

As Fowler was being carried to the cottonwood tree, his Socorro lawyer, Neill B. Field, stood on an adobe wall and shouted that if his client was a victim of mob rule, he would leave Socorro forever. The lynchers paid no attention to him. The lawyer was good to his word, as the *Albuquerque Daily Democrat* reported two days later:

> *Neill B. Field, a lawyer of Socorro who has always occupied a leading position in that burg, has gravitated to the center, and we welcome him as a new-made accession to the social residents of Albuquerque. This is a Field for enterprise.*

It was reported that Sheriff Simpson, returning to Socorro by train shortly after the hanging, sat down and cried upon learning that the prisoner had been lynched. He cut Fowler's body down at 8 o'clock that morning, and a coroner's jury was summoned, which after due deliberation issued this report:

> *We, the undersigned, justice of the peace and jury, who sat upon the inquest held the twenty-third day of January, 1884, on the body of Joel A. Fowler, deceased, found in Precinct No. 1, of the County of Socorro, find that deceased came to his death by strangulation, at the hands of persons unknown to the jury, as far as could be ascertained.*

(Signed) W.E. Kelly, justice of the peace for Precinct 1, A.J. McClusky, Thomas E. Simmons, J.L. Leavitt, G.L. Hoyt, J.H. Hilton, John Egger.

Chester D. Potter, a young member of the Vigilantes who wrote his recollections thirty years later, said that all those who signed the verdict actually were present at the hanging. In strange contrast to all newspaper accounts at the time, Potter wrote that Fowler appeared calm and collected at the time of his hanging, even laughing and joking with his captors. It also was Potter's recollection that Fowler's wife was named Belle, rather than Josie.

"Texas Ed" Rousseau and his boys threatened to "shoot up" Socorro in revenge for Fowler's lynching, but the Vigilantes escorted them to the railroad depot and placed them aboard an outbound train. A report circulated that Rousseau drew $2,500 from the bank before leaving town.

Fowler's last request was that his body be sent to his uncle in Fort Worth for burial. Before shipment, the body was first displayed to hundreds of Socorro residents, attired in a new suit and new boots Mrs. Fowler had bought for the occasion. Montague Stevens recalled that those passing by the bier could plainly see the price of the new boots, $10, chalked on the soles.

Mrs. Fowler drew what remained of her late husband's money from the bank and left town with his remains. The *Silver City Enterprise* reported on July 4, 1884, that she was living in Butte City, Montana, adding "She is well known in this city (Silver City), having dealt monte here. She went through with all the money her husband left her." The same newspaper reported on October 3, 1884, that "Mrs. Joel Fowler is again dealing monte in Santa Fe."

Finally, on March 14, 1885, the *Albuquerque Evening Democrat* published this brief item:

> *Jack Acres, a well known sporting man, has gone to Socorro where he will open the finest club rooms in the territory. He is accompanied by his wife, formerly Mrs. Joe Fowler.*

The hanging of Joel Fowler proved to be the last hanging carried out by the Socorro Committee of Safety.

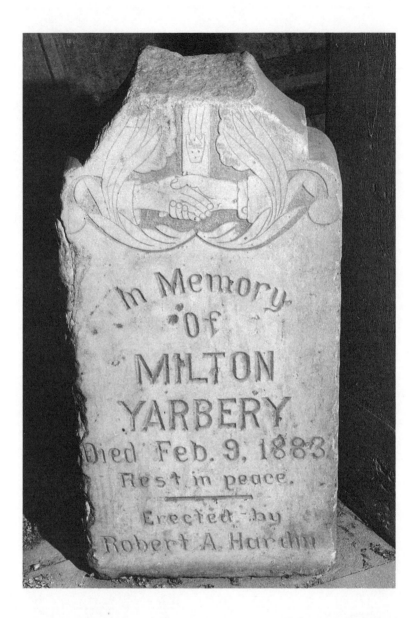

Tombstone of Milton J. Yarberry, with his name misspelled, provided by a friend after the Albuquerque town marshal was hanged in 1883 following his conviction of murdering an unarmed man. (Courtesy Andrew Gregg)

Milt Yarberry:
Trigger-Happy Lawman

Albuquerque, founded in 1706 near the east bank of the Rio Grande, gained a neighbor of the same name in 1880 when the Atchison, Topeka and Santa Fe Railroad, building south through the Rio Grande Valley, bypassed the old Hispanic community and erected a depot in some sand hills a mile or so to the east. The cluster of frame buildings that quickly sprang up in the vicinity of the depot became known as New Albuquerque, while the old community of adobe structures to the west was known as Old Albuquerque, or Old Town.

New Albuquerque, designated Precinct 12, needed a constable, or town marshal, to preserve law and order in the bustling new town, and the man known as Milton J. Yarberry, one of the first drifters to arrive on the scene, appeared to be well suited for the job. The Bernalillo County Commission appointed him constable of Precinct 12, and he was elected to the post during initial balloting in the new town.

Not much was known about Yarberry at the time he assumed his new duties, except that he had lived on the western frontier for years and appeared to be handy with a gun. Albuquerque newspapers said he was about thirty-four years old and illiterate, tall and lean with slightly stooped shoulders, had steel gray eyes and a small black mustache, and that he walked "in a shambling sort of gait."

The *Albuquerque Morning Journal*, on February 9, 1883, published a sketch of Yarberry's career on the frontier, admitting that some of the information was based on hearsay and speculation.

Originally from Walnut Ridge, Arkansas, the article said,

Yarberry left home as a young man and wandered through Texas, to Dallas, Houston, and Orange, and then north to Fort Smith, Arkansas, where he joined two notorious desperadoes, Dave Rudabaugh and David "Mysterious Dave" Mather, who were rustling livestock at the time. In attempting to help them rob a drover's house, he killed a man and fled the vicinity.

Yarberry went to Texarkana, on the Texas-Arkansas border, the article said, where he reportedly killed a man whom he thought was a detective on his trail, but who turned out to be "an inoffensive traveler." The years 1876 to 1877 found him in Decatur, Texas, where he went by the name Johnson and operated a saloon and billiards hall with a partner named Jones.

From here he went north to Dodge City, Kansas, and then to Canon City, Colorado, where he opened a variety theater with a partner, Tony Preston. The business was not a success, and he headed south into New Mexico, pausing first at Las Vegas, where he had considered opening another variety theater. Las Vegas did not look promising to him for such an enterprise, however, and he continued south to Bernalillo, temporary end-of-track for the Santa Fe line, about sixteen miles north of Albuquerque, where he opened a dance hall.

As the railroad construction continued south, Yarberry closed his Bernalillo dance hall and arrived in Albuquerque after first visiting with his former partner, Tony Preston, who was then living at San Marcial, about one hundred miles south of Albuquerque.

As New Albuquerque's first constable, the *Journal* said, Yarberry "carried things with a high hand and had the reputation of being a bully."

*   *   *

Riding high in Albuquerque early in 1881 was Harry Brown, about twenty-four, who was riding trains as a messenger for the Adams Express Company. The newspapers identified him as the youngest son of Neil S. Brown, who had served both as governor of Tennessee and as United States minister to Russia, and nephew of John C. Brown, general western solicitor for Jay Gould's railroad empire.

Brown was considered a privileged character by the express company as a result of his role in thwarting a gang of robbers, including Dave Rudabaugh, who had attempted to rob his express car on a Santa Fe train at Kinsley, Kansas, in January, 1878. Since then, it was said, he had become very reckless, and was continually drawing his six-shooter on someone.

It soon became apparent in Albuquerque that Harry Brown and Constable Milt Yarberry were rivals for the affections of a young divorcée, Sadie Preston, possibly the ex-wife of Yarberry's former partner, although the newspapers did not identify her as such.

On Sunday evening, March 27, 1881, Brown and Mrs. Preston, riding in a hired hack, drew up in front of Girard's Restaurant, on the northeast corner of Railroad (now Central) Avenue and Second Street. Mrs. Preston entered the restaurant and ordered something to eat, and Brown waited outside by the door.

Moments later, Yarberry approached the restaurant on foot, leading Mrs. Preston's four-year-old daughter by the hand. He took her into the restaurant, then walked back outside where Brown was standing on the sidewalk.

The waiting hack driver, John Clark, a black man, was the only witness to what happened next. He said he heard Brown say, "Milt, I want to talk to you," and after some conversation he heard him say, "I want you to understand I am not afraid of you and would not be even if you were marshal of the United States."

At that moment, Clark continued, he heard shots, and turned to see Brown reeling and Yarberry shooting him in the chest. He said Yarberry fired two more shots into Brown as he lay on the sidewalk.

Indicted on a murder charge, Yarberry was brought to trial and acquitted by a jury after testifying that Brown was reaching for his gun when he shot him, and producing witnesses who testified that Brown had sworn to kill him on sight.

The *Journal* said that Brown had made "numerous bad gun plays" in Albuquerque but that his friends had always kept him out of trouble, adding that he was a perfect gentleman when sober and well liked by all.

Brown's remains were shipped to Tennessee for burial.

*   *   *

Less than twelve weeks after he shot Brown to death, Yarberry gunned down yet another man in his role as constable.

On the evening of June 18, 1881, Yarberry and a friend, Frank Boyd, a prominent Albuquerque gambler, were at the Maden House, a hotel on the southwest corner of Railroad Avenue and First Street, then commonly called Front Street, when a shot was fired in the crowded R.H. Greenleaf Restaurant on First Street just south of the hotel.

Hearing the shot, Yarberry and Boyd hurried south on First Street to investigate the matter, and as they approached the restaurant, a bystander pointed to a man crossing the street and said, "There goes the man."

Witnesses said Yarberry approached the man from behind, called "Throw up your hands," and immediately began shooting him, firing more shots into him as he lay on the ground, and saying to Boyd, "I've downed the son of a bitch." Some said Boyd fired at the man, too.

The victim, Charles D. Campbell, a thirty-two-year-old Atlantic and Pacific Railroad carpenter, died with three bullet wounds, two of them in his back. No gun was found on or near his body, and it was never determined that he was the man who fired the shot in the restaurant.

Campbell, who like Brown was a native of Tennessee, was described as a quiet and inoffensive man and a loner. He had worked as a cattle herder at Dodge City in 1875, was in Leadville, Colorado, during the winter of 1879 to 1880, and then worked in New Mexico for Joe Hampson, a railroad bridge contractor. After operating a restaurant at Deming, in the southern part of New Mexico, he had arrived in Albuquerque three weeks before his death to find employment in the Atlantic and Pacific Railroad carpenter shop.

Yarberry, immediately after the fatal shooting, surrendered to Bernalillo County Sheriff Perfecto Armijo. A coroner's jury ruled that Campbell was killed "by Yarberry and another person whose name is unknown."

Interviewed by the *Journal* the next morning at Sheriff Armijo's office in Old Town, Yarberry gave a version of the killing that was quite different from that of eyewitnesses.

As he and Boyd were hurrying down the street toward the restaurant, he said, Boyd asked a man who was sitting on the sidewalk if he knew where the shooting was, and the man pointed to a man crossing the street and said, "There he goes." He said Boyd then said to him, "Milt, this gentleman says there goes the man who fired the shot."

"I got within ten steps of the man and ordered him to hold up his hands, that I wanted him," Yarberry continued. "When I said that he turned and said, 'You hold up your hands, God damn you.' Then he shot at me as soon as he got his pistol. He shot two or three times after he was down."

At a preliminary hearing on July 5, Yarberry was ordered held to await action by the grand jury. He was taken north to Santa Fe and placed in jail for safekeeping.

Boyd, meanwhile, appeared to confirm allegations that he was an accomplice to the killing of Campbell by leaving Albuquerque in a hurry the day after the killing. He headed west into Arizona along the new Atlantic and Pacific Railroad line.

On the afternoon of October 5, 1881, Boyd was on the Martin Ranch near Holbrook, Arizona, when he met two unarmed Navajo Indians on horseback. Grabbing the bridle of one of the riders, he shot him and took the horse. The other Indian wheeled his horse around and sped off.

At sundown, forty armed Navajos on horseback appeared at Armstrong's ranch near Holbrook and demanded to know the whereabouts of the man who had shot their companion. A rancher volunteered to take them in the direction taken by Boyd, and a short ride brought them to the Frank Davis Ranch, where Boyd was seen about to mount a horse. When he was identified as the murderer of the Navajo rider, all members of the avenging Navajo party, at a signal from their leader, leveled their rifles at Boyd and riddled him with bullets. They rode off, leaving his body on the ground.

★　　　　★　　　　★

Milton J. Yarberry remained in the Santa Fe jail for months before the Bernalillo County grand jury met and returned a murder indictment against him and a trial date was set. The indictment came too late for him to be tried at the October term of the Bernalillo County District Court, and the next court session did not begin until May, 1882.

Yarberry's jury trial, on the indictment charging him with the murder of Charles D. Campbell, began in Albuquerque on May 18, 1882, District Judge Joseph Bell presiding. Attorneys William Breeden and Arnet O. Owen appeared for the prosecution, and attorneys L.S. Trimble and Col. J. Francisco Chaves for the defense.

The trial lasted three days, with Yarberry insisting that he had shot in self-defense, and prosecution witnesses testifying that he had shot down an unarmed and innocent man. The jury, after a short deliberation on May 20, returned a verdict that Yarberry was guilty as charged.

Four days later, on May 24, Judge Bell sentenced Yarberry to death, ordering that he be hanged in Albuquerque on June 16.

"Judge, I have not had a fair trial," Yarberry said. "You have not treated me justly, the men in town who tried to hang me have falsely sworn my life away."

Yarberry was taken back to the Santa Fe jail, and his lawyers immediately began lengthy appeals that proved unsuccessful but served to delay for months the execution date.

On the night of September 9, 1882, Yarberry and three other prisoners, Billy Wilson, George Pease, and a man named Harris, escaped from the Santa Fe jail by overpowering a guard, throwing a blanket over his head, and knocking him down, then running up a stairway to the roof and jumping to the ground, scattering under cover of darkness. Three days later, Santa Fe Police Chief

Frank Chavez located and captured Yarberry as he was traveling with a wagon at nearby Arroyo Galisteo, and returned him to the jail.

When the New Mexico Territorial Supreme Court upheld Yarberry's murder conviction and sentence, his lawyers urged New Mexico Governor Lionel Sheldon to commute the death sentence, but the governor declined to intervene and ordered that Yarberry be hanged at Albuquerque on February 9, 1883.

Yarberry was still hoping for a last-minute reprieve when he was taken from his Santa Fe jail cell before dawn on February 9, 1883, and escorted to the Santa Fe depot for the train ride south to Albuquerque, where his execution was scheduled for 3 o'clock that afternoon. The escorting party included Romulo Martinez, sheriff of Santa Fe County; Mace Bowman, sheriff of Colfax County, and Col. Max Frost with nineteen uniformed members of the Governor's Rifles.

At the depot all boarded a special train, consisting of a single coach car drawn by a steam locomotive. The train left Santa Fe at 6:50 in the morning, was delayed for a while at Lamy Junction, and arrived in Albuquerque shortly before 10:30 that morning.

Waiting to greet the train at the Albuquerque depot was a crowd of at least 2,000 persons, including Capt. John Borrodaile with uniformed and helmeted members of the Albuquerque Guards. From the depot, all walked north on First Street to Railroad Avenue, where horse-drawn streetcars were waiting to transport the condemned man and his escort the short distance west to Old Town. Upon their arrival in Old Town, Yarberry was led to the Bernalillo County Courthouse and jail, a one-story, U-shaped adobe building that stood a short distance east of the Old Albuquerque Plaza. Here he was to be held until 3 o'clock in the afternoon, the time set for his hanging in the jail courtyard.

The *Albuquerque Morning Journal* that day, in anticipation of the execution, said of Yarberry:

> *Naturally a man of less than ordinary intelligence, Yarberry's education has not tended to improve the work of nature. Every mean instinct of his narrow brain has been fostered and nursed from childhood until now, upon his last day on earth, he will mount the scaffold and die the death of a felon, never having known the pleasures and comforts of home, always an*
> OUTCAST FROM SOCIETY,
> *from childhood a refugee from justice, and at last dispatched by his fellow men to a tribunal higher than any in existence on this earth. May the All-powerful Judge have mercy on him.*

Yarberry was served his last meal in the jail at noon, consisting of cranberry pie, a pint of whiskey, and a bottle of ale.

Among Albuquerque friends who visited Yarberry during his final hours was Elwood Maden, to whom he revealed his life story. He told Maden that his true name was not Yarberry, nor Johnson, the name he had used in Texas, but that he had changed his name to protect his respectable parents, although he did not know if they were still alive or not. He said he had three cousins living at Walnut Ridge, Arkansas. He gave his true name to Maden, who was sworn not to reveal it.

Yarberry admitted to Maden that he had been involved in some shooting scrapes over the years, but denied that he had killed anybody other than the two men he had shot in Albuquerque.

Several of Yarberry's friends brought him a new suit of black clothes to wear, which he put on, discarding what the *Journal* described as "a brown, seedy looking suit of clothes and clean white shirt without any collar."

Two priests from the San Felipe de Neri Catholic Church across the street visited Yarberry in jail, and when he expressed a desire to join the Catholic church, they baptized him.

At 2:40, Bernalillo County Sheriff Perfecto Armijo led Yarberry out into the courtyard, and the former police officer expressed surprise at seeing the scaffold, consisting of two upright poles supporting a crossbeam, together with a system of ropes, pulleys, and a heavy weight, causing death by jerking the victim upward when a rope was cut.

For the purpose of the execution, a board fence, about eight feet tall, had been erected across the one open side of the court-yard, providing a square enclosure. Admission to the enclosure was limited to one hundred persons who had been given invitations reading:

> *This entitles Mr. — to witness the execution of Milton J. Yarberry, February 9, 1883. By order of Lt. Col. Perfecto Armijo, Capt. Jno. Borrodaile, A.A.*

The audience, however, included about one thousand others, who watched the proceedings from nearby trees and flat rooftops. Some Old Town residents offered their rooftop vantage points for one dollar a head.

Placed under the scaffold, with a noose around his neck, Yarberry was asked if he had anything to say. Quiet until now, he talked for fifteen minutes, his voice loud and firm, telling of his killings of both Brown and Campbell and claiming that he was justified in both instances.

"You are going to hang Milt Yarberry," he said. "You are going to hang him not for the murder of Campbell, but for the killing of Brown."

Sheriff Armijo, looking at his watch, admonished Yarberry several times that his time was growing short, but Yarberry interrupted him each time with "let me finish this." He kept talking until Archie Hilton placed a black hood over his head.

"How near is the time, Perfecto?" Yarberry asked the sheriff. Armijo replied that his last moment had come. "Gentlemen, you are hanging an innocent man," Yarberry said.

At that moment, Armijo snapped shut his watch case, and Count Epur, described as a Polish nobleman living in Albuquerque, cut a rope with an axe and Yarberry was yanked upward into eternity.

Yarberry's remains were taken across the street to the Catholic church for services, then transported to Santa Barbara Cemetery and buried, with the rope still around his neck.

The Gage Train Robbers

The eastbound Southern and Pacific passenger train was proceeding across the flat desert terrain of southern New Mexico shortly before 4:30 on the afternoon of November 24, 1883, when the fireman, Thomas North, noticed that a rail had been removed from the track a short distance ahead of the speeding locomotive.

"My God, there's a hole in the track!" he shouted to the engineer.

The engineer, Theopholus C. Webster, quickly applied the air brakes, but the warning had come too late. The locomotive left the rails and went bouncing over the ties, the mail and express cars and two of the three passenger cars behind it also leaving the track.

The fireman jumped from the cab, and the engineer was preparing to do so when a rifle bullet pierced his heart, fired by one of a group of armed men who had made a sudden appearance next to the derailed train. The engineer fell dead from the cab, landing on the ground next to the locomotive. Several shots were fired at the fireman, who escaped by crawling on his hands and knees into the bottom of a six-foot ditch.

Leaving one man behind to hold their horses, four of the train wreckers, armed with Winchester rifles and Colt revolvers, their faces partially masked by bandanas, walked quickly to the mail car. Mistaking it for the express car, they fired several shots through the side of the car, one of the bullets passing between the arm and body of W.O. Swan, the postal agent inside the car, leaving a hole in the sleeve of his coat. Realizing their mistake, the four men moved on back to the express car and fired several shots into it.

At this moment, the conductor and a passenger arrived on the scene to investigate the trouble, and were relieved of their valuables. The *Southwest Sentinel*, a Silver City newspaper, reported on November 28 that the passenger, Charles A. Gaskill, of the U.S. Publishing House in Chicago, was robbed because "his curiosity exceeded his sense," adding:

He got off the train to "see what was going on" and very suddenly found out a great deal more than he had any desire for knowing. He was relieved of $155 in cash and a silver watch, but they gave him back his watch on his informing them that it was a present, remarking at the same time that it was "of no use to them anyhow."

The conductor, Zack Vail, was forced to hand over his gold watch and about $200 in cash. His watch was not returned. The robbers then called to the express messenger, Thomas C. Hodgkins, to come out of the express car and hold up his hands. The Silver City newspaper said "The arguments of the robbers were so pointed and emphatic that the messenger complied without waiting to argue his side of the question."

The robbers entered and ransacked the express car, opening a safe with keys handed over by the express messenger, and spending about forty-five minutes opening and examining Wells Fargo & Co. money packages. The Silver City paper said: "The leader of the gang was very particular about what he took, refusing Mexican coin and jewelry, which, he remarked, was probably intended for Christmas presents."

After obtaining about $800 in the express car, the robbers returned to the mail car and entered it. The *Albuquerque Morning*

Journal, in its report of the train robbery on November 27, said:

> *Meeting the postal agent they demanded the registered*
> *packages which were turned over to them. They only*
> *opened a few letters and remarking that they guessed they*
> *didn't care much for those things, they turned upon the*
> *clerk and demanded to know if he had any money. "I've*
> *got a little here in this drawer," said the mailman, "but the*
> *truth of the matter is I have only $7 and I need that very*
> *much." "All right," said the leader of the robbers, "let him*
> *keep it. We don't want to take everything a man's got."*

While three of the robbers were opening and examining the mail matter, the Silver City paper said, the outlaw leader busied himself cracking and eating some nuts he found in a mail drawer, picking out the meats with his bowie knife.

After sunset, the robbers left the wrecked train, mounting their horses and riding north after ordering the conductor to go into the passenger cars, which they had not molested, and not to let anybody out for at least ten minutes.

The passengers, during the course of the robbery of the express and mail cars, had been busy hiding their valuables. The Silver City newspaper said:

> *The alacrity exhibited by some of the passengers in*
> *secreting their valuables is said to have been wonderful.*
> *One gentleman from New York secreted over $1,000 in his*
> *shoe. Watches, rings and other valuables were dropped in*
> *water coolers, in the coal boxes, behind the hot water pipes,*
> *in pillow boxes and in fact in every conceivable place in the*

coaches and sleeping car. One man went so far as to
attempt to secrete himself in the linen in the sleeping car.

The fireman, who had been hiding in the ditch, returned to the scene as soon as the robbers had gone and found the body of Webster, the engineer, lying on the tracks next to the derailed locomotive. The Silver City newspaper described the touching scene:

He fell down, embraced the body and wept like a child. They had been running together over two years, and the scene is described as very affecting.

To spread the alarm and secure help for the stranded train and passengers, Thomas Scott, the brakeman, "ran with all his might," as the newspapers put it, the nearly five miles west to Gage, a small Southern Pacific station that the train had passed minutes before it was derailed. At Gage, the railroad telegrapher attempted to telegraph the news direct to Deming, twenty miles to the east, and unable to get through on a direct line, relayed the message to Deming by way of San Francisco, California, and Denver, Colorado.

At Deming, a crowd had been waiting at the depot, wondering why the train was hours late, and speculating that it had been the victim of some mishap east of Gage, where it had been last reported. When news of the derailment and robbery reached Deming, a special relief train was assembled and rushed fifteen miles west to the stricken train with two physicians and about fifty well-armed men. The relief train returned to Deming with the stranded passengers that night, while work crews remained at the robbery scene to clear the tracks.

As news of the train robbery spread up and down the line, armed posses began converging on the scene, some from as far west as Arizona. They searched the area for miles around, but no trace of the outlaws could be found.

*   *   *

Rewards totalling $8,000, or $2,000 for the apprehension of any one of the four train robbers, were offered jointly by the Southern Pacific and Wells Fargo companies, the substantial prize money resulting in a flurry of activity by New Mexico lawmen and citizens alike.

Wells Fargo detectives who arrived on the robbery scene located a campsite used by the robbers, and gathered as evidence a November 10 issue of the *Placer* (California) *Herald*, and an empty pickled pigs' feet can. The detectives telegraphed the publisher of the newspaper, asking who in the region subscribed to the paper, and the answer was Johnnie Ross, Keg Saloon, Silver City, New Mexico. Ross, interviewed at the saloon, said he could not remember if he had received that particular issue or not. He was not considered a suspect. The pickled pigs' feet can was traced to the Bigelow & Weldon store in Silver City, but the owners said they had no recollection as to who had purchased it.

The detectives were convinced that the robbers had started for the robbery scene from Silver City, seat of Grant County in which the robbery had occurred, and about forty miles northwest of Gage. Believing that the robbers had headed south for the Mexican border, they headed in the same direction.

The first break in the case came about three weeks after the train robbery when Albert C. Eaton, owner of a hay camp near

Gage, recognized a mule he saw in Silver City as one belonging to one of several men who had visited the hay camp on the early afternoon of the train robbery. Eaton told authorities that the men had visited the hay camp under suspicious circumstances, had told contradictory stories as to their business there, and that he had scrutinized their animals carefully because he thought the men were rustlers. He also noted that they had questioned him closely about the schedules and movements of Southern Pacific passenger and freight trains in the vicinity.

The authorities questioned Mike Fleming, owner of the mule, and he said that it had been given to him in trade for a horse by a young cowboy, Frank Taggart, who formerly was employed by L.A. Parker on a cattle ranch on the Gila River about thirty miles northwest of Silver City. It was learned that Taggart and three other young cowboys, Kit Joy, Mitch Lee, and George Washington Cleveland, the latter a tall, husky black man, had been "aimlessly knocking around" the Duck Creek country northwest of town where Cleveland was employed.

Convinced that these four men were the train robbers, Grant County Sheriff James Woods and former Sheriff Harvey H. Whitehill rode northwest into the ranch country and questioned ranchers along the way, but returned empty-handed.

Whitehill, however, learned that Cleveland had gone to Socorro, on the Rio Grande about one hundred and twenty miles northeast of Silver City, and traveling there alone, he found and arrested the black cowboy at a Socorro hotel. Whitehill tricked Cleveland into giving a confession by telling him that his three companions had been arrested and had "squealed" on him. Cleveland admitted his part in the train robbery, and confirmed that his companions were Joy, Lee, and Taggart. The former sheriff took him to Silver City and placed him in jail.

The *Southwest Sentinel* at Silver City, on January 24, 1884, gave some of the details of Cleveland's confession:

> *He claims, with some show of reason, that at the time the party started out he had no definite idea of their purpose other than it was to "make a raise" in some questionable manner. When the details of the plan were revealed to him, the party was already on the ground ready for action. He objected to taking part, but his scruples were overcome at the point of a gun and he was forced to participate.*

Cleveland told Whitehill that it was Mitch Lee who had shot and killed the engineer.

With one of the robbers in jail, the former sheriff now set his sights on Frank Taggart, whom he learned had been living and working on a ranch at St. Johns, Arizona, more than one hundred miles northwest of Silver City, before heading for Grant County the previous summer with a herd of cattle. Believing that Taggart might be hiding out among friends in eastern Arizona, Whitehill formulated an elaborate plan to sneak up on his prey from behind, as he knew the trails leading northwest from Silver City might be watched by Taggart's friends.

For his companions on what promised to be a long journey, Whitehill selected his seventeen-year-old son, Harry Whitehill, who knew Taggart by sight, and John Gilmo, a deputy sheriff. The trio boarded a train in Silver City, and rode a series of trains southeast to Deming, north to Albuquerque, and west to Holbrook, Arizona, where they left the railroad and hired horses. They rode sixty miles southeast to St. Johns, where they learned that Taggart had purchased a herd of two hundred cattle and was rounding them up in the extreme western part of Socorro County, New Mexico, near the Arizona border. Riding east, back into New Mexico, the trio found and arrested Taggart at the cattle roundup. It had been a seven-hundred-mile journey from Silver City, but worth the effort.

Taggart was taken to St. Johns and locked in jail while his captors sought to hire a wagon to transport him north to the railroad at Holbrook. Some of Taggart's friends converged on the town and attempted to free him on a writ of habeas corpus, contending that he had been arrested without a warrant. When the writ was denied, they managed to have Whitehill and his companions arrested on a charge of kidnaping Taggart. This charge was quickly dismissed, and the three placed their prisoner in a wagon and took him north to the railroad at Holbrook for the journey to Silver City.

The Atlantic and Pacific train carrying the captors and their prisoner arrived in Albuquerque on the night of January 13, where newspaper reporters interviewed Whitehill and got a look at Taggart, who was in a sullen mood and refused to grant an interview. The *Albuquerque Journal,* two days later, gave this description of the prisoner:

> *Taggart is a young man not over 23 or 24 years of age, about the medium height, blond complexion, and quick nervous eyes. At first sight he is rather mild looking, but closer scrutiny reveals the fact that his whole make up is that of a stubborn and desperate man. His dress is rather of the cowboy order including the broad brimmed sombrero.*

At Albuquerque, the travelers boarded an Atchison, Topeka and Santa Fe Railroad train for the remainder of their journey south to Silver City, where Taggart was placed in jail with Cleveland, his companion in crime.

Meanwhile, four ranchers in the extreme western part of Socorro County, near the Arizona border, had become convinced that two strangers who had been loitering on the range were the wanted train robbers Mitch Lee and Kit Joy. The four, Jack Best, Joe Wasson, J.S. Pitts, and Charlie Curry, decided to take them by strategy. The ranchers approached Lee and Joy on the range and suggested that they band together, ride into Socorro, the county seat, and help Joel Fowler break out of the Socorro jail. Fowler was a notorious Socorro County rancher and man-killer who had been convicted of murder and was sentenced to be hanged.

Lee and Joy took the bait, and the first morning on the trail they woke up to find themselves prisoners of the four ranchers. They were taken to Socorro and turned over to Socorro County Sheriff Pete Simpson. The sheriff and five guards placed the two prisoners aboard a train and took them to Silver City, arriving there on January 21.

The newspapers referred to Lee and Joy as "the last of the Gage train robbers," although all newspaper accounts of the November train robbery had reported that five or six men had been involved, including one or two who stood by holding the horses. No further mention was made in the papers of any train robbery participants other than the four held in jail.

The *Southwest Sentinel*, on February 16, reported that Mitch Lee's father had arrived in Silver City from his home in Williamson County, Texas, and had been granted an interview with his son in the jail. Father and son broke into tears at the meeting, the newspaper said, but when the father offered to do anything he could for him, Lee replied: "Do nothing — let me go to hell."

The Silver City newspaper, meanwhile, speculated that the Grant County jail was not secure enough to hold four such desperate men as the Gage train robbers indefinitely. Events soon were to show that these fears were not groundless.

*   *   *

Shortly before 9 o'clock on the morning of March 10, 1884, two guards at the Silver City jail took from their cells three of the accused train robbers, Kit Joy, Frank Taggart, and Mitch Lee, along with Carlos Chavez, a convicted murderer, and escorted them into the walled jail yard for their morning exercise. It was customary each morning to permit the prisoners, four at a time, to exercise for fifteen minutes.

As the four prisoners were being led back to their cells, one suddenly threw his arms around one of the guards, and held him while Lee grabbed for and secured his pistol. Lee turned to see two of his companions struggling with the other guard, and ran over and compelled him to surrender at gun point, also taking his pistol from him.

The two guards, Deputy Sheriff F.C. Cantley, the jailer, and Deputy Steve Wilson, the day guard, were locked in a cell. Searching the jail for additional weapons, the prisoners found Nick Ware, the night guard, asleep in his bed, took his weapon, and locked him in a cell.

The four released George Washington Cleveland from his cell, and invited all prisoners to join them in an escape. Only Charles Spencer, held on a charge of horse stealing, accepted the invitation. The prisoners entered the guard room and secured additional weapons, including a Winchester rifle, a shotgun, and a number of revolvers. Finding some chisels, they managed to remove some of their leg shackles, and to break the chains on the others.

The *Southwest Sentinel*, on March 15, described what happened next:

> *All this had been effected without any alarm being given upon the outside. It was now half past nine, and our six escapees were ready to move. Opening the jail yard door, and stepping outside, they started for the Elephant Corral. As they ran by the sheriff's office, just north of the jail yard, Deputy Tom Hall stepped out, when they covered him with their weapons. Tom, who had nothing but a small pistol and no arms in the office, jumped back, closed the door, and started up through the corral in the rear, toward his house, above, to secure a rifle, at the same time giving the alarm. He secured a gun, and at once set about organizing a posse.*

The six escapees ran west on Market Street to Main, then north to the Elephant Corral, where they surprised and held up the proprietor, George Chapman.

"We are the Gage train robbers and want horses," Joy exclaimed.

"You will all be killed if you try to escape," Chapman warned.

"If we stay in jail we will be hung, anyway," Joy replied, "and I would rather be shot than hung."

While one man stood guard at the corral gate, the other five began saddling six horses. As they were doing so, Jack Fleming, an unarmed citizen, started to enter the corral, unaware of what was going on, but was warned back by some bystanders who had gathered nearby. He hurried off to secure a shotgun.

The six outlaws galloped their horses out of the corral at about the same time Fleming returned to the scene with a shotgun. He blasted away at them as they rode down the street, but failed to hit any of them. The shotgun blast, however, frightened Cleveland's horse, causing it to buck and throw its rider. Cleveland got up and sprinted down the street, where his companions had pulled up to wait for him, and he vaulted to the back of a horse behind one of the riders. The six men sped out of town on five horses, pointing their weapons at citizens they chanced to meet, but firing at no one.

The escapees rode east out of Silver City on the Fort Bayard road for about three-quarters of a mile, then turned north toward the foothills of the Pinos Altos Mountains. Pursuing them this far on horseback was a single citizen, who managed to slow them down a little. The *Southwest Sentinel* account said:

> Of the citizens, J.C. Jackson was one of the most prompt to act. As soon as he heard the report that the prisoners were out, he secured a pistol, took his horse out of the express wagon, tore off the harness and jumped on for a bareback ride. He followed the retiring criminals, shadowing them, but keeping just out of bullet range. They frequently turned and fired at him, thus losing time, which was just what Jackson desired. He kept them in sight until the advance of the sheriff's party came up.

Deputy Tom Hall, meanwhile, had been busy rounding up horses from various corrals, and calling for volunteers to pursue the outlaws. Hardware dealers handed out guns and ammunition to those citizens volunteering to join the chase. He took charge in the absence of Sheriff James Woods, who was in Arkansas.

Jackson, still shadowing the outlaws alone, was joined about two and one-half miles north of town by the vanguard of the volunteers, Dan Coomer, T.E. Parks, and Frank Andrews. Coomer forged ahead, about one hundred and twenty-five yards behind the fugitives, while his companions circled around to their left.

The six escapees, spotting Coomer closing in on them, turned and charged him, firing fifteen to twenty shots at him without effect. Coomer dismounted and sought refuge among some tree stumps. From here he shot and killed the horse Carlos Chavez was riding. Chavez climbed up on the back of a horse ridden by one of his companions.

The outlaws continued north, with Coomer following them on foot, firing as he went, while Jackson, Parks, and Andrews began firing upon them from the left. The Silver City newspaper account said:

> *The fleeing gang then pushed on about a mile further, where they were driven from their horses by the pursuing party, who were then joined by Jos. N. Lafferr and C.M. Shannon. Soon after the firing became hot upon both sides, and quite a brisk little running fight was kept up, for a distance of nearly a mile. Before this the Mexican, Chavez, was killed, although it was not known at the time. His body was afterwards found under a bush, with the entire top of the head shot off.*

As the running fight continued north, Deputy Hall arrived on the scene with nearly a dozen more men, and the outlaws dismounted and took refuge on a ridge that was covered thickly with underbrush, grass, and rocks. The sheriff's party surrounded the concealed men and began moving in through the brush and grass. The newspaper account continued:

> When all came to close quarters the real fight of the day ensued. In this the Negro (Cleveland) was shot by Ed Mayer, and it is thought Coomer wounded Lee. At any rate, the latter was badly wounded, being shot from side to side, just above the hips. Fighting at close quarters ensued, the citizens firing through the bushes and making it so warm for the fugitives that Taggart finally cried out that they would surrender.

Hall ordered Taggart to come out with his hands up, which he did. While the deputy covered him with his pistol, Shannon searched him for weapons, but found none.

"Where is your pistol?" Shannon asked him.

"There in the brush," Taggart replied.

"Any loads in it?"

"No. If there had been, I would never have given up."

Lee then appeared on the scene and surrendered, so badly wounded that he could not hold his hands up, although he made an effort to do so. Spencer also came out and surrendered. The body of Cleveland, who had been killed instantly, was found nearby. Joy was nowhere to be seen, having escaped down a ravine, and it was thought at the time that Chavez was with him, it having not yet been learned that Chavez had been killed earlier.

Shannon rode back to town and returned with a physician for the wounded man and a wagon in which to transport Lee,

Taggart, and Spencer back to jail. Meanwhile, armed citizens searching for Joy, the only train robber still at large, spotted their man on a nearby hillside. The Silver City newspaper said:

> Parks, Lafferr and others, who were pushing up the opposite side of the brush-covered hill, were firing occasionally as they caught sight of their man, until he finally disappeared in the brush. Lafferr had pushed around near the head of a small ravine, close to a point whence Lee and the others had been dislodged. Parks, who saw that there was one man still in there, shouted to him not to go in, and Lafferr turned to retrace his steps. Unfortunately, however, the warning came too late, for just as the horse turned, Joy shot, killing Lafferr instantly, and wounding the animal.

Word that Joy had blasted Lafferr to death with a shotgun reached the main party of citizens just after they had placed Lee, Taggart, and Spencer in a wagon, along with the body of Cleveland, for the trip back to town. Angered by news of the death of Lafferr, a forty-three-year-old widower with six children who had been active in board of education work, they drove the wagon containing their prisoners to a tree and stopped it under an overhanging limb.

A heated discussion ensued as to whether to hang the three prisoners on the spot or take them back to jail. Deputy Cantley, the jailer, who had arrived on the scene to take charge of the prisoners, said he would not permit the hanging as long as he was armed. He was quickly disarmed. After some debate, it was decided to spare Spencer, the horse thief, as his gun had not been fired and he was not charged with a capital offense.

Two ropes were thrown up over the tree limb, and nooses fastened around the necks of Taggart and Lee. Asked if they had anything to say, Taggart admitted that he had helped rob the Southern Pacific train, but said he had not killed anybody, that Lee had killed the engineer, that the others were opposed to killing anyone, but Lee went ahead and killed the man before they could stop him.

Lee responded by denying that he had killed the engineer, but when told that he had but a short time to live, and that it would be the proper thing to confess, blurted "Well, by God! I did kill him."

The wagon was then driven out from under the two, leaving them dangling above ground. Pronounced dead, their bodies were placed in the wagon alongside the body of their companion, Cleveland. The body of Chavez, found just off the road on the way back to town, also was placed in the wagon.

Upon arrival of the wagon in Silver City, the bodies of the four men were taken to the sheriff's office for an inquest, and there displayed to the public until the next day. A coroner's jury ruled that the four "came to their death by gunshot wounds and other injuries inflicted by the sheriff's posse and citizens while in pursuit and endeavoring to recapture the prisoners after having broken jail by overpowering the guards and attempting to make their escape and committed seven miles north of Silver City, Grant County, New Mexico, on the 10th day of March, 1884."

A large crowd attended the funeral of Joseph N. Lafferr at his home, while the four outlaws were buried quietly in separate coffins in one long grave.

*   *   *

Of the four train robbers, only Kit Joy remained alive and at large, and small search parties concentrated their efforts in rugged mountains and pine forests of the Gila River country north of Silver City. The *Silver City Enterprise* cautioned that "he is a desperate young villain, and is said to have operated with Billy the Kid's gang during the halcyon days of rustlers in this territory."

About a week after the jailbreak, seven men were playing cards one evening at the home of Erichus "Rackety" Smith, at the mouth of Bear Creek on the Gila about thirty miles northwest of Silver City, when they heard somebody knocking at the door. Smith, thinking it was a neighbor, invited entry. The door was thrown violently open, and a man recognized as Kit Joy stood in the doorway, aiming a shotgun at them.

Joy asked one of the players, Sam Houston, to step outside. Houston returned to the house several minutes later and said that Joy wanted something to eat. Houston took some food back out to the fugitive, and told him of the fate of his companions. Joy repeated that he would "rather be shot than hung."

Later, Joy appeared at the house a second time, and requested some provisions, which Houston gave to him. He also stole some blankets from the cabin of Pete Jensen on Bear Creek.

Learning that Houston had been in contact with the fugitive, Silver City authorities prevailed upon him to lure Joy to Rackety Smith's house, where he could be trapped and captured. The rendezvous was set for the night of March 20, but Joy failed to keep the appointment.

The next morning, Houston decided to go out after Joy himself. He trailed him to the house of Allen Frazer, where he was told that Joy had visited the house the previous evening and asked for food. Frazer had refused to give him any, and had told him to leave and not come back, but Joy menacing Frazer with his shotgun, helped himself, and left about midnight.

Houston, believing that Joy was hiding nearby, resumed his search for him.

Shortly before noon that day, Joy was seen walking across a clearing about three hundred yards from Rackety Smith's house by Smith, Mike Maguire, and Sterling Ashby. They hurried to the house, obtained long-range rifles, and began stalking the fugitive. Joy began to run, and Smith fired at him, missing him but causing him to stop and turn around. Smith took careful aim and fired a second shot, this one hitting Joy beneath his left knee and shattering the bones in his leg.

Joy, in extreme pain, shouted that he would surrender, and Smith and his two companions approached the wounded man carefully. Smith told Joy to throw his shotgun away, and Joy complied. As the three came upon the fallen man, Joy asked Smith to kill him, saying he could not bear the pain of his shattered leg. The three carried Joy to the house, and from there he was transported to jail in Silver City, arriving there after midnight.

That morning, a physician amputated Joy's left leg above the knee. The recovering prisoner languished in jail for eight months before standing trial for the murder of Theopholus C. Webster, the Southern Pacific engineer.

The reward money offered by the Southern Pacific and Wells Fargo companies for the capture of the four train robbers was placed in court while the various claimants hired attorneys and wrangled over who was to get what. Early in September, a special master for the court ruled that Harvey Whitehill should get two-thirds of the $2,000 reward offered for Cleveland, and Sheriff Pete Simpson of Socorro County the other third. Whitehill was granted one-third of the $2,000 reward for Taggart, and John

Gilmo two-thirds, the court finding that Whitehill was not physically present at the arrest. Socorro County rancher Jack Best and his companions split the rewards for bringing in Joy and Lee.

Joy's defense attorneys, Fielder and Fielder of Deming, arguing that an impartial jury could not be selected in Silver City to try the prisoner, were successful in having the trial moved east to Hillsboro, seat of newly created Sierra County. The trial was set for the first term of court that began its session on November 10, 1884, newly appointed Judge Stephen F. Wilson presiding.

Joy, under heavy guard, was transported from Silver City to Hillsboro on November 9 to await his murder trial. After jury selection, which took most of a day, the trial began on November 17. Joy's parents and five-year-old sister, who lived near Hillsboro, sat quietly in the courtroom during the proceedings. His mother, dressed in black, was described by a correspondent for the *Silver City Enterprise* as "an intelligent looking lady of modest and retiring appearance" whose face showed signs of severe mental strain. His father had little to say to anyone, the correspondent added.

The principal witnesses for the prosecution included three members of the train crew, Thomas C. Hodgkins, the express messenger; William White, the baggage master; and W.O. Swan, the postal clerk. Questioned by District Attorney E.C. Wade, each pointed to Joy in the courtroom and said, "This is the man that came into the car and went through the express and mail matter," adding that the defendant was not masked at the time. Joy displayed no emotion, and appeared indifferent to their testimony.

Testifying in his own defense, Joy contended that he was not at the train robbery, and knew nothing about it. On the day of the train robbery, he testified, he was at Oak Springs, between

Hillsboro and Lake Valley, about fifty miles northeast of the robbery scene.

The only other defense witness was a man who gave his name as Reynolds, and who testified that he was camped at Oak Springs on the day of the robbery with two men known as Drace and Black Bill when Joy arrived during the afternoon on a dun horse and spent the night with them. The newspaper correspondent wrote that it was "obvious" that Reynolds was lying, noting that he was a stranger in the region who was staying at the home of Joy's parents during the trial. He described him as "a tall, lank, uncouth, seedy looking personage, having a reckless, lumbering, straggling gait to his walk, and a pair of eyes partially hidden behind heavy lashes with now and then an unusually bright and furtive expression peering from their hiding places."

After deliberating four hours, the jury found Joy guilty of second-degree murder, finding that it was not shown that Joy himself had killed the engineer, or that he intended with premeditation to take a life during the train robbery. Judge Wilson sentenced him to life imprisonment. While hearing the sentence of the court, Joy drew a sketch of a gallows on a piece of paper, with the words "We never sleep" underneath. If it was meant as a threat, as some thought, he was never in a position to carry it out.

Years later, after serving a portion of his life sentence, Kit Joy was released from the penitentiary, and he settled in Bisbee, Arizona, where he took care of his aged mother until her death.

Bronco Sue:
"A Shooter From Away Back"

"Socorro is a nice town. It is a lively place," the *Albuquerque Evening Democrat* reported on August 25, 1884. "There is always something occurring there to interest and amuse the populace."

What was entertaining and amusing the Socorro populace on this particular occasion was the fatal shooting of Robert Black, a handsome Socorro gambler, by his forty-year-old female partner and companion, a woman known in New Mexico as "Buckskin Sue" and "Bronco Sue." She claimed it was self-defense, but the circumstances and evidence indicated otherwise.

The remarkable but little-known story of how a young woman from Wales gained notoriety on America's western frontier is a long, varied, and eventful one, but one with many missing pages. She left a faint trail that extended from the British Isles to Louisiana, California, Nevada, Colorado, and New Mexico before vanishing.

According to biographical sketches published in various New Mexico newspapers in the 1880s, she was born Susan Warfield in Wales on September 11, 1844. As a teenager, just prior to the Civil War, she emigrated with her parents to the United States, pausing first in New Orleans. Her stay there was a short one, for it was reported that she grew up in various Nevada mining camps, where she became "a daring horsewoman and deadly shot."

As a young woman she was married to Thomas D. Rapier (or Raper), a well-to-do mining man who owned the Yankie Mine at Downieville, California. She and her husband, who had lost an arm fighting Bannock Indians in Nevada, became the parents of three sons, one of whom died young. Rapier went broke and abandoned his wife in 1870 at Elko, Nevada, leaving behind a letter in which he wrote that it was "pretty hard for a man to leave his children forever on account of damned thieves." Just what he meant by this was not explained.

Susie Rapier, as the abandoned woman was now known, took up with Col. Robert Payne, recently discharged from the Army at Fort Halleck, Nevada, and they embarked on a profitable cattle rustling business from headquarters near Carlin, in Elko County, Nevada. In this new endeavor her equestrienne and marksmanship abilities served her well, it was said, as she participated in a number of gun battles and became known as Nevada's cattle rustling queen.

Occasionally, when tried in court on various larceny offenses, she used the ploy that was to prove successful during the remainder of her career, that of sitting quietly and demurely in the courtroom with her children, sobbing and wiping away her tears with her handkerchief. Because of her "petticoat defense," as it was called, no male jury could find the heart to convict her, and they were all male juries at the time.

Her career as a Nevada cattle rustler was not a long one, however, for by 1875 she was reported living in Pueblo, Colorado, using the name Susie Stone. In 1879, she was reported living in Alamosa, Colorado, and in 1881 she was reported to be operating a stage or hack line the short distance between Conejos and San Antonio in southern Colorado, still using the name Susie Stone.

She apparently moved south to New Mexico the following year, for by June in 1882 she was in Espanola, twenty-five miles north of Santa Fe, with a new husband, Jack Yonkers, who came from Independence County, Arkansas. The two decided to open a saloon with gambling rooms at Wallace (now Domingo), a railroad town of about six hundred inhabitants on the Atchison, Topeka and Santa Fe Railroad near the Indian pueblo of Santo Domingo, about thirty miles southwest of Santa Fe. She bought a stock of liquors from Santiago Baca, an Albuquerque wholesaler, using the name Susan Yonkers.

They opened the saloon at Wallace in June and operated it until July, 1883, when they decided to move their business to the new and bustling mining town of White Oaks in Lincoln County, more than one hundred miles to the south. Loading their merchandise in a wagon, the two departed Wallace and headed south.

Susan arrived in White Oaks with the wagon, minus Jack Yonkers, plus a new friend, Robert Black, whom she said she had met along the way. According to the *Socorro Chieftain*, she gave conflicting accounts of her eventful wagon journey to White Oaks:

> *While on the road near the Alkali wells she says that Yonkers died of the smallpox, and she had to dig him a grave and bury him alone. It was here that she fell in with Black, who is supposed to have been a witness to the funeral services or the tragedy or whatever it may have been.*
>
> *On arriving at White Oaks she again assumed the name of Stone, and told that she had lost her brother at the Alkali wells with smallpox, but as there was no smallpox in this part of the country at that time, her story was regarded with considerable suspicion, and more so when she afterwards said the man was her husband and again assumed the name of Yonkers.*

White Oaks proved prosperous for Susan Yonkers and Robert Black, and with their earnings they each purchased separate but apparently contiguous Lincoln County ranches and stocked them with cattle. Joining Sue at White Oaks at about this time were her two grown sons, William and Joseph Rapier, who apparently had been searching for their mother for some time.

In 1884, for reasons not explained in the newspapers, the couple moved to Socorro, about seventy miles to the west, a ranch and ore smeltering center on the west bank of the Rio Grande and seat of Socorro County. Black opened a saloon and gambling rooms in a Socorro hotel, and Sue opened a boarding house near the Santa Fe Railroad tracks.

The two had been in Socorro but a short time when buyers offered to purchase the two Lincoln County cattle ranches in a single transaction. Sue, wanting to handle the details, persuaded Black to deed his ranch over to her, with the understanding that the proceeds from the sale of both ranches would be placed in a bank and then shared between them. Black never received his share.

On Sunday evening, August 24, 1884, Sue shot Black to death in a room of her boarding house. The first account of the shooting, published the next day in the *Albuquerque Evening Democrat*, contained a number of inaccuracies, including the identification of the victim as Richard Black, rather than Robert Black:

> *There has been a saloon for some time in Socorro which has been making money freely. The proprietors of this saloon were the man and woman who had the trouble on yesterday. His name was Richard Black, and hers was "Buckskin Sue."*
>
> *She has led a life of dissipation, and it may be added in*

a whisper, a life of unenviable reputation also. For some time past she and Dick have lived together as man and wife, but she deserves the credit of being true to the man she was pleased to call her husband.

She presided at the bar on some occasions and on others dealt "stud" to the frequenters of the saloon. She and Dick got along nicely together, and no cloud appeared on their "marital" horizon until a few days ago.

It has been said that the saloon made money and that every cent that was made was saved. With these savings a ranch was purchased. Finally some parties made the happy pair an offer to buy the ranch outright. After due deliberation the offer was accepted and the money received and in pursuance therewith placed in the bank in the same account as was the money received over the counter for wet groceries.

Some little trouble had existed between Sue and Dick prior to the sale of the ranch, which resulted in Sue swearing out a warrant and had Dick incarcerated in a dungeon cell. On Saturday last Dick gave bonds for good behavior and was released from custody.

All seemed lovely and happy on his arrival in his house and fireside Saturday evening. Dick was at home on Saturday night as usual, and on Sunday morning he left the house and returned about five o'clock in the evening a little the worse for liquor.

On entering the house he began using indelicate language, and quick as a flash picked up a goblet and threw it with brute force at his Suzie, which struck her on the shoulder. Sue attempted to make her escape, when he rushed to one corner of the room, picked up an axe and started for the woman he called his wife.

Buckskin Sue could not take time to expostulate with him, or one minute later she would have fallen a victim to Richard Black, and as if directed by providence she thought of a .38-calibre revolver that was lying on the mantel piece in the front room. She ran around the table which was near the center of the room and when nearly opposite her antagonist, she grasped the revolver, aimed and fired. The shot took effect in the left arm, passed through the heart and was extricated near the right nipple.

Richard Black lived but a few moments, Buckskin Sue was immediately arrested by Sheriff Pete Simpson, and she is now in jail awaiting a preliminary examination.

The murdered man was about six feet high, fine looking, wore a heavy black beard, and weighed about 175 pounds.

R.B. Featherstone, the town marshal of Socorro, visited Albuquerque, seventy-five miles to the north, on August 25, and gave newspaper reporters some additional details, explaining first that the victim's name was Robert Black, not Richard Black, and that the woman's name was Susan Yonkers.

The marshal said the two had arrived from White Oaks about a month before the shooting, and that nothing was known about their backgrounds. He said that Black had opened a saloon at the Walker House Hotel, and that Sue had opened a boarding house near the railroad tracks. He claimed that Sue had not led "a dissipated life," and that she was never seen in Black's saloon. Black took his meals at her house, he said, but slept in the saloon.

About a week before the shooting, Featherstone continued,

Black was closed out of his saloon by the landlord and began sleeping as well as eating at Sue's place. At about this time he deeded a ranch he owned to the woman, and until that time she had no interest in the property.

The marshal said that Sue came to him on Saturday night, August 23, and asked that Black be taken away from her house. He said he took Black uptown and registered him at a hotel, then locked him up in jail later that night at Sue's insistence. He said two of Black's friends made bail for him Sunday morning, and when releasing Black he warned him not to go to Sue's house.

Featherstone said he was informed by a hardware dealer that afternoon that Sue had purchased a .44-caliber "Bulldog" pistol, but that the dealer had given her cartridges that would not fit the gun. When he saw Sue about an hour later, the marshal said, she was looking for cartridges to fit the gun, explaining that she had a lot of jewelry in her home that needed protecting.

Featherstone said he saw Black on the street shortly afterward and warned him again not to go to Sue's place as she had purchased a gun.

"You bet I won't go to the house for she is a shooter from away back," Black told the marshal.

Featherstone said he received word later in the day that Sue had killed Black at her home after he had thrown a goblet at her and chased her with an axe and that she had been arrested by Sheriff Simpson. He said an axe was found near the corpse, but that he had no idea who put it there.

The outcome of the preliminary hearing for Sue Yonkers, date lined Socorro, August 31, was published in the *Albuquerque Journal* on September 2, the article mistakingly referring to the victim as William Black:

Mrs. Younker [sic], the murderess of William Black, a very fair account of which appeared in the Journal *of recent date, has had her examination before Justice McCuistion and [has been] found not guilty, and now she is enjoying life where the woodbine twineth, wherever that may be. Perhaps the justice could have not done otherwise as the testimony showed that she killed Black in self defense, but then we can add that she supplied the evidence, being the only living witness to the bloody deed.*

Outside evidence that was not brought out during the trial shows that Black and Younker each owned a ranch in Lincoln County and to sell one it was necessary to sell both. For the purpose of effecting the sale Black deeded the woman his property, expecting her to give him his share as soon as she received the money. She made the sale but REFUSED TO DIVIDE *and desired to get rid of him.*

When she shot him she claimed that he was attempting to brain her with an ax. The first parties in the room found him with a death grip on a bucket bail and the ax lying near by splattered with blood. Every nearby external evidence went to show that the unfortunate man had been shot while in the act of bathing.

Our citizens were greatly exasperated over the murder, and all that prevented a more searching inquiry and swift justice was the fact that Yonker wore petticoats. . . .

The article said it had been learned that the woman had left town with a black man, and that a party had been sent out by the citizens to bring both back to await the action of the grand jury. The party apparently returned empty-handed.

Tularosa, then in the northeast corner of Dona Ana County, sixty miles south of White Oaks, apparently was the place "where the woodbine twineth," for that was where "Buckskin Sue" turned up soon after her hasty departure from Socorro. Here she married Charlie Dawson, a cattle rancher, and spent most of 1885 raising horses and working with cowboys on the open range, becoming known throughout the region as "Bronco Sue."

Her marriage to Dawson proved to be a short one, however. Dawson began quarreling with a neighboring rancher, John H. Good, recently arrived from Texas, and with whom Sue was said to have had a warm and scandalous friendship. Dawson and Good, after a heated argument about some cattle business, parted with a "shoot-on-sight" understanding.

The showdown came on December 8, 1885, when the two met on a street in the village of La Luz, a short distance south of Tularosa. Both men began firing, and Sue rushed into the affray with a Winchester rifle, but she was too late. Her husband, shot three times, was dead on the ground. Good was unhurt.

Good was tried at Las Cruces, seat of Dona Ana County, and was acquitted on grounds of self-defense. Sue testified at the trial, which occurred during the last week of March in 1886.

Five months later, Sue was back in court in Las Cruces again, this time in regard to some land litigation that apparently involved her late husband's ranch. An unidentified correspondent for the *Albuquerque Journal* provided a rather enigmatic account of the doings that was published in the Albuquerque newspaper on September 4, 1886:

> Las Cruces, N.M., *September 2 – Well, gentle reader, I have something interesting to tell you. The notorious*

Mrs. Dawson, better known to the newspaper public as "Bronco Sue," is now positively and actually in Las Cruces in attendance upon a land contest in which she is contestant. She has with her a son and daughter. The son is known as young Mr. Draper (Rapier?), who has recently returned to New Mexico from South America with an indefinite amount of gold coin in the form of English sovereigns with which he is footing his mother's bills.

This same "Bronco Sue" would surprise you. She is not beautiful nor remarkably ill-favored, but her voice is as soft as the evening breeze and her manner really winsome. She converses with fluency and intelligence and manifests deep tenderness of womanly affection when her troubles and her dead husband's are alluded to.

The fact is this woman is one of three things — a rare avis, a genuine artiste, or much misunderstood and injured in reputation — possibly all three — quien sabe? At any rate it is a real pleasure to a generous mind to discover traces of good where nothing was looked for but the utterly bad. And it may be when we all get to heaven and the mist has cleared away we shall be surprised to find a great many people so much better or worse than we thought.

As to the reference to a daughter, it might be noted that Sue sometimes was accused of "borrowing" children for her courtroom appearances to strengthen her image as a devoted mother.

It was during one of her courtroom appearances in Las Cruces that Sue was arrested and taken to Socorro to face a Socorro County grand jury indictment charging her with the murder of Robert Black two years before. The indictment was brought on the basis of new information volunteered by her son, William Rapier, who told authorities that his mother and his brother, Joseph, conspired to kill Black for his money. Sue hired attorneys L.B. Hamilton and Col. Albert J. Fountain to defend her, and they were successful in getting the murder trial moved to Silver City, seat of Grant County, more than one hundred miles to the southwest.

The murder trial in District Court in Silver City began on Wednesday, December 15, 1886, and the details were published two days later in the *Silver City Enterprise*, which referred to the defendant as Mrs. Susan Yonkers, "Bronco Sue," although noting that her most recent husband had been Charlie Dawson.

The Silver City newspaper provided a biographical sketch of the woman, and said that her son, Joseph, who had been indicted as an accessory to Black's murder, had escaped from the Socorro jail after his mother had smuggled him steels from her corset. The article also said that she had paid an attorney $500 to defend her son, William, when he was tried and acquitted on a charge of assault to murder.

The article described Bronco Sue as a grey-haired woman of forty-five, adding:

> From her appearance, she was evidently used to a life of rough battling with the world; stern looking, tall, rather slender, with the hand of a man, self-possessed, respectable looking, but unattractive. During the proceedings she frequently placed her handkerchief to her eyes, and when testifying a few tears wet her cheek.

The principal witness for the prosecution was her twenty-three-year-old son, William, who testified that his mother had admitted to him that she and his brother conspired to kill Black for his money, and after shooting him she had placed an axe near his body to create the appearance that her life had been in danger.

The Silver City newspaper called the witness "a self-confessed scoundrel," adding:

> *Certainly, no one expected that a son reared as he had been should be governed by all the finer impulses, for oranges cannot be made to grow on sagebrush.*

Sue, testifying on her own behalf, repeated her original story that Black had thrown a goblet at her and was chasing her around the room with an axe when she shot him. When asked about her son's contradictory testimony, she wept and said she did not wish to prove her son a perjurer.

When all testimony had been completed, one of her attorneys, Albert J. Fountain, stood before the jury, pointed to William Rapier, and exclaimed in a loud voice, "Gentlemen of the jury — this mans wants to HANG his own MOTHER!"

The stunned jurors quickly returned a verdict of "not guilty." As the Silver City newspaper commented:

> *A jury could scarcely be had in America that would convict a yellow dog of the larceny of a beef bone upon the accusation of so depraved a witness who would have the woman hanged who gave him birth.*

A free woman, Bronco Sue walked out of the Silver City courtroom, and into obscurity.

The King of the Gypsies

An Albuquerque newspaper called him "a peculiar character on a peculiar quest." A stranger in town, he attracted much attention as he paraded the streets in a handsome coach drawn by four horses that he had rented from Johnson's livery stable.

"His fine physique and erect manner were enough to attract attention," the *Albuquerque Democrat* reported on February 18, 1896, the day after his arrival, "but his dress excited the curiosity of all spectators for the front was literally bespangled with gold coins."

The dark complected stranger soon identified himself as Col. Juan Miguel de Lacerda, and claimed, among other things, that he was a count, a much decorated officer of the Brazilian Army, the son of the Brazilian minister of war, and the King of the Gypsies. He had come to New Mexico, he said, to locate buried treasure.

During a visit to the Albuquerque residence of Amado C. de Baca, Lacerda told his host that he was a student of church history in his native Brazil, and that while delving through some old records of the Franciscan friars he had come across some ancient and mouldy papers that revealed the secret burial places in New Mexico of sixty million dollars worth of gold bars and silver bullion.

Three of the treasure troves, he said, were buried at Gran Quivira, Quarai, and Chilili, sites of long abandoned Indian pueblo and Spanish mission complexes southeast of Albuquerque, and the other at Anton Chico, a small town on the west bank of the Pecos River nearly one hundred miles to the east.

Franciscan missionaries, in the early 1600s, had supervised the construction of mission churches at Pueblo Indian towns at Gran

Quivira, Quarai, and Chilili, but these mission settlements were abandoned in the 1670s due to constant raids by nomadic Indian tribes and possibly other factors. At Gran Quivira and Quarai, the roofless stone walls of the mission churches still towered over the low ruins of the Indian settlements they had served two centuries before. Barely a trace remained of the Indian town and chapel of 17th-century Chilili, the site adjacent to a much later Mexican land grant village of the same name that was established there in the early 1840s.

Anton Chico, also a Mexican land grant village, was founded by Hispanic settlers in the early 1820s, and its small Sangre de Cristo Church was erected by the original colonists.

Lacerda said he already had a small band of gypsies digging for treasure at Chilili, about thirty-five miles southeast of Albuquerque, and claimed that they already had found some items that were described in the old Franciscan papers. He said he expected some sensational developments in the near future. A day later, Lacerda climbed into his rented coach and four and drove off toward Chilili at a rapid trot.

Residents of the Chilili area, meanwhile, had become convinced that Lacerda was a fraud.

Dr. C.F. Wilkins of Chilili, writing to the *Albuquerque Citizen* on February 24, said the gypsies there were members of a band that had been driven out of White Oaks, a New Mexico mining town about one hundred miles to the south.

"Their command of the art of sleight of hand appeals to the superstitions of the natives," he wrote, "and they can rob them with ease and impunity."

The *Albuquerque Democrat*, in an article on February 29, said it was "rumored that the colonel, while engaged in his work at

Chilili, has fallen victim to Cupid's charms and will shortly be married to one of the Dow girls."

This brought an angry response from E.A. Dow, prominent merchant of Tajique, a village about a dozen miles south of Chilili, whose letter to the *Democrat*, published on March 12, said:

> *Dear Sir: I was informed by a friend that there was an item in your paper claiming that one of my daughters was engaged to marry that man calling himself Col. Juan Miguel Lacerda.*
>
> *It is a lie, and in justice to myself and family I ask that you give publication to this in your paper and never again to couple any of our names with that man's and much less upon the liar's information.*
>
> *A few days after meeting the fraud (J.M. Lacerda) I told him to keep away from my place, but he came back under different excuses until last Friday I got so disgusted that I publicly run him off, warning him never to come near my premises again. I boldly say that he is a fraud and a liar, because proof is overwhelming.*

Dow's suspicions seemed to be confirmed when an Albuquerque resident visited the Brazilian minister in Washington and was told by the minister that he had no knowledge of a Col. Juan Miguel de Lacerda and that he certainly was not the son of the Brazilian minister of war. He said he recalled that a band of gypsies had arrived in the United States from Paris the summer before, and that their leader, who was called Lacerda, had said that he was going to the western part of the United States to buy land to establish a colony for his people.

Meanwhile, the King of the Gypsies seemed bound and determined to marry the Tajique merchant's daughter in spite of her father's objections. Albuquerque newspapers, during April and May, published reports that he planned to ride up to the Dow home in Tajique, kidnap the girl he loved, carry her off, and marry her in the traditional gypsy fashion. Dow reported that he was receiving threatening letters from Lacerda.

Lacerda visited Albuquerque periodically during this period, accompanied by three or four heavily armed bodyguards. An article in the *Albuquerque Weekly Citizen* on April 25 revealed that his travels had taken him east to Anton Chico and also one hundred miles north to Taos:

> *Juan Miguel de la Cerda [sic], who professes to be a colonel in the Brazilian army and the possessor of immense wealth and the sure clew [sic] to hidden treasures of fabulous value at Gran Quivira, has bobbed up serenely at Taos with his band of gypsies and has gained the confidence of the Pueblo Indians there to such a degree that they are alleged to have revealed to him the location of several Spanish mines on their lands. He still stoutly persists in his resolution to return to Gran Quivira and secure the hand in marriage of the daughter of E.A. Dow, of Tajique, in spite of the latter's strong declaration to the contrary. The last number of the* Taos Monitor *printed pictures of "Col." de la Cerda and Miss Anna Rosa Dow, side by side. The "colonel" is recommended to keep out of reach of Mr. Dow's long arms and righteous wrath.*
>
> *The* Las Vegas Optic, *on the subject, says:*
> *José L. Lopez and family, who have been up from Anton Chico, seem greatly encouraged over the prospects of*

unearthing treasures hidden in the earth there several hundred years ago by the Spaniards. Their faith seems based upon the fact that the Spaniards, back in the sixteenth century, took fabulous sums of gold from the country that is now New Mexico; that later, when the Spaniards were driven out of this country by the Indians, the legend goes, all that they held valuable in precious stones were buried here before they left.

Don Lorenzo Lopez and his son, José L., had given this matter considerable study and believed that the abandoned and filled up mine near Anton Chico was likely to prove the hiding place of a fortune.

No sooner had they begun work down there, when the Brazilian colonel, Miguel de la Cerda, came along and claimed that he knew of this place from a description that had come to him from Spain. He gave them a diagram of the tunnel, and their great faith is now based upon the fact that they have gone down 100 feet and the tunnel follows exactly the diagram held by the Brazilian, and if he tells the truth to the end, the treasure trove will soon be forthcoming.

The *Albuquerque Citizen*, on May 30, published a rumor that Lacerda had been mobbed and beaten to death at Tajique upon his arrival there after an absence of some weeks. It proved to be only a rumor, however, as three days later the newspaper reported that Lacerda and three armed companions had been seen in Laguna Pueblo, about fifty miles west of Albuquerque. Col. W.G. Marmon of Laguna Pueblo said Lacerda and his companions had arrived on horseback and had told him they were heading north to the Nacimiento country to seek some treasure, but that they had ridden off in the opposite direction as if heading back toward Tajique.

Marmon was correct in his assumption that Lacerda and his three companions were headed for Tajique, nearly one hundred miles to the southeast, for they were camped in the outskirts of the Valencia County village by Thursday morning, June 4. One of Lacerda's companions rode into Tajique that morning, and returned to the camp a few hours later with news that the father of Lacerda's intended bride had left home for several days. The gypsy king apparently believed that this offered him an opportunity to capture his beloved and ride off with her.

That evening, Lacerda led an ill-conceived attempt to kidnap the Dow girl, a fiasco that accomplished nothing but the death of one of his companions and the jailing of himself and his remaining companions. The story of Lacerda's abortive attack on the village was telegraphed to the *Albuquerque Citizen* from Los Lunas, seat of Valencia County, on the west bank of the Rio Grande about twenty miles south of Albuquerque:

> LOS LUNAS, N.M., *June 9 – Col. Juan Miguel de Lacerda (not La Cerda), widely known throughout the country as the man who came after the fabulous millions of Gran Quivira, is now a prisoner in the Valencia County jail, together with two of his peons, Noverto Chaves and Santa Rosa Barela. Another of the colonel's peons, Loujimio Lopez, who was wanted by the sheriff of this County for cattle stealing, is dead, and all this the result of Col. Lacerda's infatuation for a certain young lady of Tajique.*
>
> *The particulars, as far as known, are as follows:*
> *The Brazilian colonel, animated by the love he bore for the young lady above referred to, and meeting violent*

opposition from the girl's father, resolved to capture the girl in a manner worthy of the heroic ages. He therefore employed four men, presumably to work on the lost treasures, and armed them to the teeth, the preparations being perfected in western Valencia County, and Lacerda proceeded to Tajique. The colonel and his little army invaded the place (Tajique) on Thursday night last, but for some reason or other did not attack the house, which was his objective point, but stopped at one of the entrances to the town, fired several shots at different houses, narrowly missing several persons. The colonel and his party then retired to the mountains.

The next morning (Friday) the constable of the precinct was ordered to organize a mob to arrest the invaders. The latter were found in the mountains near Tajique and when ordered by the constable's posse to surrender responded with a volley of shot, whereupon the posse fired into their camp. When the smoke cleared away, Loujimio Lopez, one of the gang, was found dead with two bullets in his body. Lacerda and Noverto Chaves escaped to the mountains and eluded capture.

Other news reports said that the ten-member posse shot Lacerda's horse from under him and that Lacerda and Chaves escaped on foot and hatless into the Manzano Mountains just west of Tajique. The posse captured horses, saddles, and provisions found in the camp, the reports added.

Another of Lacerda's companions, Santa Rosa Barela, was captured by the posse and taken to the Valencia County jail at Los Lunas, about thirty air miles west of Tajique on the opposite side of the Manzano Mountains. The hatless Lacerda and Chaves, meanwhile, made their way on foot west across the mountain range and went into hiding near the village of Peralta, on the east bank of the Rio Grande opposite Los Lunas. The news dispatch from Los Lunas told of their capture:

> *On last Sunday morning (June 7) Lacerda, who was hiding in the vicinity of Peralta, sent a man to get him a lawyer, but instead of a lawyer he received a visit from our sheriff, Max Luna, and Lacerda and one of his confederates were brought to Los Lunas with all their armament, consisting of two Winchesters and several hundred rounds of ammunition, which they had succeeded in carrying away in their flight.*

Two days after his capture, Lacerda was escorted back to Tajique for a preliminary hearing before a justice of the peace:

> Los Lunas, N.M., *June 9 – It is thought here that the Tajique people will wreak vengeance upon Juan Miguel de Lacerda when he is turned over to the constable of that precinct, but still the Brazilian was sent there this morning. It is also the opinion of fair-thinking men that Lacerda is crazy on the subject of marrying the Dow girl, and that he should not be severely dealt with. He should, however, have a hearing on the charge of lunacy, and be sent to the insane asylum at Las Vegas.*

The preliminary hearing at Tajique took place without anybody wreaking vengeance upon the defendant, however, and

Lacerda was taken back to the county jail to await action by the grand jury. He was indicted on various charges, including assault with a deadly weapon, and his bond was set at $10,000. He remained in jail in lieu of bond, and according to the *Weekly Citizen*, was still in jail a month after his capture:

> LOS LUNAS, *July 6 – Col. Lacerda, the Brazilian count, is still with us, but expects to be free in a very short time, as he has sent a man to Arizona, where some of his people are, to get him enough money to deposit instead of giving bonds. Certain parties were here last week and offered to give bonds for him but the colonel would not have it. The count is pleased with this town and expects to live here for a while when he gets his millions.*

The *Weekly Citizen* reported on August 15 that Lacerda was still at Los Lunas, adding that he "acts and walks like a man who considers himself the most important being on earth." An article in the same newspaper on September 5 revealed that Lacerda had been released from jail on a bond posted by Lorenzo Lopez, the Anton Chico treasure hunter, and that both men had been to Anton Chico and back:

> LOS LUNAS, *August 28 – Col. Juan Miguel de Lacerda, the Brazilian count, arrived here last Tuesday morning from Anton Chico, accompanied by Don Lorenzo Lopez, his bondsman. They left on Wednesday morning for Tajique, where the colonel will have his hearing before the justice of the peace, as E.A. Dow accused him of being a dangerous man and wants him put under bonds to keep*

the peace. The colonel will go from Tajique to Gran Quivira, where he expects to take out the treasure which he claims amounts to $60,000,000. He took several men from here to work for him at the Gran Quivira. He will return to Los Lunas about the 10th of September.

Lacerda and his friends returned to Los Lunas a week later than expected:

LOS LUNAS, *September 17 – Col. Lacerda, the Brazilian count, arrived here this morning at 10 o'clock from Gran Quivira, accompanied by Don Lorenzo Lopez of Anton Chico, San Miguel County, and eight more friends from San Miguel and Guadalupe counties. The colonel came through Manzano and Tajique, making the trip in two days. He came in a fine yellow carriage with four fine horses hitched to it. He expects his brother, Juan Esteban Lacerda, here on the 19th of this month. The count says he is sure of finding the treasure at Gran Quivira within a month. He came here to attend court and expects to remain about two weeks and then go again to Gran Quivira.*

The *Weekly Citizen* reported on October 24 that Lacerda's District Court trial was set for November 5. But the treasure hunter, as reported by the same newspaper on November 7, failed to show up for his trial:

The hearing of the famous Brazilian count, Juan Miguel de la Cerda [sic], on two charges, assault with a deadly weapon and horse stealing, was set for this morn-

*ing, and the appearance of the romantic count was looked
on with keen interest by the attaches and hangers on of the
court. Disappointment was their portion, however, for the
doughty Brazilian failed to respond to the bailiff's call and
his bond was accordingly forfeited. These two cases with
two others against the same defendant had been set for
today and tomorrow.*

"Where is the count?" the Albuquerque newspaper asked two
weeks later, saying that Lacerda's whereabouts were shrouded
in mystery.

The answer may have come years later in the recollections of
some Anton Chico pioneers who believed that Lacerda took
advantage of their friendship to make off with a fortune in gold
and silver he found buried beneath their church. They said
Lacerda arrived in the Pecos River village in 1896 with a band of
gypsies and fourteen mules and began clearing out an abandoned
mine shaft at the foot of a bluff on which the Sangre de Cristo
Catholic Church stands, and that they had reason to believe that
he found what he was looking for.

Liberato C. Baca of Anton Chico related what he knew about
the mine shaft in an affidavit he signed in 1933. He said that his
father, Pascual Baca, had discovered traces of the shaft in 1886, and
while clearing out dirt and debris had discovered three stones with
Latin inscriptions on them, and some traces of masonry walls.

Baca said in his affidavit that the Latin inscriptions were copied
and sent to The Vatican by Father Augustin Redin, the Catholic
priest at Anton Chico, and that word came back six months later
that this particular mine had been worked centuries before by Franciscan missionaries and that it contained pure gold so rich and free

that it could be cut out in hunks with a chisel or axe.

The Franciscans had taken from three to four million dollars worth of gold and silver from the mine, according to the story, when they learned of an impending Indian attack. They put the gold and silver back in the mine shaft and filled up the entrance to obliterate all traces of it. Pascual Baca, spurred on by this information, spent thousands of dollars removing dirt and debris from the shaft, but finding nothing of value, eventually gave up the search.

José Guadalupe C. de Baca, who was a boy of sixteen when Lacerda arrived in Anton Chico, told his family that the gypsies worked day and night for some time opening the clogged mine shaft. He said Lacerda was a handsome man and always seemed to have plenty of money.

One day, he continued, Lacerda announced to the villagers that there would be a big fiesta that night, that all were invited, and that he would furnish everyone with all they could eat and drink. Everybody in Anton Chico attended the fiesta, he said, and there was dancing and merrymaking, and the celebrants gorged themselves on the food and drank the intoxicating spirits until they passed out.

When they sobered up in the morning, he said, they found that Lacerda and his gypsies had vanished. They remembered that the gypsies had not attended the fiesta, but had kept working in the mine shaft. Some had vague recollections of fourteen mules, all heavily laden, silently leaving town under cover of darkness.

Entering the mine shaft, they found a cavity where they believed the gold and silver of the Franciscans might have been concealed. The villagers reasoned that Lacerda had staged the fiesta to divert their attention while he and his gypsies sneaked off with the treasure trove.

Two Anton Chico men mounted their horses and trailed the

gypsy mule caravan many miles to the southwest. Near Gran Quivira, they learned that the caravan had passed by there heading south toward the Mexican border. One of the two men turned back at this point and headed home for Anton Chico, but the other, José Lopez, decided to follow the mule train on towards Mexico.

Lopez was never heard from again, the Anton Chico pioneers said, nor was Col. Juan Miguel de Lacerda, the King of the Gypsies.

Unless, by chance, the "Brazilian count" was the stranger who identified himself as Count Mordoff, a Russian nobleman, who arrived in the New Mexico mining town of Chloride in December, 1896, saying he was investigating the truthfulness of certain old church records that the Spaniards had worked a fabulously rich gold and silver mine in the nearby Black Range, and that concealed in the lost mine was a large amount of rich ore stored in leather sacks.

The *Black Range*, a Chloride weekly newspaper, described Count Mordoff as "a very interesting person, much above the average, with a bright active mind and the peculiar power of imparting to others in a clear and precise manner the real germ of any subject they happened to touch upon."

By January, 1897, the newspaper reported, the mysterious stranger had set up a luxurious camp near the summit of the Black Range west of Chloride, where he offered visitors fine meals and Havana cigars, and showed them a leather bag containing gold and silver ore. History appears to be silent about his fate, however, and unresolved is the question as to whether the "Brazilian count" and the "Russian count" were similar characters on a similar quest, or actually one and the same.

William "Bronco Bill" Walters

Each time William H. "Bronco Bill" Walters was admitted to the New Mexico Penitentiary at Santa Fe he gave his occupation as "cowboy." This he was, from time to time, but a more accurate job description would have been desperado, train robber, thief, and escape artist.

"Bronco Bill was the most typical western bad man I have ever known, and I have known a lot of them," Henry Brock, pioneer New Mexico cattleman, said in a 1956 interview. "He was a slender fellow, happy-go-lucky, a hard worker, and always wore a crooked smile on his face. He was cool and daring, tough but not mean, and he was absolutely without fear."

Brock's acquaintanceship with Bronco Bill and other bad men of the 1890s stemmed from his long career as general manager of the Diamond A ranches in the southwest corner of New Mexico, huge cattle ranches owned by the Victoria Land and Cattle Company and controlled by a group of California capitalists, including Col. A.E. Head, George Hearst, J.B. Haggin, and Lloyd Tevis. Many Diamond A cowboys, including Bronco Bill and some members of the Black Jack Gang, were known to have left the open ranges in the Animas and Playas valleys south of Lordsburg to follow the outlaw trail, earning the Diamond A the unenviable reputation of "producing nothing but steers and outlaws."

Brock said he first became acquainted with Bronco Bill in about 1894 when Walters was employed as a Diamond A cowhand close to the Mexican border. Walter Birchfield, a Diamond A foreman, said that Bronco Bill entered the Diamond A Ranch on foot from Mexico. Pioneer rancher John "Salty John" Cox recalled in a 1954 interview that he first met Walters when both were working as Diamond A cowboys in the early 1890s and that they both left to work for Israel King's Half Three C outfit that straddled the Mexican border south of Deming.

According to his prison records, William Walters was born in Texas in 1869, had a common school education, and had been self-supporting since age eleven. Normally a quiet man, except during periodic binges, he seldom spoke of his background, and the first two decades of his life are veiled in obscurity.

In the late 1890s, during the height of his career in crime, some New Mexico newspapers referred to him casually as "Kid Swingle," reviving the name of a young stagecoach robber along the New Mexico-Arizona border who vanished in 1888 after escaping from custody. No evidence was presented, however, that Kid Swingle and Bronco Bill were one and the same, although their descriptions and modes and areas of operation seemed to match in many respects.

A correspondent for the *Socorro Bullion*, in Socorro, New Mexico, wrote in 1888 that Kid Swingle was a smiling young man, gentlemanly in appearance, who always operated alone and "always acts square and honorable in all his personal dealings." The article said he held up some stagecoaches near Alma, in western New Mexico, but that he seemed to favor the stage line that ran between St. Johns and Camp Apache, in eastern Arizona.

In January, 1886, Kid Swingle was in a Springerville, Arizona, store, negotiating for the purchase of a pair of suspenders, when a local officer walked in.

"Kid, I have a warrant for you," the officer said.

"You have, eh," Swingle smiled. Then he turned to the clerk and said, "Did you say those suspenders were worth one dollar?"

When the clerk replied in the affirmative, Swingle put his right hand in his breast pocket as if reaching for his money, but when his hand came out it was holding a cocked Colt revolver, which he shoved against the officer's chest. The officer threw up his hands and shouted, "Don't shoot, don't shoot."

The Kid, who had been smiling all the while, burst into laughter at the officer's predicament. He backed out the door, mounted his horse, and rode off laughing.

In the winter of 1887, Kid Swingle pulled off one of his most remarkable exploits — a double stagecoach robbery.

Tethering his horse to a tree between St. Johns and Camp Apache, he waited patiently until the stagecoach bound for St. Johns came into sight. Halting the coach at gunpoint, he climbed up into the seat with the driver and ordered him to drive to a point several hundred yards off the road.

There was only one passenger in the coach, a soldier who had just been discharged and who was carrying his pay in his pocket. While Swingle was rifling the mail sacks, the soldier kept putting his hand in his pocket to feel his bulging purse. Swingle, noticing the soldier's uneasiness, smiled and said, "Be quiet, I will relieve you in a moment."

After robbing the mail and the soldier, Swingle climbed back up with the driver, ordered him to proceed, and they headed down the road a short distance until they met the oncoming stagecoach bound for Camp Apache. Swingle stepped down and held up this coach, which was carrying no passengers, and went through the mail sacks it carried.

After robbing this coach, Kid Swingle climbed up on the seat with its driver and rode back to where his horse was tied. Bidding adieu to the driver, he mounted his horse and rode away.

The sheriff of Apache County, Arizona, traced the outlaw east across New Mexico to Texas, and arrested him there in January, 1888. The sheriff placed his prisoner aboard a westbound train, and the two started back to Arizona. Swingle, handcuffed, sat next to the sheriff in one of the coaches.

Near El Paso, while the train was speeding along at a good clip near the Mexican border and not due to stop for a while, the sheriff left his prisoner alone for a moment while he went to the washroom. When he returned, his prisoner was gone, and an open car window next to his seat gave evidence that he did not plan to return. It was believed he escaped into Mexico.

That was the last heard of Kid Swingle, unless, of course, he appeared on the scene a short while later as Bronco Bill Walters.

Various newspapers in 1896 published an article indicating that Bronco Bill was playing the bad man in New Mexico as early as 1889, saying:

> *At Separ in 1889, M.P. Moore went after Walters and an associate for horse stealing. He found them asleep, but he had scarcely entered the house before Walters was up with a six-shooter in each hand, but by that time the fearless Moore had the muzzle of a double-barreled shotgun on his chest and Walters dropped his weapons. Mr. Moore said Walters unquestionably has great nerve.*

This article may be a garbled account, however, of a similar episode involving Bronco Bill at Separ that occurred in 1890. According to the same article, "Seven men once undertook to arrest him (Bronco Bill) in the Mogollons for burglary. He quit the house where he was stopping, got into a ditch and stood them off all day, only giving up at the solicitation of a friend."

It also was said that Bronco Bill, early in his career, had worked as a painter in the Atchison, Topeka and Santa Fe Railroad yards in Albuquerque, and was discharged after being accused of stealing money and a watch from a hotel room near the depot. The story is unverified, but seems to have some substance in the fact that Walters late in his career was to express quite a bit of familiarity with the Albuquerque railroad yards.

★   ★   ★

While it may be difficult, or even impossible, to document all facets of the shadowy career of William "Bronco Bill" Walters, it is a fact that he and a companion shot up and terrorized the small railroad community of Separ on the night of October 16, 1890.

According to various articles in the *Silver City Enterprise* at the time, Walters and a companion, first identified as Mike Mc-Ginnis and later as Miles McInnes, were "laying around" Hachita, on the Diamond A range south of Lordsburg, when some miners in the vicinity were discharged and paid off. The miners headed for the nearest railroad point, the village of Separ on the Southern Pacific line midway between Lordsburg and Deming.

Bronco Bill and his companion followed the discharged miners to Separ, hoping for an opportunity to rob them, particularly one named Jackson, who reportedly had $480 in his possession. All checked into the Armstrong boarding house at Separ that night.

Believing that Jackson had the money in a gripsack he was carrying, the two desperadoes reasoned that if they shot up the boarding house that night after all had retired, Jackson would flee from the house, leaving the gripsack behind. All worked according to plan, except that Jackson, running from the house in his shirtsleeves and without hat or coat, took his money with him and disappeared into the darkness. The *Enterprise* described the reaction of Bronco Bill and his friend:

> *Finding their prey escaped, they became maddened and furious, going to the telegraph office dressed only in their night clothes, they tried to kill a miner there awaiting the train and inaugurated a reign of terror at the depot, much to the annoyance of the lady operator, who during all this time had been wiring dispatch after dispatch to Lordsburg for aid.*

Grant County Sheriff Harvey Whitehill and a friend, Robert Black, both of Silver City, happened to be in Lordsburg that night, and being informed of the distress calls, boarded the next train for Separ, about twenty-five miles to the east. Upon their arrival, they found that everybody in the community was hiding out, except the two desperadoes, whom they found asleep in bed at the boarding house. Walters and McGinnis (or McInnes) awakened to find themselves looking into the muzzles of two shotguns. The *Enterprise* said:

> *Broncho [sic] Bill tried to draw his revolver which was in bed alongside of him, but it had slid out of his reach. He reviled the officers saying they had taken a sneaking advantage of them and could not have arrested him in any other way. It is hoped it will not be necessary to arrest them again for many years to come, but that they will be treated to their just deserts. Brutes who terrorize defenseless women and children, destroying their furniture and home belongings, deserve the severest penalty within bounds of law.*

The two prisoners were taken north to Silver City and placed in the county jail to await action by the grand jury, which was not scheduled to meet for some months. During their wait, the two became considered model prisoners, and were allowed the freedom of the jail corridors.

On February 16, 1891, one of Bronco Bill's Silver City friends managed to slip him a .38-caliber revolver and inform him that a horse was being held in readiness for his escape. Late that night, as Walters and McInnes were enjoying the freedom of the jail corridors, Bronco Bill pulled the gun on the night guard, A. Crowe, who had left his own gun in his desk drawer, and the two prisoners forced the guard to hand over his gun and his keys, then led him out of the jail.

Once outside the jail, Walters mounted the horse that had been obtained for him and headed south for the Mexican border, while McInnes marched Crowe three or four miles north of town, released him there, and headed west for Arizona. Crowe walked back to town in the dark, arriving there at four o' clock in the morning.

Bronco Bill rode sixty miles southeast to Deming, where he stole a fresh horse from Henry Holgate the next night, and continued south thirty miles to the Mexican border and across it to the town of Las Palomas, in Chihuahua, Mexico, within walking distance of the international border. Here he stopped, for once across the border, he was beyond the jurisdiction of United States authorities. He sent the horse back to Henry Holgate in Deming, together with a note thanking him for its use.

J.A. Lockhart, the newly elected sheriff of Grant County, learned that Walters was enjoying freedom just south of the border at Las Palomas, and began making plans to bring him to justice. To arrest him, however, it was necessary to lure him back to New Mexico soil.

To accomplish this task, Sheriff Lockhart deputized Cipriano Baca, who was well known in Las Palomas, to proceed to the Mexican town, locate and strike up an acquaintance with Bronco Bill, gain his confidence, and entice him back across the border. Baca left Silver City on March 4 and headed for Mexico.

Upon his arrival in the Mexican town, Baca located and struck up a conversation with Bronco Bill, who was suspicious of him at first, but seemed to relax when Baca told him that he was there on business, that he was a bill collector. As the *Silver City Enterprise* said, "Bronco didn't see the point until he was a prisoner and realized that about the toughest Bill in that section had just been collected." The *Enterprise*, on March 13, published the details of his capture:

> *Baca knew the fugitive's weakness and proposed to give a dance and stand the whole expense if Bronco would get the music. William fell in with the idea and as the matter was discussed over a long bottle of Mexican spirits visions of Mexican senoritas gaily tripping to the inspiring music of the violin floated before Bronco's uncertain vision and he became anxious. Kind friends suggested that a violin could be obtained about five miles away just across the line. He had no difficulty in borrowing a horse and Baca volunteered to go along for company. They took a bottle along to keep up their spirits. After having arrived at their destination while Bronco William was quite hilarious he was suddenly informed that his former associates were pining for his company. He was relieved of his revolvers and a pair of bracelets were slipped on his wrists. The visions of the dance faded away and the prodigal suddenly came to a realization of the fact that he was in the land of Uncle Sam and his disgust was intense.*

Baca delivered Bronco Bill back to the Silver City jail the next day. The grand jury indicted him on a charge of unlawfully discharging a deadly weapon, he entered a plea of not guilty, and his trial was set for the last week in May.

When the case came to trial, Walters withdrew his plea of not guilty and entered a guilty plea, in connection with his shooting spree at Separ. He was sentenced to one year of hard labor in the New Mexico Penitentiary at Santa Fe.

The Silver City newspaper said that Walters and other convicted Grant County prisoners were transported by train to the penitentiary in Santa Fe on June 10, but his prison record, unaccountably, says that he began serving his one-year sentence on August 26.

According to his 1891 prison record, William Walters was single, twenty-two years old, stood five feet nine inches tall, weighed 138 pounds, had blue eyes, brown hair, a fair complexion, several small scars on his head, and five large burn scars above his right knee. He gave his address as Silver City, his occupation as cowboy. He said he was born in Austin, Texas, that his parents were deceased, that he had no religion but that his parents had been Catholic, that he had been self-supporting since age eleven, that he had a common school education and could read and write. The record said he was temperate, used tobacco, and that the reason for his crime was drunkenness. He gave his nearest relative as one D.H. Hunter, otherwise unidentified.

The prison record said he earned good time in the penitentiary and was released on April 26, 1892, after serving eight months.

*　　　　*　　　　*

Following his release from the penitentiary in the spring of 1892, Walters apparently decided to resume his lawful occupation as a working cowboy, for it was shortly after this that Henry Brock and John Cox became acquainted with him on the Diamond A and Israel King cattle ranches along New Mexico's southern border. During this period he was considered a good hand, and loyal to his employers. He apparently stayed out of trouble, for New Mexico newspapers were silent about his activities between 1892 and 1896.

Life as a working cowboy apparently proved to be too unexciting for Bronco Bill, however, for by early in 1896 he was back in jail again, this time in Socorro, seat of Socorro County, which at the time extended west to the Arizona border. Newspapers said he was jailed for larceny, and Cox recalled that he had been arrested on a charge of stealing a horse in the mining town of Mogollon.

Shortly after midnight, on the morning of February 28, 1896, Bronco Bill and nine other prisoners escaped from the county jail by opening a cell door with a makeshift key and then pounding a hole through a two-foot thick brick wall with an axe. Once outside, they stole horses in town and rode off in all directions. They were not missed until after daylight, when a guard awoke to find the hole in the wall.

It was found that the key the prisoners had used to unlock the cell door had been fashioned from a silver-plated knife, and that it unlocked the door as well as the regular key. How the prisoners obtained the key pattern and the axe remained a mystery.

"The affair is no surprise to the people of this town," a Socorro newspaper commented, "as the prisoners have been generally allowed to go about as they pleased, without guards, especially those in for murder. Much comment has been caused by the actions of the officials in this matter."

Deputy sheriffs, with the help of bloodhounds, tracked down and captured all but one or two of the escaped prisoners during the next two weeks. Not found was William Walters, who showed up in Deming, about one hundred and fifty miles to the south, on April 1 and started on a spree. The *Albuquerque Daily Citizen*, on April 4, told what happened:

> *Two deputy sheriffs, Frank Peters and John Phillips, made an attempt to arrest him, when Walters opened fire on them, which the officers returned. As Walters was mounting his horse, it is thought that a shot struck him, as he reeled, but in any event, he got into the saddle and started out of town as fast as his horse could run.*

The newspaper described Walters as "a tough of the toughest sort," and "a horse thief, burglar and bad man generally," and made the exaggerated claim that he was thirty-five years old and that fully half his life had been spent in prison.

Two months later, in June, Walters was arrested in El Paso, Texas, and returned to the Socorro jail to face the larceny charge. Records show that in December, 1896, he was sentenced to thirty days in jail and fined two dollars cash for petty larceny. About a month later, in January, 1897, the *Deming Headlight* published this brief item:

> *Bronco Bill, who enlivened this city some months ago by shooting at Deputy Sheriff Peters and Phillips several times, has been released from jail at Socorro and taken to Silver City by Sheriff McAfee to await the action of the next grand jury.*

The *Silver City Eagle*, in June, told what happened:

*Bronco Bill, acquitted of trying to shoot officers Frank
Peters and John Phillips in Deming, afterwards arrested
on a charge of perjury, has been discharged from custody
with the understanding that he quit the territory. From
all accounts, he has followed instructions.*

If Walters quit the territory, as ordered, he did not stay away
very long.

*   *   *

Organized outlawry in New Mexico and the surrounding
region was reaching a peak in 1897 when Bronco Bill was released
from custody. Notorious robber bands, such as the Black Jack
Gang, the High Fives, and Butch Cassidy's Wild Bunch, roamed
at will over the region, robbing trains, stagecoaches, post offices,
and stores, terrorizing citizens, and fighting pitched gun battles
with officers who pursued them.

The rash of train robberies prompted New Mexico to enact a
law providing the death penalty for any person convicted of
assaulting any railroad train, railroad car, or railroad locomotive.
Many of the train robberies were never officially solved, however,
as the robbers were seldom apprehended or identified, leading to
much speculation as to the identities of those involved in each
robbery. The robber gangs were fluid, changing individual membership from time to time, and gang members seldom used their
true names and had a variety of aliases.

Bronco Bill, from time to time, was suspected of being a
member of the Black Jack Gang, using the name Bill Anderson,
but there seems to be no substantial evidence that he was ever a

member of this gang. Occasionally, he was even identified as being a participant in Black Jack Gang episodes when he actually was behind prison walls.

Thomas E. "Black Jack" Ketchum, a few hours before he was hanged in New Mexico for train robbery on April 26, 1901, identified Bronco Bill as having participated in the robbery of the post office and depot, and the attempted robbery of a Southern Pacific train at Steins, southwest of Lordsburg near the Arizona border, on December 9, 1897. In doing so, he was seeking the release from the New Mexico Penitentiary of three of his friends, Leonard Alverson, Walter Hoffman, and Bill Warderman, who had been convicted of the crimes and were serving ten-year prison terms. Ketchum claimed they were innocent, and identified the robbers as himself; his brother, Sam Ketchum; Dave Atkins; Will Carver; Ed Bullin (or Cullin); and Bronco Bill. Authorities who investigated the matter were of the opinion that Bronco Bill was not there.

Grants, on the Santa Fe Pacific (formerly Atlantic and Pacific) rail line in west central New Mexico, was the scene of a train robbery and two attempted train robberies during a nine-month period in 1897 and 1898, and it seems certain that Bronco Bill and a companion, Daniel "Red" Pipkin, participated in at least one of these episodes, although there has always been confusion as to which one. Henry Brock, who knew both desperadoes well, believed that Walters and Pipkin were the two robbers in the following episode.

*   *   *

As an eastbound Santa Fe Pacific train ground to a halt at the Grants depot at 7:55 on the evening of November 6, 1897, the fireman, Henry L. Abell, climbed down from the cab with a bucket of water to cool a hot pin on the locomotive. Suddenly, sounds of gunfire filled the air. In the darkness, nobody was quite sure what was going on.

The engineer, Harry McCarty, jumped from the cab and ran to the small depot. C.C. Lord, the express messenger, who was alone in the express car, turned out the lights in the car when he heard the gunfire, stepped out, locked the door, walked back to the passenger cars, and hid his express cap so the robbers would not know him if they came looking for him. Abell, preparing to cool the pin, turned to find himself looking down the barrel of a six-shooter.

"Hold up your hands," one of two gunmen ordered the fireman. Abell lifted his hands over his head, bucket and all. The heavy bucket slipped from his fingers and dropped on his head, spilling water over him.

The two robbers, armed with revolvers and Winchester rifles, and wearing what appeared to be false beards, ordered Abell into the cab of the locomotive. Abell noticed the bullet hole in the brim of his cap, and obeyed.

Abell's account of the train robbery was published two days later, on November 8, in the *Albuquerque Daily Citizen*. These are his words:

"When the train stopped at Grant's station, I jumped off the engine with a can of water to cool a pin. The engineer, who was in the cab, saw a man run up and fire several shots over my head and at some hobos who were hanging around. The engineer grabbed his torch and monkey wrench and started to get off the engine when a robber shot over his head, also over mine. The engineer turned, jumped off the opposite side, and ran to the station to get a gun.

"The station agent came out with a gun and fired at the robbers, who returned the fire, and the agent retreated. The engineer tried to get to the engine, crawled under the tank, was halted and fired at. He then retreated to the train.

"During this time I was held up by a robber at the side of the engine. I called out to the engineer to look out, as they saw him. I was made to get on the engine and ordered to start ahead. I started, but the air was pulled by someone on the train, and we stopped. The two robbers who were on the engine with me got mad, and thought I had stopped the engine, and threatened to shoot me if I didn't go ahead. I told them about the air, and said we could move in a few minutes when it leaked out. They threatened me again and swore, and made me open the throttle wide, so we would move ahead when the air leaked out.

"In a few minutes we started, and went about one-half mile. Then they took me back and made me cut off three cars next to the engine — baggage, express and mail cars. We returned to the engine and ran ahead about five hundred yards and stopped. They held guns on me all the time.

"We all got off, went back to the express car, held me, while one of them fixed three or four dynamite cartridges to the car door, set fire to them and blew the door to pieces. They made me open the door, and giving me some matches, pushed me in and told me to light the lamps, holding a gun over me all the time.

"One robber got in and covered me, then the other got in and located the safe and attached some dynamite cartridges to it. One jumped out, taking me with him. The other stayed in to light the fuse, then jumped out and the three of us ran to the side of the car. The explosion blew out the lights and set fire to the end of the car and some express matter. They made me get in the car with them. One rifled the safe and put a large number of packages into a long grain sack. We all got out of the car.

"One robber asked me if I drank. I replied, 'A little.' 'Well, you must drink with us,' he said. I told them I would if I had to, same as I did everything else they ordered. They produced a bottle of whisky and I took a drink.

"After this, they shook hands with me, and the leader told me that if anyone asked who they were, to say that Old Bill Dalton had come to life again. We all went to the engine, and the robbers skipped.

"I heard nothing from the rear cars, and the express car was on fire and burning lively, so I backed the engine toward the station to get help and water to put out the fire. I ran into the rear cars, the fire caught, so I pulled the mail and baggage cars ahead, while the Pullman and tourist cars were backed up by hand by the trainmen and passengers. Three cars burned up, the express, day coach and chair car.

"The robbers did not molest the baggage or mail cars. They spoke of going through them, but after filling their sack out of the express car safe they said they had enough."

The two robbers were last seen walking away from the train in a southerly direction. Officers, searching the area the next day, found that they had mounted horses and were headed southwest toward the Mogollon Mountains. The money they took from the express car, estimated to be at least $50,000, was never recovered.

In a 1954 interview, Mrs. Henry Abell, widow of the fireman, said that one of the robbers took her husband's name and address and promised to send him $1,000 after they had divided the loot. The money never came, nor was it expected. She said the robber gave her husband $15 "to eat with," then gave him a bottle of whiskey and told him to let the engineer have a drink.

A little less than five months later, shortly after midnight on the morning of March 29, 1898, five armed men attempted to rob a westbound Santa Fe Pacific passenger train at Grants when it arrived at the depot. Judson Lathrop, the fireman, said that the engineer, Ben Workman, climbed down out of the cab with a torch and oil can when the train stopped and prepared to oil a part of the locomotive. At that moment, the fireman said, he was joined in the cab by two unmasked men carrying rifles and revolvers.

When Workman called up to Lathrop to move the engine up a little, the two armed men in the cab pointed their rifles at him and told him to "look out." The engineer ran to the depot, noticing as he did so that three more armed men were standing near the train. The fireman was ordered to move the train about a mile west down the track. When the train was stopped, the two gunmen ordered Lathrop to accompany them back to the express car, holding him in front of them as a shield.

The two Wells Fargo messengers in the express car, Charles Fowler and C.C. Lord, quickly armed themselves, darkened the car, jumped out and locked the door, and took prone positions beneath the car. As the fireman and his captors approached the car, the guards opened fire, one of the bullets hitting Lathrop in the leg below the knee. The wounded fireman crawled off in the darkness and hid behind a rock.

The Wells Fargo messengers and the robbers exchanged fire for about ten minutes, during which time it was estimated that at least fifty shots were fired. The bandits gave up the battle, walked to their horses that were stationed nearby, and rode off to the southwest. Fowler said that he was sure he shot one of the robbers, and bloodstains found on the trail they left seemed to verify that at least one of them had been hit.

Red Pipkin later was indicted on a federal charge of assisting in this attempted train robbery. He hired Albuquerque attorney B.S. Rodey to defend him, and entered a plea of not guilty, but was not brought to trial as the indictment was dismissed on grounds that the government had failed to prove a case against him. Late in his life, he admitted to friends that he and Bronco Bill had held up a train at Grants.

There was yet another attempt to rob a passenger train at Grants, shortly after midnight on the morning of August 14, 1898, when two express messengers, identified in the newspapers only as Goodman and Comfort, fought off three bandits who attempted to enter their car. It is certain, however, that Bronco Bill had nothing to do with this attempted robbery.

★   ★   ★

While Bronco Bill Walters was suspected of taking part in a number of train robberies over a period of years, including at least one at Grants, there is no question about his role in the 1898 robbery of a Santa Fe Railway passenger train at Belen, thirty miles south of Albuquerque. His companion this time was William "Kid" Johnson, possibly the Bill "Kid" Johnson, alias Joe Evans, alias Ben Masterson, who had been released from the New Mexico Penitentiary on September 30, 1897, after serving more than two years for bigamy.

Santa Fe passenger train No. 21, bound from Albuquerque south to El Paso, Texas, pulled up to the depot at Belen at 1:45 on the morning of May 23, 1898, and the conductor, James Connors, stepped down from one of the cars and walked across the silent and dark platform toward the depot. He did not notice the two figures who emerged from the darkness and began walking rapidly toward the locomotive.

The two men, Bronco Bill and Kid Johnson, attired in cowboy clothing and canvas coats, climbed up into the cab and covered the engineer and fireman with six-shooters.

"All right — pull up the track," one of them ordered the engineer. The engineer obeyed, and the train began moving south from the depot. The conductor, who had just entered the depot, turned in surprise and dismay when he heard the train pulling out without orders from him. He ran back out on the dark platform and shouted to the engineer to stop the train. As the train gained momentum, he ran alongside it, still calling to the engineer to stop the train. When several bullets, fired from the cab, whizzed by his ears, the conductor retreated to the depot to give the alarm that train No. 21 was in the hands of robbers.

When the train reached a point about two miles south of Belen, Bronco Bill nudged his revolver into the engineer's ribs and ordered him to stop the train. When the train stopped, the express messenger, Edward Hicock, climbed out of the express car with a rifle and hurried back to Belen to give the alarm, not knowing that the conductor was already doing so.

One of the two robbers uncoupled the locomotive and express car from the rest of the train, and the engineer was ordered to move the locomotive and express car on down the track another mile, leaving the passenger cars behind. When the engine and its single car were stopped, Bronco Bill and Kid Johnson broke into the unoccupied express car, dragged a Wells Fargo safe to the door, and pushed it out of the car. They placed dynamite on the safe, lit the fuse, and the resulting explosion tore one side completely off the safe. Coins and currency scattered in all directions, and as Bronco Bill later told John Cox, "Paper money came floating down out of the sky like snow."

Bronco Bill and Kid Johnson loaded themselves with all the money they could carry, and tossed a shower of coins into the locomotive cab, a gesture sometimes practiced by train robbers to share excess loot with the train crew. Leaving the scene, they walked toward the west, got tangled up in a barbed wire fence, freed themselves, and disappeared on foot into the darkness. The train was reassembled and backed to the Belen depot, arriving there at 2:45 in the morning.

The alarm was given up and down the line, and lawmen from Belen and Socorro, about forty-five miles to the south, began taking to the trail of the two train robbers. Wells Fargo officials contended that only $250 was taken in the robbery, but this was a regulation estimate always given after a robbery. The silver coins the robbers had tossed into the locomotive cab alone amounted to $521. Estimates as to how much Bronco Bill and Kid Johnson realized in this train robbery range as high as $50,000.

The engineer and the fireman described the two robbers as smooth-faced young men, leading newspapers to speculate as to their identities. Names mentioned included such known outlaws as Kid Johnson and Kid Swingle, Joe Evans and Pedro Garcia, and George Musgrave. An examination of the ground after daylight revealed that the two robbers had mounted horses near where they had last been seen, had ridden southwest toward the Ladron Mountains, and then west along the sandy banks of the Rio Salado and its principal tributary, Alamosa Creek, through sparsely settled country in the northern reaches of Socorro County.

Taking to the trail of the outlaws from Belen were Frank X. Vigil, chief deputy sheriff of Valencia County, in which the robbery had occurred, and Deputy Sheriff Dan Bustamente. Leaving from Socorro, on the railroad line forty miles south of the robbery scene, were Socorro County Sheriff Holm O. Bursum; Deputy U.S. Marshal Cipriano Baca, the same Cipriano Baca who seven years before had arrested Bronco Bill after luring him out of Mexico; and two others. The small posses began converging on the small Hispanic village of Puertecito, on the Rio Salado about fifty miles southwest of Belen and the same distance northwest of Socorro.

*   *   *

In a 1956 interview, Sister Juanita, a teacher at St. Vincent Academy in Albuquerque, recalled that she was a girl of about twelve years of age, living with her family in Puertecito, when the two train robbers arrived in the village. Her father, Anastacio Baca, operated a small store in the community.

The train robbers dismounted in front of her father's store, she said, walked inside, and purchased some sardines and crackers and some feed for their horses. Baca suspected that his customers were bad men, but had not yet heard about the train robbery at Belen.

"I walked into the store while the two bandits were talking to my father," Sister Juanita said. "They were dressed in cowboy clothes, and each of them had a big money belt around his waist. One of them kept looking out the door to see if anybody was coming."

She said her father gave her an excuse to go see her mother, and she realized that he did not want her in the store while the two strangers were there. Walking outside, she noticed that a pair of thick pouches was strong across the saddle of each of the horses the men had been riding.

"The men came out and fed their horses, then went back into

the store and ate their sardines and crackers at the counter," Sister Juanita continued. "One of them paid for the food from a large roll of bills. I was sure their money belts and saddle pouches were filled with money."

Later that day, the two Valencia County deputies, Vigil and Bustamente, arrived at the village and paused at Baca's store. They wanted to organize a posse there to help them capture the two outlaws, Sister Juanita said, but were told that all the young men were out working in their fields. Baca declined an invitation to join the deputies, and suggested that they organize a posse at the Alamo Navajo community a few miles upstream. The two deputies mounted their horses and headed for Alamo.

Meanwhile, Sheriff Bursum and his three companions from Socorro were only a few miles behind Vigil and Bustamente when their horses gave out. Fresh horses were obtained for two men of the posse, while Bursum and Cipriano Baca headed back to Socorro to obtain fresh horses and more men, intending to transport them from Socorro west to Magdalena, a distance of about twenty-five miles, and from there travel north toward the Alamo Navajo community by horseback in an effort to intercept the two train robbers. Bursum said later that his attempts to organize a posse in the Puertecito area failed because young men of the region thought he was recruiting volunteers for the Spanish-American War and disappeared into the hills.

Vigil and Bustamente, after camping out for the night, arrived at the Alamo Navajo community at dawn on May 25. The Indians told them that two men were camped on Alamosa Creek nearby, at a locale known as Los Esteros, and a group of the Navajos agreed to accompany the two deputies to the site. Two of the Indians were armed with revolvers, and the others, unarmed, remained some distance behind.

The two deputies and their Indian allies proceeded the short distance to the outlaw camp shortly after 6 o'clock that morning. Topping the crest of a small hill on Alamosa Creek, near the Angelito Ranch, they discovered the outlaw camp about one hundred yards to the west of them and observed that the two train robbers were in the process of breaking camp. Their horses were picketed some distance away from them, their rifles leaning against a cottonwood tree at the edge of the camp, and their revolvers were lying on their saddles.

Silently, the possemen surrounded the camp, and one of the Navajos managed to steal unobserved to the picketed horses and lead them off. Vigil, noticing that the two outlaws had not yet armed themselves, began moving unnoticed toward the camp to make what appeared to be an easy arrest.

"Better get their guns first," one of the Indians warned Vigil.

Vigil ignored the warning, and reaching an elevation about thirty or forty yards from the robber camp, stood up, waved some papers over his head, and shouted to them that he had warrants for their arrest.

Bronco Bill and Kid Johnson, surprised by the sudden appearance of the lawmen, managed to remain calm and collected. Their arms hanging at their sides, they grinned at their visitors, throwing them off guard, at the same time inching slowly toward their rifles.

"Throw up your hands," Vigil shouted.

Suddenly, without a word, the two outlaws grabbed their rifles, threw themselves behind some cottonwood trees, and opened a quick and deadly fire on Vigil and his companions. Vigil and Bustamente fell dead under the hail of bullets, and Kid Johnson slumped to the ground with a bullet wound in his neck. Bronco Bill turned to help his fallen companion and was helping him to his feet when one of the Indians, Vicente Guerro, opened fire on him, wounding him in the hip and shoulder. Bronco Bill whirled around to see Guerro raise his head above a log, and shot him dead with a rifle bullet in the center of his forehead.

The remaining Navajos hurried south about thirty miles to Magdalena with the two horses they had captured to relate the first news of the furious gun battle in which three men had been killed and two wounded.

Bronco Bill and Kid Johnson, both suffering flesh wounds and on foot, gathered up all the money they could carry on their persons, believed to be about $7,000, buried or otherwise concealed the major portion of the robbery proceeds nearby, and began limping west. They appropriated two horses near the village of Datil, and continued west on horseback to vanish in the rugged White Mountain wilderness of eastern Arizona.

Some Navajos returned to the battle scene, gathered up the bodies of Vigil and Bustamente, and transported them on horses east to the Rio Salado village of Santa Rita, now called Riley, where both were buried in the church cemetery. Vigil's body later was removed to Belen, and Bustamente's body remained buried at Santa Rita, as his mother lived there.

The *Albuquerque Daily Democrat*, in telling of the fatal gun battle, said of Vigil:

> *He was one of the bravest officers in New Mexico but took too many chances in dealing with such desperadoes. There was not a single Winchester in his posse, Vigil having two revolvers and the rest of his men each having one. The men he attempted to arrest were fully armed with improved rifles and six-shooters.*

The newspaper predicted that the two outlaws would make good their escape, saying that Kid Johnson's father lived in the Luna Valley and that he knew every foot of the ground in the region they were crossing.

*   *   *

Bronco Bill and Kid Johnson found refuge on the Double Circle Ranch, a large cattle operation owned by railroad contractor Joe Hampson in the remote and rugged Black River country in eastern Arizona, where it was said both had previously worked as cowpunchers. Double Circle cowboys used home remedies to treat their bullet wounds, and here they were joined by Red Pipkin, Bronco Bill's companion in the Grants train robbery.

Once they had recovered from their ordeal, Walters and Johnson began displaying about $7,000 they boasted they had taken in the Belen train robbery and making plans to spend some of it. Periodically, they rode out of their mountain wilderness hideout to visit the small town of Geronimo, on the Gila River about forty miles to the south. Their escapades in Geronimo were reported later in Arizona newspapers.

One day, according to a newspaper account, Bronco Bill entered J.N. Porter's store at Geronimo, bought a new pair of pants, and paid for them from a large roll of bills. He tied the pants to the back of his saddle and rode out of town. He stopped some distance from town, put on his new pants, and threw the old ones away. Returning to town, he made another purchase, and reached down into his pants pockets to pay. His pockets were empty.

"My gosh," he exclaimed, "I left my money in my other pants!"

Running out of the store, he jumped on his horse and sped back to the spot where he had discarded his old pants. Retrieving the money, he rode back to town to pay for his purchase.

An Independence Day dance was in progress in a schoolhouse near Geronimo on July 4, 1898, when Bronco Bill, Kid Johnson, and Red Pipkin, all armed, walked in the door. While Johnson and Pipkin stood guard, Walters approached a group of young women, seated with their escorts along a wall in front of some open windows. Walking down the line, Bronco Bill asked each of the young women, "May I have the honor of this dance?" Each begged to be excused.

When the last of the seated women said that she was too tired to dance with him, Bronco Bill whipped out his six-shooter, exclaimed "Damned if I don't see that you do," and began firing bullets into the floor at her feet. Johnson and Pipkin shot out the lights, and the celebrants piled out the open windows, clearing the room in a matter of seconds.

Newspaper reports of this escapade did not escape the attention of J.N. Thacker, a Wells Fargo detective, who speculated that the train robbers were hiding out in the mountains north of Geronimo. He began making plans for their capture, and summoned to the scene two of the most efficient Wells Fargo detectives, George A. Scarborough and Jeff D. Milton, who for weeks had been concealing themselves in the express cars of various trains in Arizona and New Mexico, armed and ready in case the outlaws would try to rob yet another train.

Scarborough and Milton picked up a Diamond A cowboy named Martin in southern New Mexico, apparently for identification purposes as neither of the officers knew Bronco Bill, and traveled by train, with their horses and gear, to a point near Geronimo, where they unloaded their horses and took to the field. Granted permission to join them in the manhunt was Eugene

Thacker, youthful son of Detective Thacker, who wanted to go along for the experience. When word reached Bronco Bill that the officers were coming after him, it was reported, he sent word out asking that they bring plenty of good blankets and horses, as he needed them.

The four outlaw hunters, after disembarking from the train, rode northwest to San Carlos, then north toward the Black River into a region that was impenetrable for hundreds of miles except on foot or on horseback. For days, they made their way across rugged mountain ranges and through dense pine forests. Finding a discarded tin can with the Diamond A brand scratched on it, they guessed it had been left there by Bronco Bill, and believed they were nearing their prey.

On July 29, the four arrived at a Double Circle horse camp at the McBride crossing of the Black River. A tent stood in a clearing, and mulling around it were eight Double Circle cowpunchers and a bear hunter. The officers placed all of them under guard so that none could leave to warn the outlaws of their presence.

The four visitors spent the night at the horse camp. In the morning, Martin and young Thacker went off to look for some stray horses while the two officers remained in camp guarding their prisoners.

Milton had just walked to the bank of the river to fish for some trout when he heard some pistol shots in the distance. Looking up, he saw three men riding horseback down a steep trail off a mesa to the east. The three were shooting at a rattlesnake alongside the trail.

The man in the lead, who proved to be Bronco Bill, continued riding into the camp and paused at the tent, near where Scarborough was standing, while his two companions, Kid Johnson and Red Pipkin, lagged behind, still shooting at the snake.

"I guess I don't want to stop here," Bronco Bill said, eying Scarborough suspiciously.

"Hold on, I want to talk to you a minute," Scarborough called.

Walters whirled his horse around and started back up the trail, turning in his saddle to fire a shot at Scarborough. Scarborough and Milton both opened fire on the rider, and he plunged from the saddle and fell to the ground motionless. Johnson and Pipkin took cover behind rocks and trees and began firing at the officers, who took cover and returned the fire. A bullet downed Johnson, and Pipkin gave up the fight and disappeared into the brush.

Scarborough and Milton thought at first that both men were dead. The bullet that had downed Bronco Bill had shattered the elbow and shoulder of his extended right arm, passed through his chest, and lodged under his left arm. Kid Johnson had been shot through the middle, the bullet passing through both hips.

Milton, thinking Bronco Bill was dead, began dragging him into the camp by his heels. As he did so, blood gushed from the wounded man's mouth, and he began gasping for breath. Later, a physician told Milton that his action had saved Walter's life, as the dragging had loosened blood that was clotting his lungs.

Johnson was fading fast, and the officers sent a cowpuncher known as Climax Jim to Fort Apache, about twenty-five miles to the north, with a message reading, "Send a doctor and a coffin." But Johnson died that night, and was hurriedly buried in the camp near where he fell.

Splints were applied to Bronco Bill's shattered right arm, and he was tied to the back of a horse, his body supported by a makeshift cradle padded with blankets, for the tortuous ride of about forty miles south to Geronimo and the railroad. Here the officers escorted him aboard a train for transportation to the New

Mexico Penitentiary in Santa Fe.

The train bearing Bronco Bill and his captors to Santa Fe passed through Albuquerque on the evening of August 5, 1898, from where news of the outlaw's capture was sent out in this special newspaper dispatch, which began:

> ALBUQUERQUE, *August 6 – The notorious train robbers, "Broncho Bill,"* [sic] *whose real name is William Walters, and "Kid" Johnson, accused of the Grants hold-up on the Santa Fe Pacific in which they secured about $50,000; the Santa Fe hold-up at Belen, which netted them half as much as the first venture, and the murder of Deputy Sheriffs Vigil, Bustamente and an Indian tracker, a few days later, are not apt to make any more trouble for the present, as the rumors of their being shot and captured in Arizona a few days ago prove to have been well founded.*
>
> *"Broncho Bill" passed through this city last evening bound for Santa Fe, where he will be turned over by George A. Scarborough and J.D. Milton, by whom he was captured, to United States Marshal (Creighton) Foraker. He was shot through the right arm and shoulder, the bullet lodging in the right side. Some doubts are expressed as to his recovery. Johnson, his partner, was so seriously wounded that he died within a few hours, and the body was buried where the shooting occurred. A warrant is out from Socorro County charging "Broncho Bill" with the murders of Vigil, Bustamente and the Indian, and an effort will be made to take him to Socorro for a preliminary hearing. Detective Thacker of the Wells-Fargo Express Company and (Deputy) United States Marshal Cipriano*

Baca of Socorro also accompanied the prisoner to Santa Fe.

The news dispatch went on to describe the shooting of the two outlaws in Arizona, and added:

> *Milton all this time was shooting, but it is thought it was Scarborough's gun that got both men. The rewards offered for the two men aggregate about $4,000.*

On the following day, this news dispatch was telegraphed from Santa Fe:

> SANTA FE, N.M., *August 7* – *"Broncho Bill" [sic] has just been landed in the territorial penitentiary by J.D. Milton and George Scarborough, the officers who captured him, and his legs have been placed in shackles. In the fight with the posse at Joe Hampton's cattle ranch several days ago, "Broncho Bill," whose real name is William Walters, was shot through the right arm. The bullet entered the shoulder and passed downward, lodging in the right side. His partner, "Kid" Johnson, received two bullets in the breast and side and died within a few hours after the shooting. The body was buried on the ranch.*
>
> *J.N. Thacker, the Wells-Fargo Express Company detective, and Deputy United States Marshal Cipriano Baca, accompanied the two officers with their valuable prisoner to the penitentiary. It is unofficially learned that "Broncho Bill," feeling that his days were about numbered, has confessed to holding up the Santa Fe Pacific passenger train at Grants and also a passenger train on the*

Santa Fe road at Belen, New Mexico, wherein three deputy sheriffs in pursuit were shot and killed by the outlaws.

Bronco Bill was placed in the prison hospital, where he began a slow recovery while waiting for formal charges to be filed against him. A Socorro County grand jury returned three murder indictments against him, charging him with the murders in Socorro County of Vigil, Bustamente, and "Vincent Doe" (the Indian tracker Vicente Guerro). Socorro attorneys Elfego Baca and Judge Hamilton appeared for the defense, newspapers reported, and they succeeded in getting the case moved to Roswell, seat of Chaves County, on a change of venue. The case was moved back to Socorro, however, and the *New Mexican* at Santa Fe reported on March 3, 1899, that Baca had withdrawn from the case, leaving Hamilton to handle it alone.

On November 15, 1899, more than a year after he had been placed in the penitentiary, Walters entered a plea of guilty to second-degree murder in the District Court at Socorro and was sentenced to life imprisonment by Judge Charles A. Leland. It was said that Jeff Milton, one of his captors, appeared in court to plead for leniency for the outlaw, considering his ill health and crippled right arm.

Penitentiary records say William "Bronco Bill" Walters began serving the life sentence on December 14, 1899, gave his age as thirty, his occupation as cowboy, his marital status as single, and for his nearest relative, "none given."

★   ★   ★

As inmate number 1,282 in the New Mexico Penitentiary, Bronco Bill was assigned to duty in the prison infirmary and was considered a model prisoner. For the next eleven years he went

William Walters, alias Broncho Bill, side and front views. Photo made while in prison, about 1899.

Prison photos of William "Bronco Bill" Walters, taken in 1899 when he began serving a life sentence in the New Mexico Penitentiary for murder. (Courtesy University of Oklahoma Library, Western History Collections, Rose No. 1832) about his duties quietly, never creating any problems, and apparently causing prison guards to relax their vigilance over him even though it was remembered that he had escaped from a number of county jails in the past.

On Sunday evening, April 16, 1911, while a patient in the prison hospital, Bronco Bill found an opportunity to go over the prison wall. With the help of another prisoner, Kinch Mullen, he managed to secure a tall ladder and a rope. Under cover of darkness, the two placed the ladder against the tall brick wall, climbed to the top, and used the rope to slide down the other side. Bronco Bill made it to the ground safely, but Mullen slipped from the rope and fell to the ground, spraining his ankles. He remained at the outside foot of the wall, until found in the morning and returned to his cell, and Bronco Bill vanished on foot toward the south.

The *Fort Sumner Review*, on April 22, 1911, published the news of Bronco Bill's escape from the penitentiary, with a somewhat exaggerated account of his exploits:

> *Bronco Bill, noted murderer, train robber, crack shot, former cowboy of Grant County and desperado, with a more thrilling history than Diamond Dick or some of the other heroes of the dime novel library, and whose face has the half amused smile "that won't come off," made his escape from the penitentiary some time Sunday night and in a thoroughly thrilling manner, worthy of the man and his career.*
>
> *Bronco Bill, whose real name is William Walters, and whose number is 1282, was serving a life sentence for murder and what not, and had been in the penitentiary for the past eleven years. He was a trustie [sic] and it is said*

at the time of his escape he was at the hospital, though it seems certain that he was not a very ill man unless, perhaps, he had what the sheep herders call "the jumping sickness." His technique in getting over the "garden wall" of his terrestrial home was marvellous, especially as he had to forgo the pleasure of using his right arm which was crippled by bullets when he was arrested some time ago.

In police and other circles the escape of Bronco was the live topic of conversation all this week. It is said that he figured in no less than six train robberies in New Mexico and once landed $40,000 in Mexican silver from one of his holdups. Before he was finally captured and wounded severely in the right arm he was a great shot. He killed Deputy Sheriff Vigil of Valencia County and an Indian at a distance of 1,000 feet, and shot both in the forehead, the deputy sheriff between the eyes, and the Indian who was with him, in the temple.

It appears that Bronco Bill went to Mexico "for his health" after some of his escapades, but growing more daring, he re-crossed the border and visited a ranch in Arizona where he was finally "corralled." Before he was captured he made a rapid fire movement on his horse, wheeling around to flee and firing at his pursuers with his pistol aimed over his shoulder. The bullet, however, missed its mark that time, and his pursuers literally "pumped lead" in the cowboy bandit's right arm, putting it out of commission for any more fancy gun play.

Once outside prison walls, Bronco Bill walked south across open country about twenty miles to Waldo, a small settlement on the Santa Fe Railway, and then followed the railroad tracks another forty-five miles southwest to Albuquerque. Three posses with bloodhounds, under the command of Capt. Fred Fornoff of the New Mexico Mounted Police, followed his trail for about seven miles south of Santa Fe before losing it.

In Albuquerque, Bronco Bill bought a meal at the Mint Restaurant on Second Street, spent the night in a rooming house on First Street, and resumed his walk south along the railroad line until reaching Isleta Pueblo, an Indian town about fourteen miles south of Albuquerque.

Charles Mainz, a railroad officer, spotted Bronco Bill at Isleta, and sent word to his superior officer in Albuquerque, J.R. Galusha. Galusha proceeded at once to Isleta, and the two railroad officers concealed themselves and kept Walters under surveillance for a while, believing that he might lead them to the money he had hidden after the Belen train robbery thirteen years before. On April 19, when it became apparent that Bronco Bill was not preparing to leave, Galusha walked up to the escaped prisoner, who was squatting in the sun against an adobe wall, and arrested him without incident.

Galusha escorted him back to Albuquerque and placed him in the Bernalillo County jail overnight after informing penitentiary officials that he had captured the escaped prisoner. A search of Bronco Bill's pockets revealed $32.50 in cash, a bankbook on the Plaza National Bank in Santa Fe, some letters addressed to him in Santa Fe, and a few pictures of a niece.

Newspaper reporters interviewed Walters at the jail the next morning (April 20), and the *Albuquerque Evening Herald* that day published his story of the escape in his own words:

> *"It was spring; what little sunlight leaked down there into the prison yard seemed to get into my bones; the birds were*

singing around the place, and I saw some sparrows puttin' up a nest away up on a drain pipe.

"It was too much for Bronco. I says to myself, 'Bronco, let's see what we can do for ourselves; let's climb over the wall and try to beat 'em to Mexico.' I took another prisoner who wanted to go, got a ladder and stuck it up against the wall. It was Sunday night, a trifle cloudy, and I kept in the shade.

"Once on the wall I tied a rope and slid down outside. The other man came down, too. I had only one good arm, and the rope cut into my wrist almost to the bone. It made me wince, but I kept sliding until I struck the ground outside, and then I ran. The other man sprained his ankle and decided to return and give up.

"I started off toward Cerrillos, intending to catch a train there at night and not stop in Albuquerque. I missed my bearings, however, and when it came daylight, I was near a small station. I intended to reach El Paso, slip across the line, and then I knew I was safe, for I know Mexico.

"Fourteen years behind the bars, however, is a long time; the Rio Grande Valley did not look familiar to me. I tramped ahead, however, but I was surprised how often I ran into settlements and houses. I reached Albuquerque Wednesday night and bought a paper.

"I only knew two people here who would be likely to recognize me. One was Ben Williams of the Santa Fe (Railway); I was afraid of meeting up with Ben.

"I had $40 in cash and knew I could get through all right. I ate supper in a restaurant, and after that I went to a rooming house on South First Street and got a bed. I was worn out from the long walk. I lay in bed for a long time wondering what I had best do.

"I'll admit the old temptation was strong in me to go back to the old life. I knew none of the old boys were left, but I kept feeling like I had ought to go out and buy me a couple of good guns and make a run for it. I used to do it that way, and until they plugged me in this shoulder, I usually made good.

"I thought it over for maybe an hour, and then I says to myself, 'No, Bronco, you've been mixed up in the killing game long enough. No more guns for you. If you get away you win. If they get the drop on you, it's back to the penitentiary.'

"I rolled over and went to sleep, and it was late when I woke up. I got a snack to eat, but I didn't parade around any, and I kept my lame arm from swinging all I could.

"I then started down through the Santa Fe (Railway) yards, and it sure was a surprise to me to see the size of them. Fourteen years ago there was only one track down there, and it wasn't very long.

"I walked right into Isleta and that officer stopped me. I tried to talk him out of it, but I couldn't. I saw the game was up, and admitted who I was. Just for a minute I wished for a gun. I'm glad I didn't have one; I don't want to kill.

"I won't try it again. There isn't any use running from an officer without a gun, and I've quit using 'em.

"I will never use another gun as long as I live. I have killed enough in my time, and I will never kill another man. I could have fought my way out of New Mexico, but I've quit the bad game for good."

Bronco Bill was escorted back to the penitentiary in Santa Fe. The two railroad officers, Galusha and Mainz, split the $100 reward that had been offered for his apprehension.

*   *   *

Back behind prison bars, Walters served six more years of his life sentence in the New Mexico Penitentiary. On or about April 17, 1917, less than two weeks after the United States declared war on Germany, he was quietly released, either due to failing health, or as his friend John Cox said years later, to serve as a Red Cross volunteer in France.

Ranchers in the Magdalena region recalled years later that Bronco Bill returned to the scene of the gun battle on Alamosa Creek after his release from prison to search for the money bags he and Kid Johnson had hidden after they were wounded. Rancher Malcomb Major recalled that Bronco Bill told him that he could not recognize any landmarks in the region after the passage of years, and that he could not find the hiding place of the bulk of the currency, nor the silver coins he said he and Johnson buried between three trees on a hilltop southwest of Belen.

Giving up the search, he returned to his old haunts on the Diamond A Ranch in the southwest corner of New Mexico, where he found employment as a ranch hand and assumed the name W.C. Brown. Here he struck up a close acquaintanceship with a young boy, Jethro S. Vaught, Jr., of Deming, who periodically vacationed with his parents on the Hatchet Ranch, near the Diamond A.

In a 1956 interview, Vaught, then an Albuquerque attorney and federal bankruptcy judge, recalled that he first met Bronco Bill in about 1919. At the time, he was accompanying his parents from Deming southwest to the Hatchet Ranch, and they stopped for the night at the home of Lee Caldwell, a deputy sheriff, in Hachita.

"We went into the kitchen and were introduced to an old cowpuncher who was warming himself by the fire," Vaught said. "The man was introduced to us as Bill Brown, but we learned later that he was Bronco Bill Walters."

Vaught said that he was sent upstairs to share a room with the old cowpuncher, and when Walters peeled off his outer clothing he revealed underclothing with prison stripes.

"I was scared to death and ran screaming to my parents," Vaught said. My parents eased my fears, and Bronco was very upset that he had scared me. We slept in the same room that night."

Walters, who accompanied the Vaught family to the Hatchet Ranch the next day, developed a strong liking for young Jethro. Periodically, during the next two years, the man and boy spent many happy hours together. Walters taught Jethro how to shoot a .45-caliber revolver and a .30-40-caliber rifle, and they often rode the range together, Walters always picking a gentle and suitable horse for the boy to ride.

"Bronco Bill was the finest shot I ever saw," Vaught said. "He would shoot running jackrabbits with his six-shooter from a fast-moving Model T Ford, and would shoot the heads off ducks with a rifle."

Vaught said Bronco Bill became a second father to him.

"He always told me to mind my parents, to keep out of trouble, and to work hard in school so that I wouldn't grow up to be an old cowpuncher like he was," he said.

Vaught said Bronco Bill never spoke to him about his former life as an outlaw and desperado. Sometimes Diamond A cowboys would persuade young Jethro to ask Bronco Bill if he had any money, and was it true that he had a lot of money hidden someplace.

"Those cowpunchers have been talking to you," Bronco Bill

would answer with his crooked grin when the boy would ask him about his money.

On the afternoon of June 16, 1921, Bronco Bill was working atop a Diamond A windmill at Hachita, greasing the mechanism, when a small whirlwind, or "dust devil," struck the tower, spinning the windmill like a top, throwing him to the ground and breaking his neck. Still alive, he was carried into a ranch house and placed in bed.

"Go bring the boy to me," he gasped to the cowboys gathered at his bedside. The cowboys knew he meant young Jethro, and assumed that he wanted to tell the boy where he had hidden his money.

Vaught recalled that he was asleep that night at the Hatchet Ranch when a cowboy arrived in a Model T Ford to tell him that his friend was badly hurt and wanted to see him right away.

"I got dressed, jumped into the car with the cowboy, and we raced to Hachita," Vaught said. "When we entered the house, we were told that Bronco Bill was dead."

The *Lordsburg Liberal,* on June 23, reported that word had been received from Hachita that William Brown, aged forty-eight, known as Bronco Bill, had fallen from a windmill tower at Old Hachita and had died four hours later. The article said, erroneously, that he was the last surviving member of the Black Jack Gang, and that he had been present at the robbery of a Southern Pacific passenger train at Gage in 1883. The brief item, one of the few published about Bronco Bill's death in any newspaper at the time, said his remains were sent to his home at Big Spring, Texas, for burial, conflicting with another news report that he was buried in the Hachita cemetery.

*   *   *

Daniel "Red" Pipkin, who fled from the 1898 gun battle on

Arizona's Double Circle Ranch when Kid Johnson was killed and Bronco Bill was wounded, apparently appropriated some ranch property when he left. Records show that on October 25, 1900, he was sentenced to ten years in the Arizona Territorial Prison at Yuma on a charge of grand larceny, involving the theft of four horses and a saddle from the Double Circle Ranch. He was released in 1907.

By 1918, he was back in New Mexico, living in Gallup, seat of McKinley County, and the records show that he was sentenced to serve one to two years in the New Mexico Penitentiary from McKinley County on April 29, 1919, on a charge of assault with a deadly weapon. He was released in January, 1920.

Pipkin spent his last years as a McKinley County deputy sheriff and special officer for the Gallup American Coal Company at Gamerco, just north of Gallup. Here he worked alongside Henry Brock, who after leaving his position of general manager of the Diamond A Ranch had been working as McKinley County undersheriff and special officer for the coal company at Gamerco. Brock said Pipkin often boasted of how he and Bronco Bill had held up a train at Grants, fifty miles east of Gallup.

On July 6, 1938, Pipkin was found dead in his Gamerco home of a self-inflicted bullet wound. He was buried at Gallup.

What happened to the bulk of the money from the Belen train robbery that Bronco Bill and Kid Johnson concealed along Alamosa Creek? According to two pioneer women of the region, it fell into the hands of the Alamo Navajos shortly after the gun battle.

Mrs. Ida Mary Field, who lived on a ranch a short distance north of the robber camp, said in a 1953 interview that the Navajos found a large amount of money hidden in the crevice of a cliff.

"They certainly had a big time with it while it lasted," she said.

"They spread their blankets on the ground and gambled with it for days."

Sister Juanita, who saw the two train robbers in her father's store at Puertecito the day before the gun battle, also recalled that the Indians suddenly came in possession of a large amount of money, which they spent freely at her father's store.

"The money smelled like smoke," she said, "like it had been in a safe that had been blown with dynamite."

In the summer of 1973, Jim Williams, a Valencia County farmer, was irrigating his field near the railroad tracks a few miles south of Belen when he picked up an old and curious metal object. It was identified as a lock that had once secured the top of a Wells Fargo canvas money bag, undoubtedly an interesting memento of the Belen train robbery of seventy-five years before.

The Black Jack Gangs:
The High Fives

They called themselves the High Fives, after a card game that was popular at the time, but to the lawmen pursuing them and to the general public they were known as the Black Jack Gang, as the most notorious member was a mystery figure identified only as "Black Jack." The outlaw gang consisted of five young cowboys, all expert horsemen, marksmen, and outdoorsmen, who in the summer of 1896 left their employment on large cattle ranches near the Mexican border in southwest New Mexico and southeast Arizona to engage in organized banditry.

The High Fives soon were held responsible for robberies and murders over a wide area, extending from Texas westward across New Mexico into Arizona. Covering hundreds of miles on horseback, and eluding posses at every turn, they generally avoided large towns, their favorite targets being railroad trains and depots, stagecoaches, stores, and post offices, in or near small and isolated communities.

Authorities determined that the cowboy gang, as originally constituted, consisted of five little-known individuals of questionable backgrounds who used a wide variety of aliases, often making it impossible to determine their true identities. They were:

Cole Estes, alias Cole Young, sometimes referred to as Code Young, whose true name may have been Tom Harris, a twenty-four-year-old Texan identified as the original leader of the gang.

George Musgrave, alias Jeff Davis, alias Jesse Williams, alias Jesse Miller, alias Jesse Johnson, about twenty-two, a Texas native who grew up on a cattle ranch in southeast New Mexico. He was described as being about six feet tall, 180 pounds, dark hair and eyes, whose right leg would spring at the knee when he was standing or walking.

Bob Hayes, alias John West, alias Robert Hoy, whose real name was believed to be Sam Hassels, an Illinois or Iowa native who had fled to New Mexico after escaping from a Texas jail, where he was serving a five-year sentence for horse stealing.

Black Jack, whose identity was never definitely established, the prime candidates being Will Christian, Jr., about twenty-five, from Oklahoma, and Tom Ketchum, about thirty-three, from Texas. He was described as tall, well-built, and swarthy, with dark hair and mustache, and rather handsome. The pseudonym was attributed to nearly a dozen individuals over the years.

Tom Anderson, also referred to as Frank Anderson, also never identified, the candidates including Bob Christian, about twenty-eight, brother of Will; Sam Ketchum, about forty-two, brother of Tom; and William "Bronco Bill" Walters. Adding to the confusion were claims that there was more than one outlaw known as "Black Jack" at the time, possibly more than one Black Jack Gang.

The High Fives began their depredations on a small scale, their first target being a general store and post office in the small railroad settlement of Separ in southwest New Mexico, on the Southern Pacific line between Lordsburg and Deming, and just north of the huge Diamond A Ranch, where most of the gang members previously had been employed as cowboys. Entering the John D. Weems general store on the evening of July 20, 1896, they helped themselves at gunpoint to cash and provisions, and relieved Postmaster Robert C. Milliken of about $20 in postal receipts, for a total take of about $250 in cash and provisions.

News of the robbery was telegraphed to Silver City, seat of Grant County, forty miles to the north, bringing to the robbery scene Deputy Sheriff McAfee and a companion, Perfecto Rodriguez, who picked up the trail of the outlaws at Separ and followed it southwest across the Arizona border into the Sulphur Springs Valley. The *Albuquerque Daily Citizen* reported that the deputy discovered what he believed to be the outlaws' camp about thirty miles east of Bisbee, Arizona, adding:

> *He came upon a camp and found what he believed to be all the horses ridden by the robbers, but of the four men there he could not, from the description, identify one as having been connected with the robbery. He learned enough from their conversation and actions to establish the opinion that if they were not the real robbers, they were at least members of the gang.*

Deputy McAfee rode back to Lordsburg, telegraphed Milliken at Separ to join him at once, as he could identify the robbers, and the two rode to the outlaw camp with a posse, arriving there three days later. The camp was found to be abandoned by now, the trail of the outlaws disappearing south across the border into Mexico.

At noon on August 6, the High Fives rode into Nogales, Arizona, on the Mexican border, and stopped in front of the International Bank. Musgrave and Hayes entered the bank, followed by a third member of the gang, and held up John Dessart, the bank president, and Fred Herrera, a cashier.

As Musgrave was putting money into a bag, Dessart made a break for the door, scuffling ensued, Herrera picked up a pistol and began firing wildly, Hayes ran out the front door, and

Musgrave ran out the back door, carrying the money bag.

Musgrave tripped and fell as he ran out the doorway, injuring his leg and causing him to drop the money bag. Limping, he managed with difficulty to mount his horse and ride off, leaving the money behind.

Frank King, a local cowpuncher, realized that a robbery was in progress as he approached the bank, and drew his Colt revolver and opened fire on the bandits. The High Fives raced their horses out of town, exchanging shots with bystanders along the way. Miraculously, no one was injured in the melee, except for Musgrave, whose tripping and falling apparently was the cause of his right leg springing at the knee while he was standing or walking.

Arizona posses, led by Sheriff C.S. Fly of Cochise County and Sheriff Robert Leatherwood of Pima County, trailed the would-be bank robbers east to Skeleton Canyon on the New Mexico border and into an ambush. A telegram received the next day in Tombstone, Arizona, read:

> *Black Jack and gang ambushed us yesterday evening in Skeleton Canyon, killing Robson, custom guard. The first fire killed two horses and wounded another. They got two of our horses, we two of theirs. Think we wounded two, not certain, as they were concealed. (signed) Fly and Leatherwood.*

Posse member Frank Robson, later referred to as Frank Robinson, lone victim of the ambush, was a twenty-four-year-old U.S. Customs line rider from Tombstone. He left a wife and one child.

From Skeleton Canyon, the High Fives rode eastward through

southern New Mexico as posses from Arizona and New Mexico sought them in vain. The *Albuquerque Weekly Citizen*, on September 5, told of their movements:

> *The boldness of the bandits is something truly remarkable. After escaping from Skeleton Canyon, where they were supposed to be surrounded, and passing their pursuers at Lordsburg, traveling 110 miles undiscovered, the men came within a few miles of Deming and passed the night with a ranchman. In the morning they went into town, called at the post office, got their mail, and their presence was not even known by the officers until they had left in a northerly direction, apparently heading in the direction of Colorado.*

U.S. Marshal Edward L. Hall left his Santa Fe office to lead a posse north from Deming in search of the outlaws, the posse assisted for two days by some soldiers from nearby Fort Bayard. What was believed to be the outlaws' camp, as it showed signs of frequent use, was found in the mountains near Cooke's Peak. The posse retired from the scene when heavy rains obliterated the outlaw trail.

The *Albuquerque Weekly Citizen* said of the outlaw gang:

> *They are magnificent but cruel horsemen. When hard pressed they drove their horses at full speed down the sides of mountains so precipitous that a footman would proceed slowly.*
>
> *The notorious Black Jack, though not the leader of the band, was its most desperate member and the king of horsemen.*

Their trail was marked by dead, dying and ruined horses. One, a beautiful animal, was found with one hoof nearly entirely worn away.

But horses cost nothing, with what they were not fully supplied by sympathizing friends, they took without asking from less sympathetic ranchers.

Black Jack apparently read this news item, for in a conversation with a New Mexico rancher, reported later in the newspaper, he denied that any horses had received ill treatment, and said that any taken without permission were later returned to the owners.

Closely pursued on all sides in southern regions near the Mexican border, and having little to show thus far in their bandit careers, the High Fives headed north to try their fortunes in central regions of New Mexico, more than two hundred miles to the north.

*   *   *

Passenger trains on the Atlantic and Pacific line did not normally pause at the Rio Puerco station, which was merely a flagstop at the west edge of the Rio Puerco bridge about fifteen miles west of Los Lunas and thirty miles southwest of Albuquerque. The High Fives apparently were unaware of this, for it was at this lonely spot that they decided to hold up and rob a passenger train.

By a strange coincidence, the cowboy gang was waiting in the darkness at the station at 7:30 on the evening of October 2, 1896, when eastbound Atlantic and Pacific Passenger Train No. 2 made an unscheduled stop at Rio Puerco due to a minor mechanical problem. The engineer, Charles Ross, told in a newspaper inter-

214

view why he stopped the train and what happened next:

"I stopped at Rio Puerco on account of a hot pin, and when I got back on the engine and started to pull out I noticed three men on the tank. They came down to the cab, leveled their cocked revolvers at my head, and told me to stop as quick as possible.

"They ordered me and my fireman, Abe Reed, off the engine. We had no more reached the ground than they ordered us back on the engine. They, however, changed their mind, and kept me on the ground, telling the fireman to get back on the engine, which he did, and he was guarded by three men.

"The robber on the ground walked me to the express car to uncouple same from the train. When I started to uncouple the car, shooting commenced in general at the head end, and the man left me, going up to head end to see about the shooting. On seeing myself free, I hid in one of the coaches and could hear them hunting for me."

The shooting at the front of the train began when the brakeman, L.G. Stevens, approached the bandits, lantern in hand, and thinking they were railroad tramps trying to steal a ride, ordered them away from the train. They answered by shooting the lantern out of his hand.

Reed, the fireman, was ordered to move the train east across the bridge. When the train was stopped on the other side of the bridge, the fireman was led back to the express car and ordered to uncouple it. He said he didn't know how, but they ordered him to try anyway.

Meanwhile, the shooting had attracted the attention of Horace W. Loomis, chief deputy U.S. marshal for New Mexico, who was a passenger on the train, returning to Albuquerque from Gallup.

"I was in the smoking car when the shooting began," Loomis

said in a newspaper interview. "I got up, went to the front door of the coach, and by the whistling of bullets was convinced that it was a holdup.

"I turned and went back through the coach and secured my repeating shotgun, in which was two loads of buckshot. I jumped to the ground and laid there until I could see, it being very dark. I could see a bunch of men coming from the engine back along the front baggage car. I was afraid to shoot for fear of killing some railroad men who were being brought back to uncouple the express car.

"I crawled forward beside the day coach, when I saw a man separate from the bunch, and by his giving orders I knew him to be the leader. I fired at him, at a distance of nearly three car lengths, and he fell instantly. He got up and shot at me twice, one bullet whistling uncomfortably close. I immediately fired the other load.

"He disappeared then. I not being positive that I had killed him, and being then without ammunition, I returned to my day coach and put five or six loaded shells of duck shot into my gun."

Apparently unaware that their leader had been put out of action, the robbers tried in vain to open the door of the express car, occasionally calling out, "Cole, Cole." From a distance, a weak voice replied, "I am shot."

Two of the bandits were sent up the track to get some dynamite the gang had concealed, and they returned, saying they couldn't find it.

"I think we'll have to give this up as a bad job," one of the bandits said. His companions agreed.

"Come on Cole, we are going—we are giving it up," one of the bandits shouted.

From the darkness a voice answered, "Go ahead, boys. I am done for."

After relieving the fireman of what tobacco he had on his person, the rest of the gang mounted their horses and rode off to the south. The train moved on toward Albuquerque, leaving behind Deputy Marshal Loomis, who wanted to search for the man he had shot. Walking along the tracks, he soon found what he was looking for. As he said in the newspaper interview:

"I could see a white object at a short distance, which proved to be a shirt. It was so dark I could not make out his form, and put my hand down on the back of his neck. I knew by the feeling that the man was dead.

"I felt all around for his weapons, and found a .45-caliber Colt's revolver tightly grasped in his left hand. He wore no belt, but had a number of cartridges in his pockets. I struck a match, took a good look at his face, satisfying myself that he was Cole Young.

"Then I laid down in the weeds near the body for a short time, and afterwards scouted along the track, expecting the robbers to return and hunt for their companion, as it is not the custom of cowboys to desert each other in trouble. I remained there about three hours alone, until the special train with a posse arrived from Albuquerque."

The posse from Albuquerque took to the field, traveling miles to the south, finding the outlaw camp, but no outlaws.

Loomis said he believed the four remaining members of the gang were Black Jack, "an Oklahoma outlaw"; Jesse Williams, alias Jeff Davis (George Musgrave); Bob Hayes, alias Robert Hoy; and "Tom, probably known as Anderson."

The remains of the slain bandit leader were taken to Albuquerque and placed on public view and photographed at Undertaker Strong's. He wore a plain gold ring on one finger, and had $1.45 in his pockets. Sparsely built, he was five feet six inches tall and weighed 145 pounds.

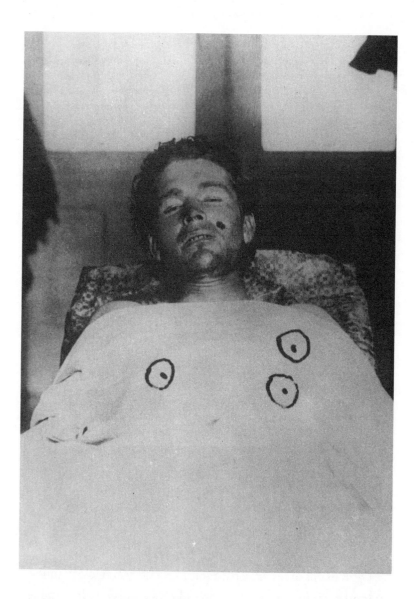

Cole Estes, alias Cole Young, original leader of the High Fives, photographed in an Albuquerque mortuary in 1896 after being shot to death during an attempted train robbery. Circles show gunshot wounds. (Courtesy University of Oklahoma Library, Western History Collections, Rose No. 2103)

Positive identification of the body was made by Albert V. Read of Deming, who said the deceased was Cole Estes, a Texan.

"For several years Cole worked for different cattle companies on the ranges around Deming and along the border, and I worked with him," Read said. "I was well acquainted with the deceased, but I cannot remember that he was known as Cole Young."

Read said Estes had left the Deming area about two months before with two men known as Tom and Jim and that he probably took the name Young at that time.

Cole Estes, alias Cole Young, was buried in potters field at Albuquerque's Fairview Cemetery. A short while later, the Wells Fargo Express Company gave Deputy Loomis a $300 reward for his killing of the outlaw leader.

With the death of Estes, the newspapers said, Black Jack apparently assumed leadership of the four-member gang, no longer calling themselves the High Fives.

*　　　　*　　　　*

Aaron Hollenbeck, owner of the San Antonio-White Oaks Stage and Mail Line, boasted in 1896 that there had not been a single robbery on the line in the sixteen years of its existence "except what was done by the stage drivers themselves." That was just before Black Jack and his three companions, remarkably unsuccessful in their bank and train robbery attempts, turned their attention to stagecoaches.

From the community of San Antonio, New Mexico, on the west bank of the Rio Grande a dozen miles south of Socorro, the stage route extended east about seventy miles to the gold and silver mining town of White Oaks in Lincoln County. It was a long and lonely stretch of road through a sparsely inhabited region, skirting rugged lava beds and winding through a low mountain pass.

Late in the afternoon on October 7, an eastbound coach driven by John Wickware had reached a point about thirty miles west of White Oaks when four armed and masked men appeared in the road and ordered the driver to stop. Finding no passengers aboard, the robbers cut open the mail sacks and took the registered mail and several express packages. Before ordering the driver back to San Antonio, they told him they were the surviving members of the Cole Estes gang, and that they intended to rob the westbound coach later that day.

The four then rode a few miles east to the Taylor Ranch, where John Mack kept a stage station for the line, and ordered him to prepare supper for them. After supper they relieved Mack of $6.00, exchanged their tired horses for some fresh company horses in the corral, and rode east to meet the westbound coach.

They met the westbound coach at about 10 o'clock that night, about twenty-three miles west of White Oaks, and ordered the driver, Ben Carpenter, to halt. Immediately, they began cutting open the mail pouches and removing anything that looked of value.

David Tinnin, the lone passenger on the coach, was ordered out of the coach at the point of a Winchester rifle, and as he stepped from the door he managed to toss his wallet on the ground behind one of the coach wheels, where it lay unobserved by the bandits. They took some of his personal belongings, including his hat, gloves, and a pipe, and when he protested that he was a "working man," they handed him $7.10 in payment for the articles.

The four relieved the driver of some tobacco and a knife, which they did not pay for, and disappeared north into the darkness. A posse from White Oaks, led by Deputy Sheriff P.S. Tate, searched for the bandits in vain.

Two weeks later, at about 8 o'clock on the night of October 21, a westbound coach, driven by Ben Carpenter again, was halted by two of the bandits at a point about twenty-three miles west of White Oaks, where the last coach robbery had occurred. The two armed but unmasked men told Carpenter that they wanted nothing from him, but would take anything of value from the mail and express shipments, and began cutting open the mail sacks. There were no passengers aboard.

After unhitching and appropriating the two coach horses, the two robbers held the driver captive while they waited for the eastbound coach to put in an appearance, which it did about two hours later. There were two drivers aboard this coach, William L. Butler and Joseph J. Carpenter, and as the coach slowly approached the holdup scene, one of the drivers said to the other, "Here is where they held us up two weeks ago."

At that moment, one of the two bandits stepped out from a place of concealment and said, "And here is where we hold you up again."

There were no passengers aboard this coach, either, and the two armed men proceeded to slice open the mail pouches. Noticing an express box on the floor of the coach, the robbers asked Butler what it contained. Butler kicked the box with his foot, and said it contained a clock, so they did not open it. Actually, the box contained $2,100 in silver bullion.

The robbers told the drivers they were the same who had held up the two coaches two weeks before, claiming they had obtained $785 from those robberies.

"And we are going through the outfit again in a few days," one of them added, although the threat failed to materialize.

The bandits also unfastened and appropriated the two horses from the second coach, and told the drivers they would have to walk the more than twenty miles to White Oaks.

"Tell the postmaster that if they will put the mail in baskets it will save cutting up all these government pouches," the departing drivers were told.

Again, posses took to the field in vain, and the *White Oaks Eagle* published these descriptions of the two robbers:

> *One of the men is described as wearing a gray suit and blue overalls, about five feet eleven inches high, weight about 170, dark brown hair, grey eyes, sandy complexion, wore a large plain ring on left hand, wore boots and had a large crimson negligee shirt. He appeared to be about 23 or 24 years old and was called by the other man "Rube."*
>
> *The other man was addressed as "Hand." He was of dark complexion, heavy black mustache, five feet nine inches high, weight about 150 pounds, wore a black suit, slouch hat, and appeared to be about 30 years old.*

It soon became apparent that these two were the gang members known as Black Jack and Tom Anderson, for by this time George Musgrave and Bob Hayes had left their companions to ride more than one hundred miles to the southeast on a mission of vengeance.

*   *   *

A cattle roundup was in progress on the Rio Feliz, about forty-five miles southwest of Roswell, when two men on horseback, their clothing ragged and torn, were seen approaching the Circle Diamond wagon camp at about 9:30 on the morning of October 19. The first to greet them were two Bloom Cattle Company cowboys, Harry and Dan Welch, who recognized one of the approaching riders as George Musgrave, who formerly had worked with them. They did not know his companion, Bob Hayes, described as "a tall man with mean eyes."

Conversations and actions that followed were recalled years later by A.H. Aguayo, a New Mexico cowboy who was among those at the wagon camp that day. His recollections coincided with newspaper accounts at the time.

"Hello, Harry, are you still here?" Musgrave asked Harry Welch as he pulled his horse to a stop. "You must be a good hand."

"No, but I'm still here, though," Welch replied.

"Who is the boss here?"

"George Parker."

"Where is he?"

"He is out on the drive."

"About what time will he be in?"

"In a short time."

"Who is the cook?"

"Sam Butler, the same as when you were here with us."

"Do you think he will give us something to eat?"

"Sure he will."

"We laid out last night, and haven't had anything to eat."

Musgrave and Hayes rode into the roundup camp and stopped at the chuck wagon, where the cook set out some food for them. After eating, they sat down on some bedrolls close to a water barrel, pulled some Bull Durham tobacco from their pockets, rolled cigarettes, and closely observed incoming riders. As small groups of cowboys arrived with bunches of cattle, Musgrave asked the cook to identify each man. In a short while, three men arrived whom the cook identified as Les Harmon, a Block Cattle Company man; Billy Phillips, a Bar V man; and George Parker, the cattle boss.

Parker dismounted and approached the water barrel, where Musgrave and Hayes were seated. He nodded at Musgrave, whom he apparently did not recognize.

Musgrave stood up and walked toward Parker with outstretched hand, as if to shake hands with him, and said, "Hello, George." Then, quickly drawing his .45-caliber revolver, Musgrave said, "I have come all this way across this territory to kill you, and now I'm going to do it." He fired four shots into Parker's body at close range, and the cattle boss fell dead at his feet.

Hayes drew his gun and warned the fifteen to twenty cowboys in the camp that "the first man who makes a flash dies." The cowboys, none of them armed, stood quietly.

Musgrave turned and addressed the stunned cowboys:

"Boys, I don't want to hurt any of you, but I've come a long ways to kill this son of a bitch. He had caused me a lot of trouble. He reported me to the law for the things he had done himself. In other words, for branding mavericks when we were partners a few years ago. He caused me to go into hiding for several years."

Musgrave also claimed that Parker has swindled his mother out of her cattle, falsely telling her that he had given her son $500 to leave the country, for which he was to take her cattle in payment.

Musgrave and Hayes walked to the roundup remuda and began selecting the two best horses and saddles they could find. Hayes picked up a saddle belonging to young Kirk Johnson.

"Are you going to take my new saddle?" Johnson asked. "I will have to have it, as it is all I have."

"How much did it cost you?" Hayes asked.

"Sixty dollars."

Hayes put his hand in his pocket as if to pay for the saddle, then changed his mind.

"I'll tell you what I'll do," he told the young cowboy. "What is your name? The first time I get to a town where I can send you the money, I will send it to you."

After roping and saddling the two horses they wanted, the two outlaws rode off across the plains. As they were disappearing from view, the cowboys in the camp noticed a wisp of smoke coming from Parker's clothing, it having been ignited by the closeness of the pistol shots. Several of the cowboys, including Lycurgus Johnson and Frank Parks, were sent to Roswell to report the killing to authorities. After an inquest at the scene, Parker's body was placed in a cattle company hack and transported to Roswell for burial.

Musgrave and Hayes rode to the V Ranch headquarters, where they ate supper and exchanged their horses for fresh ones. After pausing at Cedar Hill, to visit Musgrave's father and brothers, they headed on west.

New Mexico newspapers, telling of the killing of George Parker on the Rio Feliz, published another brief item saying that a George Parker had been killed by a young man named Clements on the Rio Hondo between Lincoln and Roswell, but speculated that this was merely a garbled account of the Parker killing about twenty miles to the south.

*   *   *

On the evening of October 27, 1896, two members of the outlaw gang returned to Separ, scene of the first robbery by the High Fives three months before, and proceeded to rob and terrorize every man in the railroad village. The two robbers variously were identified as George Musgrave and Bob Hayes, George Musgrave and Black Jack, and as Black Jack and Tom Anderson.

The first report of the unusual robbery was published a few

days later in the *Deming Headlight*:

> *Last Tuesday evening about 6 o'clock, two men held up the entire population at Separ, this county, and took everything available in sight. One of the men was recognized as Black Jack, and the other, it is said, is none other than Jeff Davis [George Musgrave].*
>
> *The robbers first entered the telegraph and express station, robbed the operator and pumpman, marched them to the boarding house, relieved the inmates of all their available cash, [and] making them get into position in the procession, marched from there to [the] J.D. Weems store, where there were about eight armed cowboys.*
>
> *Black Jack and his first lieutenant disarmed the cowboys and borrowed all their loose change, and then turned their attention to Col. Robert Milliken, postmaster and assistant in the store, who making some resistance received an ugly scalp wound from the back end of a gun, the front end of which was held by one of the bandits, which convinced him that his proper place was in line with the operator, pumpman, lodging house keeper and cowboys.*
>
> *After securing about $100 in money, a lot of whisky, tobacco, cigars and merchandise, the bandits gave the order to march, and what proved to be the entire population of Separ was marched about two miles from the depot, where the robbers mounted their horses which were stationed there, and after bidding the citizens a fond farewell, departed. When the passenger train going west pulled into the station, the crowd was just returning from their forced march into the country.*

Other details of the drama began to unfold after lawmen and

postal inspectors reached the scene and interviewed the victims. The first victim was the station agent, a man named Ellis, who said he was sitting in his office in the depot when two masked men walked in the door with drawn guns. He said they took $20 from his person, and another $56 belonging to the Southern Pacific Railroad and the Wells Fargo Company.

The two bandits then placed a mask and cowboy hat on Ellis and made him walk in front of them as they made their rounds of the village, so that if any of the villagers started shooting, they would shoot first at Ellis, believing him to be the outlaw leader.

The bandits marched the people to the only saloon in town and set up the drinks, Black Jack paying the barkeeper with money taken from the post office. Each citizen, in turn, was permitted to approach the bar, lower his raised hands, take a drink, raise his hands again, and return to the lineup.

During this little social get-together in the saloon, the two bandits boasted that this was their second visit to the town, that they had been among those who had held up the Separ post office in July. The *Albuquerque Citizen* said:

> They then marched them all out in the dark to the stockyards and again stood them up in a line just as the Southern Pacific train was coming in.
> After asking them whether they thought one Winchester bullet would go through the bodies of the entire thirteen, they told them to stand still while the bandits mounted their horses and rode off.

*   *   *

Sometimes working together, sometimes in pairs, the four

surviving members of the High Fives embarked on a campaign of robbery and terror, covering hundreds of square miles in southwest New Mexico and southeast Arizona. Writing from Bowie Station, Arizona, on November 11, 1896, G.H. Waterbury, chief regional postal inspector, said the gang had attempted to hold up a Southern Pacific mail train at Deming, and listed their other depredations:

"These same bandits have successfully held up and robbed four stages on the San Antonio and White Oaks, New Mexico, stage line, cutting open the pouches and rifling the registered mail; robbed the Separ post office a second time; held up the postmaster and robbed the post office at San Simon, Cochise County, Arizona, sixteen miles east of here; made an attempt to rob the Nogales, Arizona, bank at midday, and last Saturday night held up and robbed the agent and all of the citizens at Huachuca (Arizona), nine miles from the United States fort of the same name, besides numerous stockmen and ranchmen, whose horses they have stolen and carried off.

"They have killed three men — a Mr. Parker near White Oaks, who had informed on them; another cattleman on the Gila River, whose name I have not yet learned, and one of the United States customs officers, who was in the sheriff's posse following them above the Mexican boundary line after the attempt on the Nogales bank, and named Robinson.

"In their attempt to rob the post office at this place (Bowie Station), Postmaster Wickersham took a shot at one of them, the bullet going within a few inches of Black Jack's head, since which time the gang sent word to the postmaster that they would come back and kill him on sight. When they robbed the post office at San Simon (Arizona), they brutally pounded the postmaster over

228

the head with a revolver when down and kicked him into insensibility. . . .

"They are that bold that they no longer pretend to wear masks, and openly tell how they held up the White Oaks stages, the Atlantic and Pacific railway mail train, the Separ post office; also of the San Simon and Teviston (Arizona) post offices and the Nogales bank, and they declare that they will rob every small post office they come across until they get a sufficient 'stake,' when they will leave the country, but not until they have killed Deputy Marshal Loomis, who shot and killed their first leader, Cole Estes, alias Cole Young, in the Atlantic and Pacific train robbery, and the postmaster at this place who took a shot at their new leader, Black Jack, a few days ago, while they were attempting to rob this office.

"They also acknowledge that Black Jack shot and killed Customs Officer Robinson in the mountains below here, and they boldly tell the cowboys where they stop that they will kill anybody who informs on or opposes them in any manner, and which has, as you may imagine, terrorized the whole country.

"The names of these bandits are George Musgrave, alias Jeff Davis, alias Jesse Williams; Bob Hayes; Black Jack, whose right name is also said to be Williams, and the gang was formerly led by Cole Estes until he was killed, but is now led by Black Jack, all of whom are cowboys who have ridden this and the New Mexico ranges for years past, hence are thoroughly familiar with the country from White Oaks to Arizona, and who will ride 100 miles in twenty-four hours with ease, stealing fresh horses whenever they need them and terrorizing people along the route into silence for fear of their lives and stock. Thus you will see that these bandits are as bad as the Apaches, and that something desperate must be done to stop these outlaws or it will be hard to say what the end will be."

229

On November 17, the *Tombstone* (Arizona) *Prospector* published an interview with an Arizona rancher who had been paid a visit by Black Jack and his companions:

> *A rancher who is in town today on court duty, and who does not desire his name made public, informed the* Prospector *reporter that the band of robbers, after robbing Huachuca Siding, next appeared at our informant's ranch in the valley, where they dismounted and remained for dinner.*
>
> *They made no attempt to conceal their identity and seemed well informed as to the movements of the posse in pursuit.*
>
> *During the meal the robbers became quite loquacious, recounting all their deeds and various hold-ups which would furnish an interesting topic for a blood and thunder novel, narrating some particularly ludicrous episodes of some unfortunate who was scared to death and begged pityingly for his life when there was no intention of harming him at all, would break out in a most hearty laugh; this would recall another incident followed by more peals of laughter, until apparently forgetting all precautionary dangers and usual grave demeanor and watchfulness turned the hour into one of veritable mirth, seemingly enjoying it to the utmost.*
>
> *Upon taking their leave, the rancher was informed that they were using quite a number of horses found on the range, but would steal none nor ride any to death. They asserted that they did not care to harm any individual.*
>
> *In regard to the posse or officers after them, it was their duty to follow them, but they would not concern themselves much about it should they meet, as they intimated*

they would not be taken alive.

The newspapers credited Black Jack with exhibiting a "chivalrous nature" at times, reporting that he refused to rob post offices or stores that were managed by women, and that he sometimes compensated his victims for items taken from them. As the *Albuquerque Weekly Citizen* reported on November 14:

> *A cowboy sporting a dream of a cowboy hat, with all the spangles and trimmings that made its owner prouder than a president and envied by every knight of the lariat who saw it, was met by the robbers. All hands stopped. Black Jack's covetous eyes fell on the hat and simultaneously the spirits of its possessor also fell as he reluctantly complied with the former's polite, but commanding request, to let him see the hat, adding that if it would fit there would be a change of ownership.*
>
> *The cowboy made one last appeal, and said familiarly, addressing him as "Jack," that he was broke and supplicatingly asked that he not be deprived of his treasured sombrero. Whereupon Black Jack inquired the price of the headgear, which proved to be $12. The money was paid to the cowboy and Black Jack rode on decked out with the gorgeous hat, evidently well pleased with his bargain.*

★   ★   ★

Among the New Mexico posses searching for Black Jack and his companions was a four-member Grant County party led by Sheriff Baylor Shannon of Silver City. His companions were Deputy Sheriff Frank M. Galloway of Silver City, and two special deputies, Steve Birchfield and Frank McGlinchy of Deming, the latter a deputy U.S. marshal.

From Separ, scene of the October 27 robbery spree, the sheriff's posse trailed the outlaws west into the San Simon Valley, on the Arizona border, where they camped on the night of October 31. Fearing that the bandits were nearby and might attack their camp, the four deputies agreed to take turns standing watch through the night, each sentry remaining awake while seated on his bedding.

During the early morning darkness, Birchfield was awakened by a noise outside the camp. Springing up and grabbing his rifle, he woke up Shannon and McGlinchy, who reached for their rifles, Shannon unable to get possession of his immediately because it was stuck in his saddle. Peering into the darkness, the three saw a dark object about fifty feet away approaching the camp.

"Who is there — Who is there?" McGlinchy shouted. When there was no answer, Shannon told his companions, "Shoot — Shoot!"

McGlinchy and Birchfield fired simultaneously, and the figure dropped. Shannon then glanced around the camp and noticed that Deputy Galloway, who was on watch at the time, was nowhere to be seen.

"My God, boys, we have killed Galloway," the sheriff exclaimed.

Sure enough, Galloway was found dead outside the camp, a rifle bullet having passed through his head. It was not determined why he had left the camp, or why he had not answered the "Who is there?" call, although it was speculated that he did not hear the challenge because he had his overcoat pulled up over his head to protect him from the cold.

The three embarrassed officers took Galloway's body to the ranch home of J.A. Chenowith, from where it was transported to Lordsburg. A coroner's jury ruled that the shooting was accidental. Galloway was buried at Deming, leaving a wife and four children.

*   *   *

Returning to Separ, Sheriff Shannon and his two surviving deputies, Birchfield and McGlinchy, met three lawmen from the Roswell area who were on the trail of George Musgrave and Bob Hayes, wanted for the October 19 murder of George Parker at the cattle roundup near Roswell. The newcomers were J. L. "Les" Dow, a deputy U.S. marshal and sheriff-elect of Eddy County; Charlie Ballard; and Fred Higgins.

It was known that the outlaws were in the vicinity on November 14, when they held up and robbed a store at Steins, a tiny railroad village about thirty-five miles west of Separ. The lawmen learned that the outlaw gang, when in the vicinity, was in the habit of visiting and eating breakfast with cowboy friends at the Deer Creek horse camp on the Diamond A Ranch, near the Mexican border about fifty miles south of Separ. The horse camp consisted of a small house, a large corral, and an earthen water tank surrounded by a picket fence. The combined posse headed south for Deer Creek.

Later, in relating to a newspaper reporter the events of that fateful expedition, Dow made no mention of the Grant County possemen, who failed to take an active part in the action that followed at the horse camp. Dow's account, as published in various newspapers at the time, follows:

"On the evening of Tuesday, the 17th (of November), after following the trail of Black Jack's gang for several days, we struck the place where they had recently broke camp, and from that point their trail led towards Deer Creek. We knew the robbers were out of provisions, and concluded they would go into the

233

Diamond A Ranch next morning to secure supplies. In order to get there ahead of them, we went around the trail and by hard riding reached the Diamond A Ranch at daylight.

"After getting breakfast we did not have long to wait before, just as we expected, two of the robbers came riding into the ranch. They were Bob Hayes and a large, dark complected man with heavy black moustache, and I knew he was Black Jack from the description given me of the leader of the gang.

"I had only two men with me but they were dead game. When the two robbers got within sixty yards of us we covered them, and I called out for them to throw up their hands. That, however, was not their game. Both men snatched out their pistols, jerked their horses' heads up between us and themselves, and leaning back in their saddles opened fire, which we returned with interest.

"In pulling his horse back, Black Jack jerked the animal to his haunches, and then set him wild by clinching his spurred heel in the animal's flank to keep him from falling off. The horse began plunging, and seeing Hayes fall, Black Jack headed for the brush.

"Seeing he was about to get away, I shot his horse, killing him. The animal rolled over on Black Jack's rifle, but he swiftly lifted the horse sufficiently to secure his gun, and then he disappeared in the bushes.

"Bob Hayes, though mortally wounded, fought to a finish, firing two shots at us while he was lying on his back dying. I don't think any of us touched Black Jack, his confounded horse was cavorting around at such a rate. He rejoined his men, who had remained some distance out in the bushes.

"I had to return to Eddy [County] to file my bond and qualify as sheriff, but left Charlie Ballard in charge of the posse to follow the trail of the gang. Black Jack will be hard to catch, as his men can get fresh horses whenever they need them, and they have more friends out there than the officers have."

Among those who witnessed the battle at the Deer Creek horse camp was Henry Brock, superintendent of the Diamond A Ranch, who was working in the corral with about a dozen of his cowboys. In a 1957 interview, more than sixty years after the event, Brock gave his recollections of what happened at the camp on the morning of November 18, 1896.

Brock said the officers and the cowboys had just finished breakfast that morning when four mounted men were seen approaching the camp from the northeast, riding down from a ridge on what was known as the Old Smugglers Trail. Sheriff Shannon and his two deputies concealed themselves in the small house, he said, while Dow, Ballard, and Higgins took up defensive positions in the empty water tank, the earthen walls of which were about four feet high.

Brock said that Black Jack and Hayes were riding some distance ahead of their two companions and entered the camp unaware of any danger, while the other two, Musgrave and a man Brock did not recognize, were still some distance back, near the foot of the ridge.

"The Roswell posse opened a heavy fire on Black Jack and Hayes when they were only a few yards from the water tank," Brock recalled. "Hayes went down in the first volley, fatally wounded, but lived just long enough to raise himself up and empty his six-shooter at the posse, making them keep their heads down.

"Black Jack's horse was hit and started pitching toward the open corral gate. Not wanting to be cornered in the corral, he whipped off his hat and slapped his horse along the side of its head with it, causing the horse to veer to the left of the gate. His pistol fell from its holster as the horse was pitching. The horse fell on its side near the corral, pinning Black Jack's rifle, which was in the saddle scabbard, beneath it.

"Black Jack jerked the saddle around, dislodged the rifle, then whirled around and opened fire on the posse. He fired that rifle so fast you would have thought it was a machine gun, and you should have seen the splinters fly around the posse members. After emptying his rifle, Black Jack ran down an arroyo, climbed part way up a hill, and hid behind a small bush. The posse searched the area for him, but did not see him, even though they passed to within about twenty feet of him.

"When the officers left, Black Jack walked twenty miles west to the Gray Ranch, stole a Diamond A horse, and disappeared into Arizona or Mexico."

As to the identity of Black Jack, Brock said he definitely was Tom Ketchum, regardless of later accounts that claimed that this Black Jack was the Oklahoma outlaw Will Christian. He said that Ketchum, on a later visit to the ranch, joked with him about the battle.

"I didn't know you had a posse at the camp," Ketchum told Brock. "When all the shooting started, I thought the Diamond A cowboys were trying to get me."

Brock said Black Jack also joked about hiding behind a bush when the posse was searching for him.

"When I noticed how far my behind was sticking out," he laughed, "it seemed to me as big as a mountain."

The Grant County posse returned to Silver City triumphantly following the gun battle, McGlinchy reporting that they had battled the Black Jack Gang and had killed Bob Hayes and wounded George Musgrave. He made no mention of the Roswell posse that had done all the fighting.

The body of Hayes was taken north and buried at Separ, scene of some of his earlier exploits. The *Deming Headlight*, a few weeks later, reported that the dead outlaw had been identified by a friend as Sam Hassels, a fugitive from Texas, adding:

> *Hassels was a resident of Gonzales county, Texas, and was sent to the Texas penitentiary for a term of five years for horse stealing. He had served his time with the exception of about four months when he made his escape....*
>
> *Until his recent escapades, he was known in this section as a hard-working, peaceable cowman, and his associates never thought that he would adopt the course that finally cost him his life.*

The Deer Creek battle marked the end of what was believed to be the "original" Black Jack Gang, the three High Fives survivors going their separate ways. The *Albuquerque Weekly Citizen*, on December 26, 1896, told of the disbanding of the cowboy gang, citing reports from Tombstone, Arizona:

> *Word received in Tombstone of the whereabouts of the Black Jack band is to the effect that the terrorizing band has pretty much disbanded and have left the territory.*
>
> *The* Prospector *says: After the Deer Creek fight Jesse Williams and one other of the band whose name is not known left in one direction, and neither hide, hair nor track of either of these have been heard of since, while Black Jack, whose horse was shot from under him, hid around until he could make his escape. He flocked by himself, going towards Mexico. He was traced to different ranches and followed across the line.*

Later he made tracks toward Nogales, where it is presumed he disguised himself and boarded the New Mexico & Arizona for a ride out of the country. It is known that he had considerable money as he offered to pay for some victuals at the last ranch and was anxious of the whereabouts of his two partners, being apparently as much at sea of their location as the officers.

The supposition that Black Jack had disguised himself and left Nogales on the train is arrived at by different facts traced to reliable sources, all of which point to his intention of so doing. It is believed he went to San Antonio, Texas.

★   ★   ★

The mystery as to the true identity of Black Jack appeared solved, at least to the satisfaction of some, by a brief article that appeared in the *Eddy County Current* at Carlsbad, seat of Eddy County in southeast New Mexico, and picked up by various other New Mexico newspapers in January, 1897. The article said:

Black Jack was for a couple of months a resident of Eddy County. He was well known to Bob Brogdon, with whom he attended school in the Pan Handle of Texas some 10 or 15 years ago.

Brogdon says Black Jack's real name is Will Christian, that he is one of two brothers who tarried near Seven Rivers from July to September, 1895. He says Christian is a simple and ordinary bad boy who has become reckless.

This appears to be the only newspaper article of the period identifying Black Jack as the Oklahoma outlaw Will Christian.

William Christian, Jr., and his older brother, Robert, were born near Fort Griffin, Texas, Will in 1871 and Bob in 1868. Their parents were William, Sr., and Sallie Christian; the father, known as "Old Man" Christian, being a Kentucky native who reportedly had been one of Quantrill's Raiders during the Civil War. The Christian family moved to the Texas Panhandle in about 1883, and left Texas in about 1891 to settle in Indian territory near Tecumseh, Oklahoma. Here the two brothers were described as "nervy and reckless men," engaged in robberies, horse stealing, and peddling whiskey to the Indians.

On April 27, 1895, Deputy Sheriff Will Turner of Pottawatomie County approached the Christian brothers and two of their companions with a warrant charging Bob Christian with grand larceny. A gunfight ensued, the officer was shot to death, and the Christian brothers were convicted of first-degree manslaughter and sentenced to ten-year prison terms.

On June 30, while being held in an Oklahoma City jail, the two brothers, armed with weapons smuggled to them by friends, broke out of jail and escaped in a hail of gunfire. For a while, it was reported, they embarked on a robbery spree in Oklahoma and fought several gun battles with pursuing posses before vanishing from the region.

Several widely differing accounts have been given as to the fate of the two Christian brothers.

Oklahoma authorities eventually came to the belief that they had fled to Cuba, joined the Cuban Army, and remained there until after the Spanish-American War in 1898. From Cuba, it was reported, they had gone to Mexico.

Years later, reports surfaced that the Christian brothers had fled not to Cuba, but to New Mexico and Arizona, pausing first in the

Pecos River Valley in southeast New Mexico before moving on west to work as cowboys in Cochise County in southeast Arizona. While working for the Erie Cattle Company in Arizona, it was said, Will Christian used the name Frank Williams, but was known to the cowboys as "202," because that is how much he weighed. As members of the High Fives outlaw gang, it was believed, Will Christian was known as Black Jack, because of his swarthy appearance, and Bob took the name Tom Anderson.

The belief also has been expressed that Will Christian was never known as Black Jack, and that the Christian brothers never operated as outlaws in New Mexico or Arizona.

According to Texas author Ed Bartholomew, long a noted authority on western outlaws, Will Christian was struck and killed by lightning in the Palo Duro country of the Texas Panhandle within three months after he and his brother escaped from the Oklahoma City jail. In a letter to the author, Bartholomew provided this sequence of events:

After escaping from jail on June 30, 1895, Will and Bob Christian, accompanied by their father, returned to their former farm and ranch home at Antelope, in Jack County, Texas, northwest of Fort Worth. Another brother, Jim Christian, was working at the time for the Goodnight-Adair outfit, the JA Ranch, in the Palo Duro country, and he got his two brothers jobs as cowboys at the ranch.

Will Christian and another cowboy, Warner Reid, were holding about a dozen head of cattle on a small elevation during a drizzling rain when a bolt of lightning struck the horns of the cattle, bounced off, and killed the two cowboys, who were seated on their horses.

Bartholomew said that Mrs. Cordelia Adair, widow of John

Adair, owner of the JA Ranch, drove to the spot in a buggy, picked up the bodies of the two men, and had them buried in a single grave at Silverton, Texas.

A "Black Jack Christian" never existed, Bartholomew concluded, and Will and Bob Christian were never outlaws in New Mexico and Arizona.

*   *   *

With the death of Bob Hayes at Deer Creek, the three surviving members of the High Fives, Black Jack, George Musgrave, and Tom Anderson, went their separate ways and nothing more was heard from the original Black Jack Gang for several months. There were reports that Black Jack and Anderson were hiding in Mexico, and that Musgrave was working on a Socorro County ranch near Magdalena under the name Jesse Johnson. In January, 1897, the Post Office Department offered rewards totaling $2,000 each for the capture of the three bandits, and an additional $1,000 was offered for the capture of Musgrave, wanted for the killing of George Parker near Roswell.

In March, 1897, newspapers reported that Black Jack had ridden north out of Mexico with six companions and had picked up four more in Arizona, bringing the strength of the new Black Jack Gang to eleven. If there were that many members of the new gang, they apparently operated independently in much smaller numbers, for there were no reports of as many as eleven bandits ever seen together.

Adding to the confusion was the fact that by this time there were a number of outlaw leaders using the name Black Jack, otherwise unidentified. William French, owner of the WS Ranch in western Socorro County at the time, wrote in his book, *Some*

Recollections of a Western Ranchman, that the cognomen Black Jack was a favorite among the border outlaws, derived from "the original Black Jack Davy, celebrated in song by every cowboy, and who was no doubt the founder of the dynasty."

Newspapers speculated that the place of rendezvous of the new Black Jack Gang was Joe Hampson's Double Circle Ranch at the head of Eagle Creek in eastern Arizona, as the bandits usually fled in that direction when pursued.

In what New Mexico newspapers described as "a general pillaging expedition," members of the Black Jack Gang swept through western regions of Socorro and Grant counties in March, stealing horses and robbing stores. First seen in the Datil Mountains and on the San Agustin Plains, they headed southwest through what is now Catron County. They stole four saddle horses from the WS Ranch near the village of Alma on March 21, and the next evening held up and robbed William Heather's general store at Cliff, near Silver City, taking $300, a gold watch, several suits, and an overcoat. Heather said the robbers were two masked men, one of them Black Jack.

On the evening of April 3, 1897, two horsemen in cowboy attire arrived at the home of ranch manager George Smith at Horse Springs in western Socorro (now Catron) County, dismounted, went to the door, and asked Smith if they could spend the night there. The two visitors later were identified as Black Jack and Sid Moore, the latter a new member of the gang who formerly had served as foreman on the Double Circle Ranch in Arizona.

Smith, manager of the Z-P Ranch for the Horse Springs Cattle Company, of which he was a stockholder, told them they were welcome to spend the night in the small home he shared with his cook, Frank L. Melville. He told the two to put their horses in the stable, and told Melville to go into the kitchen and prepare supper for the guests.

The two put their horses in the stable and entered the living room. One was tall, dark, and swarthy, and the other was short, light, and stocky. In the light of the room, Smith recognized one of the visitors, the shorter one.

"Hello, Sid, I thought I left you in Arizona," Smith said to him.

"You did," he replied, "but I thought I would come over here and look around."

The two visitors followed Melville into the kitchen, sat down at the table, and ate the meal that had been prepared for them, gulping down the food and engaging in but little conversation.

When they had finished their meal, Black Jack walked into the living room, and without saying a word, drew his revolver and shot Smith five times, killing him instantly. At the same moment, Sid Moore drew his revolver and shot Melville in the back. The shot extinguished the kitchen lamp, leaving the room in darkness. The wounded cook fell to the floor, and his assailant fired four more shots in his direction, all of them passing over the prone man.

Melville got up, pushed his way past the gunman, and ran out the door into the yard.

"Did you get him?" Black Jack asked his companion.

"No, I got him down, but he got up and got away from me," Moore replied.

Both men opened fire from the porch at the wounded man in the yard, one of the bullets striking Melville again. Under cover of darkness, he dragged himself a quarter of a mile from the house, then dropped exhausted.

Unable to move, the wounded cook lay helpless for two days

and two nights, until his cries attracted the attention of "Doc" Higgins, who was passing by on a nearby road. Smith was found dead in the house, with five bullet holes in him. His remains were taken to Albuquerque for burial in Fairview Cemetery.

Melville, who survived his ordeal and two bullet wounds, related to authorities the details of the shootings, and identified the assailants as Black Jack and Sid Moore.

Although a motive for the murder of Smith was never officially determined, George Stevens, a Horse Springs pioneer, said in an interview in the 1970s that Black Jack killed the ranch manager as a favor for a neighboring ranchwoman, who told the outlaw when he stopped at her place that Smith had been causing her some sort of problems.

*   *   *

Soon after the killing of Smith, a storekeeper in Clifton, Arizona, became suspicious when a cowboy entered the store and bought some .45 – 90 ammunition. There were few guns in that part of southeast Arizona that used this type of ammunition, one of the few exceptions being a gun used by Black Jack. Suspecting that Black Jack was hiding in the area and sending for ammunition, the storekeeper notified authorities.

Deputy U.S. Marshal Fred Higgins, still on the trail of Black Jack and his companions, arrived on the scene, and was approached in Clifton by Jim Shaw, who said he had been a member of the Black Jack Gang until a recent falling out with the outlaw leader. Shaw, fearing that Black Jack was out to get him, offered to lead a posse to a place where he said Black Jack could be ambushed and taken. He told Higgins that Black Jack and several members of his gang were hiding out in a cave in Cole Creek Canyon, about twenty miles east of Clifton, and about a quarter-mile up the narrow canyon from the Charlie Williams goat ranch. He said the outlaws were in the habit of riding to the ranch house for breakfast every morning, and that he could position a posse among some rocks close to where the outlaws would pass on their way to their morning meal.

A five-man posse was organized, consisting of Higgins, Deputy Sheriffs Ben Clark and William "Crookneck" Johnson, Charlie Paxton, and Billy Hart. They rode to the spot selected for the ambush on the night of April 27, 1897, concealed themselves among the rocks, and waited for morning. Breakfast time came and went, without any sign of the outlaws, and the possemen had given up and were starting to leave when Paxton noticed three men riding out of the narrow defile. He shouted a warning to his companions, and all fired at once at the three riders.

Sam Jones, who was sleeping in the nearby ranch house, was awakened by the gunfire, and ran outside. He reported later that all he could see were "two outlaws running up the canyon, and five officers running down the canyon."

The posse rode quickly back to Clifton, reporting that it had fought a gun battle with Black Jack, but that it was not known if anybody had been shot, as the outlaws had disappeared from view when the shooting began.

Later that day, as Jones was taking his team of horses to a spring for water, he found a man lying on the ground, shot through the abdomen, and begging for water. He gave the wounded man some water and took him to the ranch house, where he died within two hours.

Jones sent word to the officers in Clifton that they had killed one of the outlaws, and asked that they come get the body. Fearing that this might be a trap, the officers refused to return to the scene, and offered Charlie Williams $15 if he would bring the body to town in a wagon. Williams conveyed the body to town, but refused to give up possession until he had the $15 in hand. The officers took up a collection among themselves, paid him the money, and got their first look at their victim.

Hurriedly, they telegraphed word that their victim was Sid Moore, "one of the killers of George Smith," but after others had viewed the body, they sent out telegrams saying the victim was not Sid Moore, but Black Jack himself. There was much confusion as to the true identity of the slain man, however, some claiming he was Jack Barrett, others Jack McDonald, both little-known stock rustlers.

The confusion heightened during the next two weeks as various newspapers in New Mexico and Arizona published contradictory accounts as to the identity of the slain outlaw. The *Lordsburg Liberal* said, in part:

> *The body was positively identified by several people as being the redoubtable Black Jack himself. Among others who identified him was James Speck, who claimed to be his brother-in-law, and who had known him from childhood. He described many marks and scars on the body, and said his true name was Thomas Ketchum, and that he was wanted in Kickapoo, Texas, for a murder committed some nine years ago.*
>
> *When the body was brought in, Black Jack's guns, money, ring and everything else of value about his person had disappeared. It is known that he had been wearing a valuable diamond ring, and the mark of it could be seen on his finger.*

The *Phoenix Gazette* told yet another story, saying in part:

> *The killing of this outlaw is regarded of momentous importance in the Southwest, for during the past year the operators of his band have terrorized the settlers from the Texas Panhandle to Nogales, Arizona.*
>
> *Black Jack's true name was McDonald, and he came into New Mexico in June last, according to Tom Anderson. Their first two victims were merchant Herzstein, a young Philadelphian, who was postmaster and storekeeper at Liberty, 100 miles south of Las Vegas, N.M., and J.M. Trujillo, member of a sheriff's posse....*
>
> *The outlaw was a college graduate, finely educated and remarkably handsome. He came to the New Mexican border about two years ago, from where no one knows. He made a specialty of running things to suit himself, and gained the goodwill and assistance of cowpunchers and cattlemen of the entire region owing to his respect for poor men and ladies.*
>
> *In no case would he tackle a poverty-stricken rancher, and he was faultlessly polite to members of the gentle sex. Yet, with all this, he was considered the coolest and most daring man in the country.*

In June, newspapers in New Mexico and Arizona were contending that the slain man was not Black Jack, but were at a loss to explain who he was. Henry Brock, who knew most of the gang members, said late in his life that he believed the victim was a brother of George Musgrave, a young man who wanted to join the Black Jack Gang but was turned down as he was considered too undependable.

Members of the Clifton posse never collected any of the reward money offered for Black Jack, as they could not prove who it was they had killed.

During the remainder of 1897, some New Mexico newspapers periodically referred to the slain outlaw as Tom Ketchum. Years later, after it was known that the victim definitely was not Tom Ketchum, it was decided, for obscure reasons, that the man killed in Cole Creek Canyon was Will Christian, Jr., believed by some to have been the original Black Jack.

The *Phoenix Gazette* reported in 1897 that with the death of the man believed to be Black Jack, the remaining members of the gang included George Musgrave, Tom Anderson, Van Musgrave, brother of George, described as "a border cow thief late of Deming," and Sid Moore, whose true name was believed to be Ef Hillman. All had vanished into obscurity by the end of the year, but one of them turned up a dozen years later under unusual circumstances.

*　　　*　　　*

In December, 1909, while visiting Grand Junction, Colorado, Frank Parks of Roswell spotted a familiar face, and notified Chaves County Sheriff Charles Ballard at Roswell that he had found George Musgrave, still wanted for the killing of George Parker near Roswell thirteen years before. Parks had been among the cowboys at the cattle roundup on the Rio Feliz when Parker was killed on October 19, 1896.

Sheriff Ballard proceeded north to Grand Junction and learned that Musgrave was not in town, but he was able to trace his movements. On December 30, the fugitive was apprehended aboard a passenger train at North Platte, Nebraska, while returning to Colorado from a trip to Omaha. With Musgrave on the train was his wife, whom he had married nearly two years before.

They were the parents of a year-old child.

Sheriff Ballard identified Musgrave as the wanted man and escorted him to Roswell to face the murder charge. In Roswell, Musgrave told news reporters that he had been in and out of the country since leaving New Mexico years before, but had spent most of his time buying and selling cattle in Colorado and Nebraska under the name Mason, making frequent trips to eastern cattle markets. He said he was a member of the Elks Lodge at Grand Junction, and had served as a deputy sheriff in one Colorado town. He repeated to reporters his grievances against the man he admitted killing, saying that when he was a boy of fifteen, Parker had traded him some stolen horses for his cattle, advised him to skip the country, and had then swindled his mother out of her cattle.

Musgrave entered a plea of not guilty to the murder charge, posted a $10,000 bond, and was released from custody on January 25, 1910, pending his trial, scheduled to begin in May.

Musgrave returned to Roswell from Colorado in May, accompanied by his wife and child, and his murder trial began in the Chaves County District Court on May 27, Judge William Pope presiding. The jury on May 3 returned a verdict of acquittal, on grounds of self-defense, after hearing testimony from two cowboys at the 1896 roundup, Lycurgus Johnson and one identified in the newspapers only as "Les Miserables," who said Parker had pulled a gun on Musgrave when he was shot. Their recollections were in sharp contrast to eyewitness accounts at the time.

Musgrave, a free man, returned to Colorado to continue his business career, living under an assumed name, it was reported, until his death in 1947, the last surviving member of the original Black Jack Gang.

The Black Jack Gangs:
The Ketchum Brothers

Soon after the outlaw Tom Ketchum was captured in northeast New Mexico in the summer of 1899, he claimed that he was "the original Black Jack," and he has been referred to as Black Jack Ketchum ever since, even though two years later he recanted his statement and said that he was never known as Black Jack, that Black Jack was alive and at liberty, but that he would not reveal his identity.

His older brother, Sam Ketchum, also captured in 1899, told authorities that he was "a brother of Tom Ketchum, the original Black Jack," but changed his story a short while later and said that Black Jack was dead. At one point, Tom said that Sam was Black Jack.

New Mexico newspapers seldom referred to either of the Ketchum brothers by name prior to their capture, and never to a "Black Jack Ketchum," although noting in 1897 that a man believed to be Black Jack who had been killed in Arizona that year had been identified as Tom Ketchum.

If Tom Ketchum was the original Black Jack, as he claimed for a while, and if his brother used the name Tom Anderson, they, then, were the two mystery figures of the High Fives outlaw gang that was organized in the summer of 1896. If not, the identity of those two individuals remains in doubt.

It has been claimed that the original Black Jack and Tom Anderson were the Oklahoma outlaw brothers William and Bob Christian, and that Tom Ketchum "appropriated" the Black Jack title from Will Christian after the latter was ambushed and killed near Clifton, Arizona, in April, 1897. The outlaw slain in Arizona was never positively identified as Will Christian, however, or as anybody else, for that matter.

Considering the similarity of the names Ketchum and Christian, and the fact that the descriptions, personalities, and characteristics of the Christian brothers were almost identical to those of the Ketchum brothers, it does not seem beyond the realm of possibility that the Ketchum brothers mistakenly were referred to as the Christian brothers early in their careers, and that Black Jack Ketchum and Black Jack Christian actually were one and the same.

Thomas Edward "Black Jack" Ketchum was born in 1863 in San Saba County in central Texas, the youngest of five children of Green Berry Ketchum and his wife, Constance, owners of a small stock farm at the mouth of Richland Creek, a few miles west of San Saba, the county seat. Although newspaper reports sometimes referred to Samuel Ketchum as Tom's younger brother, census records indicate that he was nine years older, born in 1854. Another brother, Berry, was two or three years older than Sam, and there were two sisters, Elizabeth and Nancy.

San Saba County was sparsely settled when the Ketchum boys were growing up, and the few families living along Richland Creek often were the targets of Comanche Indian raiders. Later, as other settlers moved into the area, the region became notorious for lawlessness.

Tom's father died when he was a child, his mother died when he was nine, and he grew to manhood under the care of brothers Berry and Sam. As a teenager, he worked as a hand for cattle outfits at nearby Richland Springs. There is evidence that Tom and Sam, both considered "wild" by their older brother, engaged in some livestock rustling in San Saba County, escaping on fast racehorses when approached by authorities.

Tom and Sam were both tall and physically strong, and considered fine specimens of manhood, but were otherwise dissimilar in appearance. Tom, who stood about six feet two inches tall, weighed about 180 pounds, and had a swarthy appearance with dark eyes, hair, and mustache. Sam was about two inches shorter than Tom, and was fair-skinned with blue eyes and reddish-blond hair.

In the 1880s, Berry moved west one hundred miles to establish a horse and cattle ranch in Tom Green County south of San Angelo, near the village of Knickerbocker. His two younger brothers followed him west to work on the ranch.

Robert W. "Bob" Lewis, pioneer New Mexico lawman and rancher, recalled in a 1949 interview that he was a neighbor of the Ketchum brothers in Texas before he moved to New Mexico in 1885. He had kind words for Sam, but said Tom was a mean individual who enjoyed such diversions as pulling the legs off grasshoppers.

"Black Jack was the most cold-blooded individual I have ever met, and would not hesitate for a moment to kill a man or even a boy," Lewis said. "He was a coward at heart, though. I wouldn't have been afraid of him in a fair fight, but I sure wouldn't turn my back on him.

"Sam Ketchum, on the other hand, was a brave and courageous man. If it hadn't been for the bad influence of his brother, he would have been a fine man."

Lewis recalled an episode illustrative of Tom's early career in Texas:

"One day Black Jack sat down at a table in a restaurant with three strangers. The strangers decided to play a little joke on him, and kept passing the butter among themselves without offering any to Black Jack. Finally, Black Jack drew his six-shooter and commanded the strangers to eat all the butter remaining on the table. When they had finished gulping it down, he ordered the waiter to serve them a couple of more pounds, seeing that they seemed to like it so well."

In New Mexico, Lewis had a number of encounters with his former Texas neighbors. As an example, he recalled an incident that occurred while he was employed on the Bar-N Ranch in western Socorro County in the late 1890s:

"Several of us were standing by a corral where a ranger station now stands when Black Jack and two others rode up on tired mounts. Black Jack said, 'Bob, I need three fresh horses,' but I told him we didn't have any to spare. Black Jack told me that if I didn't cut out three good horses at once, he would take the bunch. I was never foolish enough to argue with Black Jack, so I cut him out three horses. The three men saddled them and jumped on, and as they dashed away Black Jack threw $320 on the ground at my feet. I found the three horses wandering on the range several days later and recovered them."

Lewis recalled another incident in which Black Jack paid for what he had taken:

"I arrived at my home in Socorro County one evening when a young boy came running out to tell me that Black Jack had been there earlier and had stolen some of my flour and bacon. I went in and examined the larder, and there, left where I was sure to find it, was a $20 gold piece."

Another pioneer lawman who knew the Ketchum brothers early in their careers was Frank Shelton, onetime sheriff of Martin and Midland counties in Texas, who was living in Santa Fe in 1932 when he gave some of his recollections to the *Albuquerque Tribune*.

Shelton said that Tom Ketchum, as a boy in Texas, was caught stealing pecans from a pecan grove, and the owner of the grove gave him a whipping. This didn't set well with the boy, and he swore revenge.

"Then he got friendly with an old Irish well-driller, and the well-driller taught him how to use dynamite," Shelton said. "So Tom stole some dynamite and blew up the whole pecan grove. That started things."

Shelton said the first time he heard of Tom Ketchum being in trouble with the law was in connection with the robbery of a store at Knickerbocker, Texas, and his part in the stealing of some mavericks. He said he believed that Tom took the name Black Jack from Jack Gregg, an old-time outlaw who disappeared into Mexico.

While Berry Ketchum settled down on his ranch near San Angelo to enjoy a long and successful career in the livestock business, his two younger brothers left the ranch to become roving cowboys and trail drivers. Little is known of their movements from the mid-1880s to the mid-1890s, as they left no detailed itineraries. There are reports that they operated a small ranch in southeast Utah in the late 1880s, where they dealt in stolen livestock. Leaving Utah after a short stay, they spent years working as cowboys and trail drivers for various cattle outfits in the Texas Panhandle and throughout eastern New Mexico, returning periodically to Texas between jobs.

During one of his trips home, Tom was arrested in Texas on a charge of disturbing the peace after he allegedly disrupted a Sunday church service by chasing a dog down the aisle. In about 1894, Sam opened a saloon and gambling hall in San Angelo in partnership with William "Cowboy Bill" Carver, who had been a hard-working young cowboy until taking up drinking and gambling following the death of his wife.

On December 12, 1895, John N. "Jap" Powers, a farmer living near Knickerbocker, was shot and killed from ambush a short distance from his house, reportedly at the instigation of his wife. Later, a grand jury returned murder indictments against Tom Ketchum, Dave Atkins, and Bud Upshaw in connection with the slaying, but no warrants were served as the three defendants could not be found. By this time, Tom Ketchum was back in New Mexico, in the Pecos River Valley near Roswell, and Atkins and Upshaw had proceeded farther west to Cochise County, Arizona.

It was at about this time that Sam Ketchum and Will Carver closed their saloon and gambling hall in San Angelo and headed west. Sam joined Tom in New Mexico, and Carver joined Atkins and Upshaw in Arizona.

Eventually, Tom and Sam Ketchum were to become prime suspects in two unsolved murders that occurred in New Mexico during the first six months of 1896, murders that created quite a sensation at the time.

✴   ✴   ✴

It was on the afternoon of February 1, 1896, that Col. Albert J. Fountain and his eight-year-old son, Henry, were last seen alive, traveling by buckboard along a lonely stretch of road near the broad expanse of the White Sands in southern New Mexico. Father and son were returning to their home at Mesilla, just outside Las Cruces, from a grand jury session at Lincoln, where the colonel, as special investigator and prosecutor for the Southeastern New Mexico Stock Growers Association, had managed to secure thirty-two indictments charging various individuals, some of them prominent ranchers, with stealing cattle and altering brands.

As Fountain was leaving the Lincoln County Courthouse on the afternoon of January 30, he was handed a note reading: "If you drop this we will be your friends. If you go on with it, you will never reach home alive." Undaunted, the flamboyant lawyer, no stranger to dangerous situations, climbed to the seat of his buckboard, and with his youngest son at his side, embarked on the one-hundred-fifty-mile journey southwest to his home.

They spent the first night at the home of Dr. Joseph H. Blazer at Mescalero, and while traveling on down the road the next morning they met an Apache Indian who insisted that Fountain accept the gift of a pinto pony in exchange for a debt of gratitude. The pony was tied to the rear of the buckboard. They paused in Tularosa, where Fountain bought some oats for his team of horses and the pony, and continued the short distance south to La Luz, where the two spent the night with Dave Sutherland, a local merchant.

The next morning, February 1, they left La Luz for the last leg of their journey home, a seventy-mile stretch of lonely road that skirted the White Sands and wound through San Agustin Pass before descending to Las Cruces. They had covered about half the distance, reaching a point where the road cut through a natural landmark known as Chalk Hill, when they met a mail carrier, Saturnino Barela, who was driving a mail stage in the opposite direction toward Tularosa. They paused to chat.

Barela noticed that Fountain was carrying his Winchester rifle across his knees, and seemed apprehensive. Fountain asked the mail carrier if he recognized three men on horseback who were watching them from a distance, saying that they had been shadowing him for some time off of and parallel to the road.

Barela answered that they were cowboys, but that he could not recognize them at that distance. He suggested that Fountain turn back to La Luz, but Fountain said that he was determined to push on.

As Barela was returning to Las Cruces the next day, he noticed that the tracks of Fountain's buckboard turned off the road a short distance from where he had talked to him the day before, and that these tracks were joined by the tracks of three horseback riders. Upon his arrival at Las Cruces that night, the mail carrier asked if Fountain and his son had reached home, and the answer was that they had not.

The *Albuquerque Weekly Citizen,* under a headline reading "Murdered!," published an early account of the unfolding mystery on February 8, 1896:

> LAS CRUCES, *February 4 – The citizens of Las Cruces were thrown into considerable excitement Sunday evening on the arrival of the mail carrier from Tularosa, who reported that he feared Col. A.J. Fountain had met with foul play.*
>
> *Col. Fountain is the prosecuting attorney of the Southwest Cattlemen's Association and has hounded the cattle thieves of this section and brought many of them to justice. In consequence he has earned the enmity of these law breakers, and the report that foul play was suspected had good grounds.*
>
> *The colonel has lately been in Lincoln where he secured indictments against a number of cattle thieves. He went by team and the mail carrier reports having met him coming home while he, the carrier, was bound to Tularosa.*
>
> *On returning the carrier met three men on horseback*

going toward Tularosa. Upon seeing him approach the men took the plain toward the hills, thus averting meeting the carrier. Further down the road he saw the track of Col. Fountain's buggy making toward the hills.

He alighted and examined the tracks, following them for some ways. The foot prints of three horses, evidently those ridden by the men previously met, appeared to be following Col. Fountain's buggy.

The carrier came on to town, did not pass Fountain on the way, and on learning on his arrival that Fountain had not yet appeared here, told his story.

The fact that Fountain has prosecuted these thieves, the lonely section of the country in which he met the three men, and the suspicious actions of the men, give credence to the theory of foul play, and a posse immediately started out in search of the colonel.

The first posse to reach Chalk Hill found a pool of dried blood and a bloodstained handkerchief on the ground where the buckboard tracks left the road. Following the tracks east, they found the carriage standing abandoned twelve miles off the road, with no sign of life around it. Missing from the scene, in addition to the father and son, were the team of horses, the pinto pony, and Fountain's rifle and blankets. His legal papers were strewn over the ground, and his necktie, tied to a wheel spoke, fluttered in the breeze. Among items found were the note that had been handed to Fountain as he left Lincoln, and his son's hat.

The posse followed the tracks of three horsemen miles to the east from the abandoned buckboard before losing the trail in a maze of cattle tracks. All evidence indicated that Fountain and his son had been ambushed and murdered.

For weeks, parties searched the region in vain for any trace of the missing pair, and rewards for the arrest and conviction of any of those responsible for the murders of Fountain and his son eventually totaled a staggering $20,000. The huge bounty reflected Fountain's two decades of public service in New Mexico as a soldier, statesman, militia leader, newspaper editor, prosecuting attorney, and speaker of the New Mexico House of Representatives.

No trace of the prominent and colorful lawyer and his son was ever found, and the trial of a prominent cattle rancher accused of being implicated in the murders ended in a verdict of acquittal.

In his 1949 interview, Robert W. "Bob" Lewis revealed that Sam Ketchum had confided to him in 1899 that he watched as his brother, Black Jack, shot and killed Fountain and his son and burned their bodies to destroy the evidence. Lewis, who was a Socorro County deputy sheriff at the time, said he visited the dying Sam Ketchum at the New Mexico Penitentiary in Santa Fe while delivering a prisoner to the prison.

"Sam told me he was present when the Fountains were killed," Lewis said. "He said there was a third man in their party, too, but he would not reveal his name. He told me Black Jack wanted to get rid of Fountain because of his success in prosecuting their outlaw friends."

Lewis quoted Sam as telling him: "I tried to persuade Black Jack not to kill the boy, but he said he wanted to destroy all the evidence. I told him they would break all our necks if they caught us, anyway, but Black Jack insisted and shot them both. He built a large fire and destroyed the bodies. Then we stood back on a hill and watched it."

Lewis had an excellent reputation for truthfulness, much more so than either of the Ketchum brothers, and if the Ketchums had nothing to do with the Fountain murders, one can only wonder why Sam would confess to such a crime.

Officially, the strange disappearance of Col. Albert J. Fountain and his eight-year-old son remains an unsolved mystery.

*   *   *

Cowboys on the huge Bell Ranch in northeast New Mexico were highly suspicious of the two strangers who joined their ranks in the spring of 1896. Both men were secretive, kept pretty much to themselves, refused to give their names, and one of them, at least, enjoyed demonstrating his prowess with a six-shooter, twirling it around his trigger finger, cocking and firing it at each turn with speed and accuracy.

One of the newcomers was referred to as Welch, as he carried a gold watch with the name Welch, or Welsch, engraved on it, and his companion was referred to only as Steve. Descriptions given later of the two matched the descriptions of Tom and Sam Ketchum.

On June 8, the two killed and butchered a ranch steer and prepared themselves a meal. That night, they broke into the small Bell Ranch storeroom and helped themselves to some supplies. They rode off to the south, followed at a distance by Tom Kane, the wagon boss and part-time deputy sheriff.

On the evening of June 10, the two reached the village of Liberty, about thirty miles to the south, near present-day Tucumcari. Before daylight the next morning they broke into the store and post office operated by the brothers Morris and Levi Herzstein, German-Jewish immigrants who had lived in Philadelphia before settling in New Mexico a few years before. They took some provisions, including clothing and blankets, and about $250 in cash.

Levi Herzstein, about twenty-two years of age and the younger of the two brothers, took to the trail of the robbers, accompanied by Merejildo Gallegos, Placido Gurule, and Atanacio Borque. The four-man posse caught up with the robbers the next day just below the Chavez Ranch, about thirty miles southwest of Liberty. The robbers were camped on the plains and had just finished a meal when they saw the four riding down upon them.

The two robbers quickly grabbed their rifles and opened fire on their pursuers. Herzstein, Gallegos, and Gurule went down in the hail of bullets, along with several of their horses. Borque managed to escape on foot.

The robbers approached the prone figures of their three victims and emptied their rifles into the bodies of Herzstein and Gallegos. Gurule, only slightly wounded, remained motionless on the ground, feigning death, and escaped the fate of his companions. A horse ridden by one of the outlaws was killed in the battle. The robbers secured another that had been ridden by one of the posse, and the two rode off to the south.

Two men in the vicinity, Sam Goldsmith and Harry Edwards, upon hearing the gunfire, hurried toward the scene. They met Borque about a quarter of a mile from the battle scene, and he told them that his three companions had been killed. Proceeding on to the battle scene, they found that Gurule was very much alive, having suffered only a flesh wound. Herzstein, they found, had been shot eleven times. The bodies of Herzstein and Gallegos were taken more than one hundred miles northwest to Las Vegas for burial.

The *Las Vegas Optic* published descriptions of the two gunmen:

It is supposed that the men are two men who were

employed on the Bell ranch and that the following is a description of them:

The first has a dark complexion, dark brown hair, brown mustache, about six feet tall, weight, 185 to 195 pounds, stoop shouldered, brown eyes, very quick tempered, heavy built, and carries a 45-70 Winchester rifle.

The second is of light complexion, sandy mustache, red face, hair inclined to be red, blue eyes. He is about six feet tall, weight about 170 pounds, carries himself very erect, wears about No. 9 boots. His name is supposed to be Welsch, as he carries a fine gold watch with the name of Welsch engraved upon it.

A.J. Tisdall, manager of the Bell ranch, offers $200 for the arrest and imprisonment of these men in either the Clayton or the Las Vegas jail, and M. Herzstein, the merchant at Liberty, offers $1,000 for the delivery of the men in any jail in New Mexico.

As for their conviction there can be no question, if they are caught, as the murder was witnessed by several men.

Tom Kane, meanwhile, trailing the outlaws south from the Bell Ranch, arrived at Fort Sumner, on the Pecos River about sixty miles southwest of Liberty, where he learned that the two gunmen had exchanged their tired horses for fresh mounts at the nearby Carson Ranch. He organized a posse, consisting of Mike McQuaid and several other men, and followed the trail of the outlaws on down through the Pecos River Valley until the trail vanished into Texas. McQuaid said that the man known as Steve used the alias Red Buck, and that he had arrested him in Colorado some time before for stealing cattle. He said he believed both men were wanted in Texas.

The identities of the two men who killed Herzstein and Gallegos were never definitely established. More than four years after the killings, however, in November 1899, while Tom Ketchum was a prisoner and being escorted to a court appearance in Las Vegas, Placido Gurule saw him at the Las Vegas depot, and said that he was one of the two men who had wounded him and killed Herzstein and Gallegos. No formal charges were ever brought in connection with the murders, however.

*   *   *

History is silent as to the movements of Tom and Sam Ketchum from the spring of 1896 to the spring of 1897, unless, of course, they were members of the High Fives outlaw gang that operated during that period as the original Black Jack Gang. It was shortly after the dissolution of the High Fives, and reports of the death of the original Black Jack, that the Ketchum brothers, sometimes working together, sometimes separately, embarked on outlaw careers devoted almost exclusively to robbing trains.

Their most constant companions in crime were Will Carver, Sam's former partner in the saloon business; and Dave Atkins, sometimes called Tommy Atkins, who had been indicted along with Tom Ketchum in connection with the 1895 ambush slaying of the Texas farmer, J.N. "Jap" Powers.

Carver was described as being fair complected with light hair, of medium height, weighing about 140 pounds, and possessing a quiet, retiring nature. Frank Shelton, the former Texas sheriff, recalled in 1932 that Carver was one of the fastest drawing, quickest shooting men in the Southwest, adding:

"He was a pretty decent youngster. He was working steady and making good. He got married — a nice girl that he thought the world of. She died giving birth to their child. After that, Carver went to pieces. Drinking and gambling led him to outlawry. He became one of the toughest hombres that ever carried a gun. He could shoot faster and straighter than any member of the gang."

Atkins, believed to be part Indian, was described as being dark complected with very dark brown hair and a thin mustache, about five feet eleven inches tall, very slender and weighing about 150 pounds. Like Carver, he was said to be quiet and rather sullen.

Tom Ketchum, Carver, and Atkins were identified as the trio that held up and robbed a Southern Pacific train in southwest Texas, near the Mexican border, during the early morning hours of May 14, 1897. The train had stopped at the isolated depot of Lozier, between Dryden and Langtry, and was leaving the small depot when the robbers climbed aboard, made their way to the locomotive cab, and ordered the engineer to halt the train a mile or so west of the depot. Forcing their way into the express car, they placed dynamite on top of a large safe, placed a small safe on top of the dynamite, lit the fuse, and waited outside the car for the resulting explosion.

The explosion blew both safes apart, and the robbers filled three bags with money, said to be as much as $42,000, and rode off under cover of darkness, the money bags secured to a fourth horse they had brought along.

During the course of the robbery, an elderly woman stuck her head out of a coach window and demanded to know what was going on.

"Get your head back in there, grandma," Ketchum shouted.

"Young man, you keep a civil tongue in your head," she replied as she closed the window.

Ketchum, Carver, and Atkins were reported seen later at

Knickerbocker, leading to speculation that they had concealed at least part of the loot on or near Berry Ketchum's ranch. Leaving Texas that summer, they headed west into New Mexico.

Sam Ketchum, meanwhile, had been earning an honest living working for Eugene Manlove Rhodes on the Rhodes Ranch along the northern fringes of the San Andres Mountains in south central New Mexico, and it was to this ranch that Tom Ketchum and his two companions made their way. Tom persuaded his brother to join the outlaw band, and the four headed more than two hundred miles north to the once boisterous community of Cimarron in Colfax County. In Cimarron, it was reported, they put up at a boarding house, and for weeks frequented the saloons and gambling rooms in Cimarron, Elizabethtown, and other nearby communities. The four strangers were greeted with suspicion, as they were rough looking characters who displayed quantities of money at the gambling tables, including numerous gold coins. Tom Ketchum, at least, did not step up to the bars, as he was not a drinking man, but sometimes displayed generosity by buying drinks for the house.

It apparently was at this time that the four established what has been known ever since as Black Jack's Hideout. This secret rendezvous was a shallow cave in a canyon wall, in the isolated, upper reaches of narrow Turkey Creek Canyon, about ten miles northwest of Cimarron. They erected log barricades at strategic locations near the cave, and built a corral just below the cave, next to a pool of clear water fed by a tiny stream. Here they felt secure, as this portion of the rocky and wooded canyon was difficult to access from any direction. This was one of several cave hideouts the gang reportedly used in New Mexico and Arizona.

By the end of August, the four decided that it was time to get down to business. Mounting their horses, they rode about seventy miles northeast to the small community of Folsom, a short distance south of the Colorado border, where they planned to meet a train and relieve it of some of its valuables.

★   ★   ★

A southbound Denver and Gulf passenger train was leaving the Folsom depot shortly after 10 o'clock on the night of September 3, 1897, when two men climbed onto the outside of one of the cars and began making their way toward the locomotive. The train had reached a point about four miles south of Folsom when the two jumped into the locomotive cab and took possession of the train. At gunpoint, they ordered the engineer to stop the train two miles on down the track, where their two companions were waiting with four horses. The train was stopped where the tracks cut through a hill, known thereafter as Robbers Cut, within a sweeping double curve of the railroad line at Twin Mountain, a natural landmark.

Charles Drew, the express messenger, believing that the train had halted at the small community of Des Moines, the next stop, opened the door of the express car, and was confronted by two armed and masked men. Entering the car, they ordered Drew to hand over the keys to the way safe. When he resisted, they clubbed him with their rifles, forcing him to produce the keys. They opened the safe, took money from it, and ordered Drew to open the larger, through safe. When the express messenger protested that he could not open this safe even if he wanted to, the two robbers secured dynamite from their companions, placed the dynamite on top of the safe, placed a quarter of beef on the dynamite to soften the explosion, lit the fuse, and waited outside the car. The terrific explosion wrecked the safe and most of the express car. After gathering up scattered money and valuables, the four rode off in the darkness.

The *Albuquerque Morning Democrat*, on September 5, published a brief report from Denver that a Gulf passenger train had been held up and robbed at Twin Mountain. Apparently not realizing that Twin Mountain was in New Mexico, the editor headlined the story "Train Robbery in Colorado." Early news reports estimated that the amount taken in the robbery was from $4,000 to $15,000. Posses from Folsom and Trinidad, Colorado, attempted in vain to pick up the trail of the four robbers, whose identities were unknown at that time. The two Ketchum brothers, Carver and Atkins, gloating over their success, apparently headed back to Cimarron, from where it is believed they traveled far to the southwest to a cave hideout in southeast Arizona.

During the next two years, bandits robbed or attempted to rob at least seven more trains in New Mexico, in spite of the fact that the territory had enacted a law providing the death penalty for anyone convicted of assaulting a railroad train. Eventually, the Ketchum brothers were suspected of having taken part in most of these robberies and robbery attempts, although it is certain that they had no part in some of them.

Grants, on the Atlantic and Pacific line, was the scene of a successful train robbery on November 6, 1897, and of two train robbery attempts on March 29 and August 14, 1898, and the Ketchums became suspects in at least one of them. Shortly before his death in 1901, Tom Ketchum claimed responsibility for an 1897 train robbery attempt at Steins, in southwest New Mexico, in which he had not been a suspect.

★   ★   ★

A group of at least six men on horseback appeared in the railroad village of Steins, about twenty miles southwest of Lordsburg, shortly after dark on the evening of December 9, 1897, about two hours before a westbound Southern Pacific passenger train was due to arrive. Several of the men remained in the village, while their companions rode west along the railroad tracks about two miles to a point near the Arizona border, where they stopped and began preparing two bonfires.

Those remaining in the village, apparently to kill time, held up and robbed the Steins postmaster, obtaining two dollars, and relieved the station agent of another $9.20. When the train arrived, they climbed aboard the locomotive and ordered the engineer to proceed west and to stop where their companions had built two bonfires, one on each side of the track.

When the train was stopped, the engineer, Thomas North, probably the same Thomas North who had been the fireman on a Southern Pacific passenger train that was wrecked and robbed between Lordsburg and Deming fourteen years before, was ordered out of the cab and told to uncouple the train behind the express car. Before leaving the cab, he set the air brakes so that the train could not be moved.

Eating supper inside the express car at the time were Charles Adair, the express messenger, and two novice Wells Fargo guards, C.H. Jennings and Eugene Thacker, son of Wells Fargo detective John Thacker. Realizing that the stopped train probably was in the hands of robbers, they darkened the car, picked up shotguns, threw open the door, and began blasting away at figures of armed men they could see in the light of the bonfires. All but one of the bandits quickly took up defensive positions on the locomotive and coal tender, while the other concealed himself at one corner of the express car.

A gun battle raged for about thirty minutes with little harm to any of the combatants, and came to an end when Jennings fired a shotgun blast into the head of the bandit standing by the express car, killing him instantly. The remaining robbers gave up the battle, mounted their horses, and rode off in the darkness.

The dead man, left behind on a railroad tie, was identified as Edward Cullen, believed to be the leader of the outlaw band, and said by newspapers to have come from Colorado City, Texas, where he was known as J.A. Hespath. There also was speculation that his name was Bullion, and that he was a brother of Laura Bullion, Dave Atkins's girlfriend in Texas. Among his cowboy friends he was known as "Shoot 'Em Up Dick," stemming from an incident in which he refused to pay for a meal in a Chinese restaurant, warning the oriental cook that he was "Shoot 'Em Up Dick," whereupon the cook picked up a six-shooter and shouted "I'm Shoot 'Em Up Sam! You pay."

Combined posses, which included such federal and railroad officers as Jeff Milton, George Scarborough, Cipriano Baca, and John Thacker, trailed the robbers southwest across the southeast corner of Arizona. Arriving at the John Cush Ranch near the Mexican border, a known gathering place for outlaws, they rounded up Cush, also known as John Vinadge; Walter Hoffman, also referred to as Walter Hovey and as Fatty Ryan, who had a fresh gunshot wound in his leg; Leonard Alverson; W.H. Warderman; Henry Marshall; and Tom Capehart, the latter referred to in the newspapers as T.S. Kephart.

The lawmen returned to New Mexico with their six captives, and a grand jury in Silver City, seat of Grant County, returned federal indictments charging Alverson, Hoffman, and Warderman with attempting to rob a U.S. mail car, with conspiracy, and with robbing the Steins postmaster. Cush, Marshall, and Capehart were named in the indictments as accessories.

All six stood trial in Silver City on charges of attempting to rob the mail car, during which the engineer and other members of the train crew identified Alverson, Hoffman, and Warderman as being among those who held up the train. The jury, on March 8, 1898, returned a verdict, finding all of the defendants not guilty, much to the surprise and anger of Judge Frank W. Parker. Alverson, Hoffman, and Warderman remained in custody to face trial on the charge of robbing the Steins post office, and the lesser charges against Capehart, Marshall, and Cush were dismissed.

In September, a jury in Las Cruces convicted Alverson, Hoffman, and Warderman of the charge of robbing the Steins post office, and they were sentenced to serve ten years in the New Mexico Penitentiary at Santa Fe. They began serving their sentences on September 28.

Later, Tom Ketchum was to claim that these men were innocent, contending that the robber gang at Steins consisted of himself and his brother, Sam; Ed Cullen; Dave Atkins; Will Carver; and William "Bronco Bill" Walters. Ketchum's "confession" apparently was greeted with some doubt, however, as it did not win immediate release of the three prisoners.

*   *   *

Tom and Sam Ketchum spent at least part of 1898 in Texas, as they were identified as among the robbers who held up two trains in Texas that year.

On the night of April 28, 1898, with Will Carver and Dave Atkins, they took possession of a Southern Pacific passenger train at Comstock, near the Mexican border between Langtry and Del Rio, dynamited the safe in the express car, and escaped with an undisclosed amount of money. The robbery scene was about fifty miles southeast of Lozier, where they had robbed a Southern Pacific train the year before.

Pioneer Texas lawman Frank Shelton recalled in 1932 that while he was sheriff of Martin County, Texas, he received word at his home in Stanton on July 2, 1898, that Tom and Sam Ketchum and Will Carver had held up a Texas Pacific train between Stanton and Midland the night before and robbed the express car of $5,000 in currency consigned to the Roswell (New Mexico) National Bank. He said that he and Deputy U.S. Marshal Jim Baggot took to the trails with a posse, going first to the scene of the robbery, where they found that the safe had been blown through the roof of the express car, and what remained of it was lying on the ground about eighty feet from the railroad tracks.

Members of the train crew told Shelton that watermelons in the express car had been broken open by the explosion, and that the three train robbers sat down alongside the tracks and filled up on watermelon. One of the trainmen warned the outlaws that they had better head for Cuba, and Tom Ketchum replied, "We're doing pretty well in this country."

Shelton said that one of the three robbers was riding a horse with a bad foot, and the posse was able to trail them for eighty-five miles, then found that they had driven a herd of horses for ten or twelve miles to cover their tracks.

"We went on, but never caught up with them," Shelton said. "I learned later that once when we stopped to debate which way to go, we were within three hundred yards of where they were hiding."

Since Atkins was not mentioned in connection with this train robbery, it is possible that he had left the gang by this time, for the dissolution of the gang as it had existed soon became apparent. There is evidence that gang members had grown tired of Tom Ketchum's brutal ways, moodiness, and violent rages, rages that sometimes saw him punish himself by beating himself over the head when things did not go to his liking.

Tom and Sam Ketchum split up and went their separate ways, their movements veiled in obscurity for months to come; Atkins left, reportedly because he had grown tired of the outlaw life; and Carver left to turn up later as a member of Butch Cassidy's Wild Bunch, a notorious gang of train and bank robbers that operated principally in Wyoming, Utah, Colorado, Montana, and Nevada.

★   ★   ★

William French, manager of the large WS Ranch near the village of Alma in western New Mexico, was quite impressed with the new ranch hands who went to work for him in 1899. The newcomers, strangers to the locality, demonstrated great skills in the handling of cattle and horses, and brought an end to the thievery of WS cattle by local rustlers, whom the new hands referred to as "the petty larceny crowd."

The leader, who introduced himself as Jim Lowe, was described by French as a fair complected, stoutly built man of medium height who proved to be the best trail boss he ever had. Lowe was placed in charge of the WS cattle.

Working closely with Lowe was William McGinnis, taller and darker than Lowe, described by French as a good-looking young man, debonair, gentlemanly, with a bit of a swagger. An expert bronc buster, McGinnis was placed in charge of the WS remuda.

French said that another newcomer, Tom Capehart, was

Lowe's right-hand man whenever he was on the ranch. He apparently was the Tom Capehart who had been implicated in the attempted train robbery at Steins in 1897.

All the new hands proved to be excellent cowpunchers, French said, and Lowe maintained strict discipline over the group, forbidding any drinking, gambling, or shooting up the town. French was particularly pleased that rustlers now avoided his livestock, still complaining that Tom and Sam Ketchum, on a previous visit to the ranch, had taken off with his best saddle horse and one of his two buggy team horses.

French learned later that his new hands were members of Butch Cassidy's Wild Bunch, hiding out in New Mexico after a series of train robberies far to the north. This revelation came about when French was visited by a Pinkerton detective, who told him that some currency taken by the Wild Bunch in a Wyoming train robbery had turned up at the general store in Alma.

The detective showed French an old and faded photograph of three men in cowboy clothing and asked if he recognized any of them. French replied that he recognized one of them as his cattle boss, Jim Lowe, and that he thought one of the others might be Tom Capehart. The detective told French that the man he recognized as Jim Lowe was actually Robert Leroy Parker, alias George L. Parker, better known as Butch Cassidy, leader of the Wild Bunch.

It also developed that William McGinnis, French's expert bronc buster, was Elza (or Elzy) Lay, sometimes referred to as William Ellsworth Lay, one of Cassidy's lieutenants in the outlaw gang.

The true identity and background of Tom Capehart was never definitely ascertained, some believing that he was Harvey Logan, alias Kid Curry; or Harry A. Longabaugh, alias The Sundance Kid;

or merely a roving cowboy from New Mexico's Diamond A Ranch.

Questioned by the Pinkerton detective, the Alma storekeeper said the stolen currency traced to his place was given to him by a WS cowboy, Johnny Ward, in exchange for some goods. Ward admitted having the money, but said that he had received it from a former WS cowboy, known as McGonigal, who bought some horses from him when he left the ranch.

No arrests were made, even though Cassidy reportedly was at the ranch at the time and had spotted the visitor as a Pinkerton detective.

McGinnis, called "Mac" by his associates, announced in June (1899) that he was leaving the WS Ranch, saying that there were no more horses left for him to break, and offering to help with some cattle that French was shipping to a new pasture near Cimarron in Colfax County, more than four hundred miles to the northeast. Quitting the ranch at the same time, to accompany McGinnis and the cattle shipment to Colfax County, most of the way by rail, was Bruce "Red" Weaver, said to be a loud-mouthed braggart.

Weaver came down with smallpox soon after his arrival in Colfax County, and was taken to a pest house near Springer, about twenty-five miles southeast of Springer. McGinnis loafed around Cimarron for several weeks, staying at the St. James Hotel, and was soon seen keeping company with two other men, later identified as Sam Ketchum and G.W. Franks, who had been hanging around the vicinity for about two months. The three often played poker at the hotel, arousing suspicion by flashing $50 and $100 bills.

The true identity of the man known as G.W. Franks remains an unsolved mystery. There is some evidence that he was Sam Ketchum's old friend Will Carver, but William French had reason to believe that he was Tom Capehart. Others have had other candidates.

It probably was Sam Ketchum's idea that the three hold up and rob another passenger train near Folsom, at the exact spot where he had participated in the 1897 train robbery. Early in July, the three departed Cimarron and headed east to meet another train.

*   *   *

A Colorado and Southern (formerly Denver and Gulf) passenger train was rounding one of the wide curves near Twin Mountain south of Folsom late on the night of July 11 (1899) when two armed men suddenly appeared in the locomotive cab and ordered the engineer to stop the train. The train was stopped close to the point of the previous train robbery of September 3, 1897.

A third armed man appeared on the scene, and the trio went to the express car and ordered the express messenger to open the door and get out. The three entered and looted the car, produced some dynamite, and blew a large hole in the through safe. The explosion peeled back the roof of the car and scattered debris in all directions. Gathering up a large number of packages and bundles, the three bandits mounted their horses, which were hitched near the tracks, and rode off in the darkness.

As soon as the robbers had left, passengers clambered out of the cars and collected pieces of the wrecked safe as souvenirs. Reports of what was taken by the robbers ranged from "nothing of value," as the express messenger put it, to a large amount of money, as much as $70,000.

Among the passengers on the train was Fred Higgins of Roswell, sheriff of Chaves County, who was long familiar with the operations of the Black Jack Gang. Interviewed by the *New Mexican* at Santa Fe, the sheriff told of his movements during the robbery:

275

"As quick as we discovered what was the matter, I asked the conductor (Frank Harrington) to turn out all the lights, which he did. The robbers' horses were hitched near the track, and with the conductor, I crawled to the place and made as close an examination of the horses, saddles and so forth as the darkness would permit, and remained near the spot until the robbers returned.

"They seemed to have a great many packages and bundles, and were some time getting them tied on their saddles, and I think I recognized all three of the parties. I was armed only with a pistol and could not afford to fire in the open, exposing myself and the conductor to the guns of the gang.

"The passengers were badly frightened, and asked me not to shoot from the car, which would have been useless, as I could not see the robbers from that position. By looking out of the window I could see a couple of men, but they were moving about and I could not tell whether they were robbers or trainmen, it being dark, and the parties seemed to avoid the light."

Posses from northern New Mexico and southern Colorado soon converged on the robbery scene. The Colorado contingent was led by Edward J. Farr of Walsenburg, Colorado, sheriff of Huerfano County. U.S. Marshal Creighton M. Foraker left his Santa Fe office to establish temporary headquarters in Springer, and sent deputies Wilson Elliott and J.H. Morgan west to Cimarron.

Those following the trail of the bandits from the robbery scene found that it led southwest toward Springer. At a campsite used by the robbers they pieced together some shreds of paper they found scattered on the ground. According to one account, it proved to be an envelope addressed to William McGinnis at Cimarron, while another account said that it was a bill of sale from a Cimarron store made out to G.W. Franks. Sheriff Farr and W.H.

Reno, special agent for the Colorado and Southern, hurried on to Cimarron.

James K. Hunt, Cimarron postmaster and storekeeper, told authorities that he believed the train robbers were three men who had been hanging around town until shortly before the robbery, and predicted that they would return. He gave detailed descriptions of them.

On Sunday, July 16, word was received in Cimarron that three men on horseback, believed to be the train robbers, were seen riding toward Turkey Creek Canyon west of town, and a posse was organized to search for them. The seven-member posse consisted of Wilson Elliott and J.H. Morgan, both deputy U.S. marshals; Edward J. Farr, the Colorado sheriff; W.H. Reno, the railroad officer; Henry M. Love, a young cowboy from the Charles Springer Ranch; Perfecto Cordova, an area resident; and F.H. Smith, a young man from New York who was visiting the nearby McCormick Ranch and who volunteered to go along for the fun of it. Elliott, an Albuquerque resident and former Wells Fargo guard, led the posse.

Shortly after 5 o'clock that afternoon, a telltale column of smoke from a small campfire in the upper reaches of Turkey Creek Canyon attracted the posse to the outlaw camp that was to become known as Black Jack's Hideout. Seen moving about the camp were three men, who proved to be Sam Ketchum, William McGinnis, and G.W. Franks. Silently, the posse split into three forces. Farr, Reno, and Smith took an elevated position in front of the camp, while the others took positions in the canyon and behind the camp. At least seventy-five yards separated the lawmen from the bandits.

Ketchum and Franks were standing by the fire, and McGinnis was walking to a small water pool with a coffee pot in one hand, when the posse opened fire on the camp, with or without warning, according to conflicting accounts. McGinnis fell to the ground with bullet wounds in his left shoulder and the lower part of his back. Ketchum and Franks grabbed their rifles and began returning the fire. A bullet slammed into Ketchum's left arm just below the shoulder, putting him out of action. Franks continued firing, joined by McGinnis, who managed to struggle to his feet and pick up a rifle.

Sheriff Farr and Smith, the young New Yorker, sought protection behind a small pine tree. Smith caught a bullet in the fleshy part of his left leg, and fell to the ground next to the tree. Another bullet grazed Farr in the wrist. He bandaged the wound with a handkerchief and kept firing until a .30- 40 caliber rifle bullet tore through the tree and into his chest. He fell down on top of Smith, gasped "I'm done for," and died.

Love, the young cowboy, was hit by a bullet that drove the blade of his large pocketknife deep into his thigh. Two of the four horses in the outlaw camp were killed in the exchange of gunfire.

By 6 o'clock the fierce gun battle was over and it was beginning to rain. The casualties consisted of one posse member dead and two wounded, and two outlaws wounded. Franks and his two wounded companions disappeared during the night, leaving behind some provisions, camp equipment, thirty pounds of dynamite, and a pack saddle identified as one taken from the express car during the train robbery.

Reno, unscathed but with bullet holes in his clothing, left the posse after dark and made his way to Cimarron, arriving in the morning with the first news of the battle. Some claimed that he fled the scene before the battle was over. U.S. Marshal Foraker apparently received a garbled account of the affair, for he sent a telegram to his office from Springer on July 17 reading: "Had fight with train robbers last night. Think all my men killed or wounded except one."

Early reports of the battle indicated that one of the bandits had been killed, and when the body of Sheriff Farr was brought into Cimarron, a rumor circulated that he was one of the bandits, prompting a false newspaper report dispatch that read: "The dead man was known by the name of William McGinnis, alias G.W. Franks, and he came from Magdalena, N.M., where he was known as a broncho [sic] buster."

A heavy rainfall obliterated the trail of the retreating outlaws.

Love, the young cowboy who was wounded in the battle, died in Springer on July 20. While the bullet wound itself was not particularly serious, the pocketknife the bullet drove into his thigh was one with which he had been treating cattle that were victims of blackleg, an infectious disease. The infected knife blade caused his death.

*   *   *

A stranger, pale from exhaustion and loss of blood from a bullet wound in his left arm, appeared at the Ute Creek headquarters of the Lambert Ranch west of Cimarron on July 18 and asked for food and medical attention, saying that he had been shot in a hunting accident. Cowboys at the ranch, managed by James McBride, had no reason to doubt him, as they had not yet heard of the gun battle that had occurred two days before in Turkey Creek Canyon, about five miles from the ranch headquarters.

One of the cowboys at the ranch, Pearl Claus, accompanied by Mrs. McBride, led the wounded man to a saddle room, dressed his wound, fed him, and put him to bed on a spare cot. Later that day, Claus rode into Cimarron for supplies and the mail, and upon his arrival learned of the recent gun battle with outlaws. He told Henri Lambert, owner of the St. James Hotel and the Ute Creek Ranch about the wounded man at the ranch, and Lambert said he was certain that the wounded man was one of the three outlaws. He notified authorities.

W.H. Reno, the railroad officer, organized a small posse and proceeded west to the ranch headquarters to apprehend the suspect. Upon their arrival at the ranch, Claus and Jack McBride entered the saddle room, and noticed that the wounded man had placed his gun, a .45-caliber revolver with a stag handle, on a chair next to his cot, within easy reach.

Casually, so as not to arouse suspicion, Clause picked up the gun while saying to his companion, "Jack, look at this. This is a mighty fine gun."

At that moment, Reno and other members of the posse entered the room. The wounded man sprang from his cot, trembling and cursing, and was quickly taken into custody. The posse placed him in the back seat of a spring wagon to begin the first leg of a trip to the penitentiary in Santa Fe.

Upon reaching Cimarron, the wagon was halted in front of the St. James Hotel long enough to change the team of horses. A crowd of Cimarron residents gathered around the wagon, including James Hunt, the postmaster, who asked the prisoner who he was.

"Who do they think I am?" the prisoner said.

"Sam Ketchum," the postmaster replied.

"That's my name," he admitted.

Reno, who had been seated next to Ketchum in the back seat of the wagon, climbed down and walked toward the hotel, forgetfully leaving his .30-30 Winchester rifle on the wagon floor behind the front seat. Ketchum reached for it with his good arm, only to have the rifle yanked away by one of the onlookers, George

"Black Jack" Tom Ketchum

Newpaper artist's sketch of Tom "Black Jack" Ketchum, copied from an 1899 photo at the time of his capture. (Courtesy Museum of New Mexico, negative 128887)

Crocker.

The postmaster told Ketchum that he liked him better than he did some of his companions.

"I'm not a bad sort of fellow," Ketchum told him. "I haven't done anything bad." Then, pointing to Claus, who had led the posse to him and disarmed him, Ketchum said, "There's a meaner man than I am. I'd have his hide hung on the fence if he hadn't worked it just right."

Much of the dialogue between Ketchum and Hunt was recalled fifty years later by George Crocker, who had snatched the rifle from Ketchum's reach.

A waitress at a Cimarron boarding house was sent for, and she identified Ketchum as one of the men who had stayed at the boarding house just prior to the 1897 train robbery near Folsom.

After a fresh team of horses was hitched to the wagon, Ketchum was driven on east to Springer, on the Atchison, Topeka and Santa Fe Railway line, and taken aboard a train for the trip south to Santa Fe. A newspaper reporter on the train described Ketchum as "a muscular looking fellow, nearly six feet in height, heavily built and wears a mustache." Ketchum gave the reporter this account of his recent ordeal:

"They (McGinnis and Franks) placed me on my horse twice, but I could not sit there. I was the first one shot. When I saw I could not ride, I told the kid to pull out and leave me. If they want my gun and ammunition, it is hid up there in the rocks.

"When they (the posse) commenced firing I threw up my hands and then is when I was shot. If they had ordered us to throw up our hands, we would have done so.

"After they (McGinnis and Franks) had left me I was wet through. I could not cut kindling to build a fire, and my matches were all damp and I could not light one after trying the whole box.

"I suppose they have me now. I am a brother of Tom Ketchum, the original Black Jack."

Ketchum's reference to "the kid" as one of his companions led to speculation that he was referring to Kid Curry or The Sundance Kid, using the alias G.W. Franks.

Ketchum was received at the New Mexico Penitentiary in Santa Fe on July 20, where he was to be held while awaiting trial. The prison physician, Dr. M.F. Desmarais, told him he could not survive unless his wounded arm was taken off, but Ketchum refused to have it amputated. Dr. Desmarais told Ketchum on July 23 that he probably would not survive, and attempted to trick him into giving details of the train robbery by telling him that his two partners, who were still at large, had been captured.

"Well, Sam, the jig's pretty near up with you," he told Ketchum. "You're hit hard and can't get well. You might as well tell what you know about these things, as your two confederates are in prison here, safe and sound."

"Well," Ketchum replied, "let them tell about it."

Sam Ketchum was found dead on the floor of his prison cell the next morning, July 24. William "Bronco Bill" Walters, who occupied an adjoining cell, told guards that he had heard Ketchum get up and move about during the night, but had heard nothing that would indicate that he was dying. Blood poisoning was given as the cause of death.

Shortly before his death, Ketchum reportedly retracted his earlier remark that his brother was "the original Black Jack" and claimed that the original Black Jack had been killed several years before.

Sam Ketchum was buried near the edge of a Santa Fe cemetery near the prison, in a spot that eventually became an unkept portion of the cemetery that was paved over in a road construction project. His remains lie today under the pavement of Cerrillos Road, one of Santa Fe's busiest thoroughfares.

*   *   *

Reward money amounting to $1,400 was offered for the capture, dead or alive, of William McGinnis and G.W. Franks, who had disappeared at the close of the gun battle in Turkey Creek Canyon. The Wells Fargo Express Company and the Colorado and Southern Railway offered $1,000 of the amount, and the remainder was offered by the brothers of Sheriff Ed Farr, who was killed in the battle.

It was determined later that the two fugitives, upon leaving the battle scene, had ridden all night and part of the next day to the ranch home of an Hispanic couple, and that Franks had given the couple a considerable amount of money to take in his badly wounded companion and care for him until he recovered his strength. Franks headed south toward Roswell and Carlsbad, and McGinnis remained with the ranch family for about a month before heading south to meet Franks at Carlsbad, a Pecos River town previously known as Eddy.

From Carlsbad, the two rode about twenty miles east to the Chimney Wells ranch of Virgil H. Lusk to retrieve some stolen horses that gang members had left there previously. Lusk sent word to Eddy County Sheriff M. Cicero Stewart in Carlsbad that there were two outlaws at the ranch, and the sheriff left at once with two deputies, Rufus Thomas and John D. Cantrell. Riding all night, they reached the Lusk Ranch at daylight on August 16 (1899).

McGinnis was eating breakfast in a camp tent, and Franks was rounding up some horses, when Sheriff Stewart and his two companions dismounted and converged on the tent. McGinnis, who was armed with a revolver with only two bullets in the chamber, darted from the tent when he heard the three men approaching and ran toward his horse in an attempt to get his rifle, which was in a scabbard on the horse. Opening fire on the three men with his revolver, he hit Thomas in the shoulder and Lusk in the wrist before a bullet grazed the top of his head, stunning him momentarily and giving Stewart the chance to seize him after a desperate struggle. Newspaper accounts said that McGinnis "continued to fight after he surrendered and was knocked on the head."

"At the time McGinnis was captured," the *Albuquerque Citizen* reported later, "Franks was away from camp hunting horses. He returned while the fight was in progress, but seeing that the battle was going against his partner, watched it from a hill half a mile away, and at the end of it waved his hat to the officers and galloped off."

Sheriff Stewart did not know the identity of the man he had captured, but assumed that he was one of the wanted train robbers when he saw bullet wounds in his body and bullet holes in his clothing. Jailed in Carlsbad, McGinnis insisted that his name was John Thomas, but a positive identification was made by James Hunt, the Cimarron storekeeper, who went to Carlsbad to view the prisoner.

Wilson Elliott, who had led the posse at the Turkey Creek Canyon battle, interviewed McGinnis at the jail and told reporters he was of the opinion that the outlaw "is an educated easterner, knows very little about cowboy life and developed into an outlaw by becoming associated with the Ketchums." He added that he found McGinnis "unwilling to talk, and thoroughly silent when the subject of train robberies was brought up."

William French, manager of the WS Ranch, wrote later that

Tom Capehart arrived at the ranch three days after McGinnis was captured, both he and his horse in the last stages of exhaustion, having ridden nearly four hundred miles from Eddy County, changing horses periodically along the way. He said Capehart told him he had been with McGinnis until the time of his capture, leading French to believe that Capehart must have been the man the authorities called G.W. Franks, but believed by some to be Will Carver.

McGinnis stood trial in Raton, seat of Colfax County, during the first week of October, 1899, on an indictment charging him with murder in connection with the deaths of Sheriff Farr and Henry Love near Cimarron. Cowboy friends of McGinnis took up a collection to pay his defense attorneys, Edwin B. Franks of Trinidad, Colorado, and A.A. Jones of Las Vegas, New Mexico. District Attorney Jeremiah Leahy of Raton prosecuted the case.

The jury convicted McGinnis of second-degree murder after hearing conflicting testimony as to whether he had taken an active part in the gun battle at Turkey Creek Canyon after being wounded in the opening gunfire. Judge William J. Mills on October 10 sentenced him to life imprisonment in the New Mexico Penitentiary at Santa Fe. New Mexico Governor Miguel A. Otero, a courtroom spectator at the proceedings, wrote later that he did not believe McGinnis received a fair trial.

Upon entering the penitentiary, according to prison records, McGinnis gave his age as thirty-four and his birthplace as Coles County, Illinois. He said he was single, did not know if his parents were living, gave his occupation as a laborer, and said he had been self-supporting since the age of twenty-one. He said he had a common school education, but no high school or college. He listed E.A. Cunningham of Mogollon, New Mexico, near Alma, as his nearest relative or friend. The record said he was temperate, and used tobacco.

His prison record also shows that he was five feet nine and one-half inches tall, weighed 164 pounds, had a light complexion with light brown hair and eyes, had bullet marks on his left shoulder and the back of his loins, and a small scar on the top of his head.

In July, 1905, Governor Otero commuted McGinnis's life sentence to one of ten years, permitting his early release from prison the following December. The New Mexico governor, in explaining his move, said that McGinnis had been a model prisoner, never violating any penitentiary rules; that he had been a trusty for some time and night engineer in the prison power plant, and had twice assisted prison authorities in suppressing convict uprisings. Upon his release from the penitentiary, McGinnis headed at once for Alma, where he had friends, and where he was put up by Louis and Walter Jones, owners of an Alma mercantile store.

McGinnis visited William French at the nearby WS Ranch, and French wrote later that his former bronc buster had grown fat and had lost his athletic figure, was clean shaven, and wore a long, black frock coat that gave him "rather a clerical appearance." Asked by French where Jim Lowe (Butch Cassidy) and Tom Capehart were, McGinnis replied that they had gone to South America. French said a picture of the two appeared in newspapers later, the caption identifying Capehart by a different name.

McGinnis bought a good saddle horse, told his merchant hosts that he knew where there was a cache of money in a box buried under the root of a juniper tree on the Mexican border, and rode off, saying he would be back in about two weeks. He returned thirteen days later with $58,000 wrapped in a slicker, which he dumped in the corner of a utility room at the store. About $1,100 of the amount was in silver, which McGinnis graciously exchanged for currency whenever the store ran short of change. The source of the money, and where he obtained it, was never determined.

After a stay of about eighteen months in Alma, McGinnis headed north for Wyoming, the money tied to his saddle. Later, he wrote his friends in Alma that he had invested $40,000 in a Wyoming cattle ranch and intended to go straight, apparently resuming the name Elza (or Elzy) Lay. He opened saloons in Shoshoni and other Wyoming communities, and was married for a second time, a much earlier marriage of short duration having ended in divorce.

In 1916, he served as a guide for an oil geologist, studied with him, and reportedly became an expert oil prospector and the discoverer of the important Hiawatha oil field on the Wyoming-Colorado border. Later, he and his wife and two children moved to California, where he managed a waterworks or irrigation system prior to his death in Los Angeles in 1933.

*   *   *

It was on August 16, 1899, the day that William McGinnis was captured near Carlsbad, that Tom Ketchum appeared alone in Folsom, a community now gaining some notoriety as being near the scene of two train robberies that had occurred in less than two years. According to some reports, Ketchum spent part of the day at a gambling table in Jim Kent's saloon, losing all of the nearly $1,000 he had taken into the saloon.

Shortly after 10 o'clock that night, a southbound Colorado and Southern passenger train left Folsom, apparently with Ketchum hiding in the coal tender. A short distance south of town he entered the locomotive cab, armed with a rifle and a revolver, and ordered the engineer to stop the train at Twin Mountain, scene of the two previous train robberies. When the train was stopped, Ketchum ordered the engineer, Joe Kirchgrabber, and the fireman, Thomas Scanlon, out of the cab, and marched them at gunpoint to the express car. Ketchum pounded on the door of the express car and ordered the express messenger, Charles Drew, to "fall out of there damn quick," which he did, joining the engineer and fireman next to the car.

Ketchum ordered the three to uncouple the train behind the express car, but as the train was stopped on a curve, the trainmen worked in vain to unfasten the coupling device.

"I'm going to shoot to kill now, pretty soon," the impatient Ketchum warned the engineer.

"Well, now, partner, don't be in a hurry, we can't do these things all at once," Kirchgrabber replied.

Fred Bartlett, the mail clerk, stuck his head out the door of the mail car to see what was going on.

"Get your damn head in there," Ketchum shouted to him, at the same time firing a rifle shot that shattered Bartlett's left jawbone and caused him to fall to the floor of the car.

Frank E. Harrington, the conductor, who was in one of the passenger cars, was certain that the train was being robbed, as he had been the conductor on the two previous passenger trains that had been robbed at this very spot south of Folsom. Only several days before, he had taken out a $10,000 insurance policy on his life and had loaded a double-barreled shotgun with 0.5 buckshot, telling his wife, "Well, if they try to hold up the train again, I'll either kill them or they will kill me. They've held us up twice, now, and I'm getting tired of it."

Picking up the shotgun, Harrington walked through the train

Newspaper artist's sketch of Sam Ketchum, copied from an 1899 photo at the time of his capture. (Courtesy Museum of New Mexico, negative 150945)

into the mail car, where he found the prone figure of the wounded Bartlett on the floor. Peering out the car door, he saw a man with a rifle, about ten or fifteen feet away, covering three men who were attempting to uncouple the train.

Harrington and Ketchum saw one another at the same moment, and both fired instantaneously. Ketchum's rifle bullet grazed Harrington in the fleshy part of his arm, and Harrington's shotgun blast mangled Ketchum's right arm above the elbow, some of the buckshot entering his chest. The badly wounded Ketchum staggered off into the darkness, and the train went on its way.

Early the next morning, a northbound freight train proceeded to the scene of the attempted train robbery, the crew members instructed to keep an eye out for a wounded man near the tracks. Among those aboard the train was Saturnino Pinard, sheriff of Union County, who boarded it at Clayton, the county seat.

As the train approached Twin Mountain, John W. Mercer, a railroad brakeman who was seated on the roof of the locomotive cab, spotted a man sitting on the ground about three hundred yards from the tracks, calling attention to himself by waving his hat in the air with his left hand. The train was stopped, and crew members and Sheriff Pinard walked across the prairie to find the would-be train robber sitting on his feet, his legs doubled beneath him, and nursing an arm wound. A Winchester rifle and a .44 Colt revolver, partially concealed under his legs, were taken from him.

"Can you walk?" Sheriff Pinard asked Ketchum.

"If I could, I wouldn't be here," Ketchum growled.

Ketchum, a stranger to all those around him, admitted that he had been shot while trying to hold up a train, complaining at the same time that the train crew "had no business" shooting him, that he only wanted money and did not want to hurt any of them. He told his captors that he was "hard up" and needed money, and "if I could get $500 I would leave the damn country and go to South America."

A cot was brought from the train, and Ketchum was carried to the caboose and placed inside. As the train moved north with the unidentified captive, Ketchum told those in the caboose that his name was George Stevens, that he was a peace-loving cowboy from "the Panhandle country," where he had a brother and a sister, and that this had been his first attempt to rob a train, "and a damn poor one." These statements prompted the *Albuquerque Journal-Democrat* to publish a news article about his capture under a headline reading "Bandit Was An Amateur."

When the train paused at Folsom, a physician bandaged Ketchum's arm, and preparations were made to transport him on north to the nearest hospital, at Trinidad, Colorado. Ketchum told authorities that he and two others had planned the train robbery, but that his two companions had "decamped" the moment the train stopped, leaving him to finish the job alone.

A posse, searching in vain for his supposed confederates, found Ketchum's horse and saddle, a pack saddle, coffee pot, frying pan, and a Navajo blanket. Some dynamite, wrapped in a gunnysack, was found under a cattle guard at a railroad crossing near the holdup scene.

When the train carrying the wounded Ketchum reached Trinidad, he was admitted to a hospital under the name George Stevens.

*   *   *

In an effort to make a positive identification of the man who called himself George Stevens, photographs of the wounded prisoner were taken at the Trinidad hospital and circulated throughout the Southwest. W.H. Reno, the Colorado and Southern Railway officer, took one of the pictures with him as he headed south to Carlsbad to take custody of William McGinnis. In Carlsbad, Eddy County Sheriff M. Cicero Stewart identified the man in the photograph as Tom Ketchum, saying he had once worked as a cowboy in that vicinity.

Arizona authorities examined the photograph of Ketchum and said he matched the description of the lone gunman who had shot to death R.M. Rogers and Clinton D. Wingfield in a store they owned at Camp Verde, Arizona, on the previous July 2. The two partners had been shot down in cold blood for no apparent reason, as the killer, who seemed to know his victims, made no attempt to rob the store. Efforts by Arizona authorities to remove Ketchum to Arizona to face murder charges were unsuccessful.

Ketchum was told at the Trinidad hospital that his arm should come off, but he refused to permit the amputation. Becoming depressed and suicidal, he asked one of his guards to give him a gun so he could shoot himself. The request, of course, was refused. That night, the guard found Ketchum trying to kill himself by another method. He had taken the bandage off his arm, tied one end around his neck, looped the other end around his foot, and was attempting to strangle himself by drawing the noose tight with his foot. He also tried to swallow the pins from the bandage.

Reno and Stewart arrived in Trinidad with their prisoner, McGinnis, on August 23, and Stewart visited Ketchum at the hospital to verify his earlier identification of him. Confirming the identification was Fayette Baird, of Carlsbad, who said he had worked with Ketchum on the cattle ranges.

Ketchum finally admitted his true identity and "acknowledged that he was the original Black Jack," the newspapers said, although quoting him earlier as saying that "he knew Sam Ketchum, the original Black Jack." Thus began a flood of contradictory statements that was to continue for the remainder of his life.

Ketchum said that he had written the story of his life and intended to publish it in a three-hundred-page book. There is no record of any such manuscript. He also told authorities that he did not know there had been a train robbery at Twin Mountain only five weeks before his attempt, nor that his brother, Sam, was dead, explaining that "I am not in the habit of reading the newspapers."

Ketchum and McGinnis were placed aboard a train at Trinidad and transported south to Santa Fe, where both entered the New Mexico Penitentiary on August 24. The *New Mexican* at Santa Fe, referring to the two prisoners, said "There is no sign given when the two men meet that they have previously known each other."

Arriving from Texas to visit Ketchum in prison were his older brother, G.B. (Green Berry) Ketchum of San Angelo; his brother-in-law, Bige Duncan of Knickerbocker; and G.B. Shields, sheriff of Tom Green County. According to some reports, Tom refused to see Berry, claiming that he had started his two younger brothers on their outlaw careers before settling down to become a wealthy and respected rancher. The Santa Fe newspaper, in telling of Berry Ketchum's brief visit, said:

> *He came a few weeks ago upon a similar errand to see Sam Ketchum, who died in the prison from a wound in the arm. The San Angelo man is wealthy and has several times aided his outlaw brothers with funds upon their promise to reform. While here he offered to pay any debts incurred by the prisoner and to provide burial in case of death as he did when Sam Ketchum died. . . .*

When (Tom Ketchum) was being brought to Santa Fe
he asked that if he died his body should not be given to G.B.
Ketchum but should be buried beside that of Sam Ketchum,
whom the prisoner declared was "the best of all the family."

The *New Mexican* article, reprinted in the *Albuquerque Jour-nal-Democrat* on August 30, went on to say:

There is a marked resemblance between the two Ketch-um outlaws. Tom says he planned nearly all the train rob-beries that were committed by the gang, but hardly ever took an active part in them. He left the execution of his plans to his brother Sam, who seldom failed to carry them out to the letter.

According to Tom's story, he would go over the ground of a proposed robbery, noting minutely the lay of the land, and figure at what rate of speed the train would be going at certain points on the road; on where the gang would go and strike certain trails that would lead them to safety.

Then he made his report to his brother Sam, and in a few days the paper would record another successful train robbery in Colorado or New Mexico, wherever it chanced to happen, and tell all about the Black Jack Gang.

Sam Ketchum was considered a much deeper thinker than Tom, and that's the reason he always took charge of the hold-ups himself. Tom was vicious and would rather shoot at a man than at a target, while Sam was cool and avoided killing men as much as he could, only shooting when he thought it was absolutely necessary for his own safety, while Tom would shoot at the slightest provocation.

It is alleged that the original "Black Jack" was Jack Anderson, a cowboy of very dark complexion, who was known as "Black Jack" long before he committed any robberies. Anderson first started out robbing post offices in 1893, and then went to holding up stages and trains. He kept this up until about one and one-half years ago when he dropped out of sight and is supposed to have been killed.

When any member of the gang got killed his place would be filled by someone else who was called "Black Jack," the title descending to each successive leader. In this way Ketchum obtained it and he had been piloting the gang successfully for the past six months. Before Sam Ketchum died from his injuries received in a train hold-up he said that the original "Black Jack" had been killed long ago.

U.S. Marshal Creighton Foraker, after questioning the prisoner at length, told news reporters he was certain that Tom Ketchum was "the original Black Jack." The prisoner did not deny the assertion, and gradually appeared to relish his new found notoriety as Black Jack Ketchum.

On September 3, Ketchum permitted Dr. M.F. Desmarais, the prison physician, to amputate his shattered right arm, reportedly "thanking" the doctor after the operation with the remark, "I hope I can do the same for you, some day." Dr. Desmarais said that Ketchum's recovery was certain, attributing this to the fact that Ketchum had never touched alcoholic liquors in his life, even refusing alcoholic stimulants after the operation.

Ketchum's spirits rose sharply after the operation, only to be dashed when his plans to escape from the prison hospital were foiled with the discovery of a steel saw, fashioned from a clock spring, that he had concealed in his bandages; and a dummy pistol, made of wood and covered with tinfoil, in the hospital water closet. Ketchum broke down and cried when the items were taken from him, and he was promptly removed from the hospital to a prison cell.

On November 15, Ketchum was taken by train east to Las Vegas, where he entered a plea of guilty to federal charges of interfering with the U.S. mails in connection with the attempted train robbery. Sentencing was deferred pending the outcome of New Mexico indictments charging him with assaulting a railroad train, territorial charges that provided the death penalty upon conviction.

It was during Ketchum's brief appearance in Las Vegas that Placido Gurule saw him and identified him as one of the two men who killed Levi Herzstein and Merejildo Gallegos south of the village of Liberty in July, 1896. Gurule had escaped a similar fate by feigning death.

A large crowd of Las Vegas residents gathered at the railroad depot as Ketchum and his guards were preparing for the train ride back to Santa Fe, all hoping for a glimpse of the notorious Black Jack. Ketchum concealed his face from the crowd, offering to uncover it only if they would take up a $25 collection for the privilege of seeing him.

Ketchum remained in the penitentiary at Santa Fe for nearly a year while awaiting trial on New Mexico charges brought in connection with his attempted train robbery near Folsom. During this period, visitors to the penitentiary who wanted to see the notorious train robber often found him seated in a corner of his cell with his shirt pulled over his head, a crude sign reading "25 cents to see Black Jack."

*   *   *

A New Mexico indictment was returned against Thomas E. Ketchum charging him with assault on a railroad train with intent to commit a felony, and with the wounding of two members of the train crew. He was ordered to stand jury trial beginning September 6, 1900, at Clayton, seat of Union County in which the attempted train robbery had occurred.

On September 3, guards removed Ketchum from the penitentiary and escorted him northeast to Clayton aboard a passenger train. Special precautions were taken, as authorities feared that an attempt to rescue the prisoner might be made by members of Ketchum's gang, they apparently not realizing that Ketchum no longer had a gang.

During the train ride to Clayton, a passenger, unaware of Ketchum's identity or even that he was a prisoner, struck up a conversation with him and asked him how he had lost his arm.

"Oh, railroading," Ketchum replied.

Upon his arrival in Clayton, Ketchum appeared to be in a jovial mood. As U.S. Marshal Creighton Foraker was removing his leg shackles in the county jail, Ketchum said, "Foraker, you are the first man that ever put shackles to me. One of these days I'll do the same thing for you, and I'll take you way off on the prairie and leave you."

Ketchum kept his guards and spectators amused with various accounts of his outlaw career. Only one of his stories, unfortunately, was recorded by the newspapers:

"We got into a fight, Sam and Tommy Atkins and me, down in the Territory, and it was getting pretty hot for us. Tommy Atkins exclaimed, all at once, 'Sam, I'm shot.' 'Where?' says Sam. 'In the leg,' says Tommy. 'Well, you white-livered dude, says

Sam, 'go on shooting. I'm shot twice in the head.' "

Ketchum, who had never denied his single-handed attempt to rob the Colorado and Southern passenger train, entered a plea of guilty to the indictment when he appeared for trial on September 6. The presiding judge, Chief Justice William J. Mills of the New Mexico Territorial Supreme Court, refused to accept the guilty plea, due to the gravity of the offense and the fact that it carried the death penalty upon conviction, and ordered that he stand trial under a plea of not guilty.

Appointed by the court to represent Ketchum at the trial was William B. Bunker, a Las Vegas attorney, assisted by John R. Guyer. Prosecuting the case was District Attorney Jeremiah Leahy of Raton, assisted by L.C. Fort of Las Vegas.

The prosecution presented testimony from a parade of witnesses who were present at the attempted train robbery or at the subsequent capture of Ketchum. Joe Kirchgrabber, the engineer, testified that Ketchum climbed out of the coal tender into the locomotive cab with a rifle strapped to his back about three miles out of Folsom, poked a gun in his ribs, and ordered him to stop the train. Fred Bartlett, the mail clerk, his face disfigured by Ketchum's bullet, told of the circumstances of his misfortune. Frank Harrington, the conductor, testified that he had sneaked up through the train with his shotgun, saw Ketchum standing in the moonlight through the partly open door of the express car, and blasted him with the shotgun.

Ketchum's attorneys, at a loss to present much of a defense, argued unsuccessfully that Ketchum was a federal prisoner, not subject to prosecution in the territorial court, and that capital punishment was "unusual and excessive" punishment for assaulting a railroad train. The jury, after deliberating less than ten minutes on September 8, found Ketchum guilty of all the charges.

Judge Mills denied a defense motion for a new trial, and sentenced Ketchum to be hanged by the neck until dead on October 5, 1900, in an enclosure to be erected on the courthouse grounds in Clayton. Asked by the judge if he had anything to say, according to one report, Ketchum replied, "I'd like to shave the district attorney."

Ketchum's attorneys filed notice of appeal, which automatically granted a stay of execution, as the New Mexico Territorial Supreme Court, which would consider the appeal, was not due to meet until the following January.

Ketchum was returned to the penitentiary in Santa Fe to await a ruling by the higher court.

*　　　　*　　　　*

During its January session in 1901, the New Mexico Supreme Court sustained Tom Ketchum's conviction and sentence, ruling, among other things, that death was a suitable punishment for train robbery, and that hanging was not cruel or unusual punishment, as would be such torturous punishment as drawing and quartering, cutting off noses, ears, and limbs, burning at the stake, starving to death, or boiling to death. After more legal maneuvering by Ketchum's attorneys, which proved unsuccessful, New Mexico Governor Miguel A. Otero set April 26, 1901, as the date for Ketchum's execution at Clayton.

As the date for the execution neared, word was received that Will Carver, former member of the Ketchum gang, had been shot to death in Sonora, Texas, about sixty-five miles south of San Angelo.

After leaving the Ketchum gang in 1899, Carver had joined

Butch Cassidy's Wild Bunch. On September 19, 1900, Cassidy, Carver, and Harry Longabaugh, "The Sundance Kid," held up the First National Bank at Winnemucca, Nevada, and escaped with more than $32,000. The three turned up later at Fort Worth, Texas, where they were joined by Harvey Logan, alias Kid Curry, and Ben Kilpatrick, known as "The Tall Texan." The five posed for a group photograph at a Fort Worth studio, then went into hiding at San Antonio, Texas.

On March 27, 1901, Carver and Logan were at the Kilpatrick farm in Concho County, Texas, with Ben, Ed, and George Kilpatrick and a man named Walker when a neighboring farmhand, Oliver Thornton, approached the outlaws as they were playing croquet in the yard. Thornton complained that Kilpatrick hogs were straying into the property of his employer, Ed Dozier. One of the men, said to have been Walker, shot Thornton dead, and all but Ed Kilpatrick began to hurry off, heading southwest into neighboring Sutton County.

On the evening of April 2, Carver and George Kilpatrick were buying grain in a Sonora bakery shop, while their companions were waiting outside town, when Sutton County Sheriff Elijah Briant and three other officers entered the shop and ordered the two to throw up their hands. Carver and Kilpatrick reached for their guns, and the sheriff and his men opened fire, felling both of them before they could get off a shot.

The two were carried to the courthouse, where Carver died, having been shot seven times. Although shot five times, George Kilpatrick survived. Before dying, Carver said his name was Franks, but he was identified as Carver by those who knew him.

Less than a week later, on April 8, Bruce "Red" Weaver, the WS Ranch cowboy whose connection with the Ketchum or Cassidy

Thomas E. "Black Jack" Ketchum, photographed shortly before his hanging in 1901. (Courtesy University of Oklahoma, Western History Collections, Rose No. 2239)

gangs remains unclear, was shot to death on an Alma street by Pad Holomon, a local rancher, following a minor dispute. Some believed that Weaver took part in the second Folsom train robbery and the ensuing gun battle in Turkey Creek Canyon.

*   *   *

On the afternoon of April 23, 1901, three days before his execution date, Tom Ketchum was taken from the New Mexico Penitentiary at Santa Fe by armed guards and placed in the mail car of a northbound Santa Fe Railway passenger train to begin a journey of more than two hundred and fifty miles northeast to Clayton.

New Mexico authorities took extraordinary precautions to guard the condemned man, fearing that Ketchum's outlaw friends or sympathizers would make a last ditch effort to free him. Ten guards, including several sheriffs and railroad officers, were assigned to accompany him on the journey, and his sudden removal from the penitentiary came two days sooner than the announced time for his departure. To maintain secrecy as to what train they were on, the guards and their prisoner changed trains at Glorieta, and again at Las Vegas.

At Trinidad, Colorado, Ketchum was taken from a Santa Fe train and placed aboard a Colorado and Southern train for the last leg of the journey. The train arrived in Clayton early on the morning of April 24, and as Ketchum was being escorted from the train to the county jail, he asked and was granted permission to examine the tall scaffold that had been erected near the courthouse for his execution. The scaffold was enclosed by a stockade, erected to shield the hanging from all except those who had been given tickets to enter the enclosure.

"It's a good piece of work," Ketchum told his guards after examining the gallows, "but gentlemen, I wish you would take the stockade down so the boys can see me hanged."

Ketchum suggested that they try the gallows first on Frank Harrington, the railroad conductor whose shotgun blast had ended his outlaw career, to see if it worked right. It soon became obvious that Ketchum blamed Harrington for all his problems.

At least twenty guards were assigned to duty in and about the Clayton jail as Ketchum awaited his execution. On April 25, eve of the execution, the sheriff's office in Clayton received a telegram from Santa Fe reading: "By request of President McKinley, defer execution of Thomas Ketchum to May 25, 1901. Otero." An immediate check with Governor Miguel Otero in Santa Fe revealed that he had not sent the telegram, and knew nothing about any postponement of the hanging. The telegram was put down as a practical joke.

Although Ketchum had been reared in a Baptist environment, and professed no religious affiliation, a Catholic priest was sent to the jail to visit with him. When invited by the priest to confess his sins, it was reported, Ketchum answered that he would do so only if the priest would confess to him.

"I don't know if there is a hell," Ketchum said, "but if there is, there will be a lot of people out of this Territory (of New Mexico) that will go there."

On the morning of April 26, Ketchum ate a hearty breakfast and chatted with friends and newspaper reporters after taking a bath and donning a new suit of black clothing. Newspapers reported that Ketchum was "cooler than anyone who met him" that morning. He posed for two photographs, asking that one be sent to Lee Smith in San Saba County, Texas, and the other to Eva Prodman, of Lodi, California, believed to be a relative.

Ketchum rambled on about a variety of subjects all morning, his remarks characterized later by railroad officer W.H. Reno as "mostly lies." He declined to discuss his outlaw career, claiming that he had written a three-hundred-page manuscript about it.

He said he thought hanging was "a little unjust" for the crime of assaulting a railroad train, but that he thought death was preferable to imprisonment. He said New Mexico laws were designed principally to protect the railroads and other large corporations, and contended that the Colorado and Southern had paid for his prosecution.

Ketchum denied that he was the original Black Jack, said the man killed near Clifton, Arizona, in 1897 was not Black Jack, and that Black Jack was still alive and enjoying freedom. He declined to reveal Black Jack's identity.

Although newspapers were estimating that Ketchum had killed as many as sixteen men, he claimed that he had never killed a man in his life, and had "only shot three." He said he knew who killed Levi Herzstein near Liberty in 1896, that these men were alive and free, but that he did not wish to say who they were.

Ketchum requested that he be buried face down, "so Harrington can kiss my ass."

Shortly before noon, Ketchum conferred with his attorney, John R. Guyer, and asked that he send a letter to President William McKinley saying that three men serving ten-year sentences in the New Mexico Penitentiary for robbing the U.S. mail at Steins on December 9, 1897, were "as innocent as a newborn babe." The three inmates were Leonard Alverson, Walter Hoffman, and W.H. Warderman.

Ketchum claimed in the letter that the crime was committed by Ed Cullen, Sam Ketchum, Will Carver, William "Bronco Bill"

Walters, Dave Atkins, and himself. He said in the letter that he had given his attorney means by which articles taken in the robbery could be found, and the names of witnesses in the vicinity who would testify that he and his companions were in the neighborhood before and after the robbery.

Those identified by Ketchum as the robbers had nothing to lose by his "confession," true or not. Cullen, Sam Ketchum, and Carver were dead, Walters was serving a life sentence for murder, the whereabouts of Atkins was unknown, and he (Tom Ketchum) was about to die on the gallows. Ketchum's letter did not bring an immediate response, for it was to be another three years before the three penitentiary inmates were released.

After dictating the letter, Ketchum asked to hear some music. Guyer sent for a fiddle, and together with a guitar player, identified only as Epimenio, they serenaded Ketchum with "Just as the Sun Went Down," which he had requested, and several other selections. As Guyer was leaving the jail, Ketchum called to him, "Say, tell Harrington I'll meet him in hell for breakfast."

Shortly after 1 o'clock that afternoon, Union County Sheriff Salome Garcia informed Ketchum that his time had come. Ketchum told the sheriff to hurry up with the hanging, so he could get to hell for dinner.

Ketchum was led out of the jail to the scaffold, where about one hundred and fifty ticket holders had gathered inside the enclosure to witness the execution. Mounting the scaffold steps, he looked at the noose above him and said, "The rope looks like a good one." As a black hood was being placed over his head, he said, "Goodbye, please dig my grave very deep." A moment later, he uttered his final words, "All right, hurry up."

Sheriff Garcia cut a control rope with an axe, the trap door

Execution of Tom "Black Jack" Ketchum at Clayton in 1901, photographed by the John Wheatley Studio. At top, the noose is placed around Ketchum's neck. (Courtesy Museum of New Mexico, negative 128886)

beneath Ketchum sprang open, and he plunged downward. The seven-foot drop, coupled with Ketchum's two-hundred-pound weight, resulted in his decapitation. The crowd gasped as Ketchum's headless body hit the ground beneath the scaffold, alongside the black hood containing his head.

A news reporter on the scene provided this graphic account of the gruesome execution for the *Albuquerque Journal-Democrat*:

CLAYTON, N.M., *April 26 – Thomas Edward Ketchum, alias "Black Jack," the notorious outlaw who terrorized the Southwest for the past fifteen years, was hanged here this afternoon for the last of his many crimes and his head was severed from his body as if by a guillotine. The headless trunk pitched forward toward the spectators and blood spurted upon those nearest the scaffold. The execution took place in a side stockade built for the occasion.*

The enclosure was crowded, 150 witnesses having been admitted. When Ketchum mounted the scaffold at 1:17 p.m. his face was pale, but he showed no fear. A priest stood at his side as the rope was being put around his neck. The condemned man consented to this at the last moment. Ketchum decided not to make a statement. He muttered "Goodbye" and then said, "Please dig my grave very deep," and as the cap was drawn over his head shouted "Let her go." His legs trembled but his nerve did not fail.

At 1:21 the trap was sprung, and his body shot through the air, his head being torn from the trunk by the tremendous jerk. His head remained in the sack and fell into the pit, while the body dropped to the ground, quivering and bleeding.

Some men groaned, and others turned away, unable to

A black hood is placed over his head. Bottom, Ketchum's decapitated body beneath the gallows. (Courtesy Museum of New Mexico, negative 46086)

Ketchum's decapitated body beneath the gallows. (Courtesy Museum of New Mexico, negative 46084)

endure the sight. For a few seconds the body was allowed to be there, half doubled up on the right side, with blood issuing in an intermittent stream from the severed arteries as the heart kept on with its mechanical beating. Then with cries of consternation the officers rushed down from the scaffold and lifted the body from the ground.

Before going to the scaffold Ketchum acknowledged that he planned and led his gang in many robberies, but declared that he was not the original "Black Jack" and said that that outlaw was still alive and enjoying liberty.

Ketchum said that Frank Harrington, the conductor who shot him, causing him to lose his right arm, and Nick Fort, the Wells Fargo detective, and W.H. Reno, the Colorado and Southern railway special agent who effected his capture, will be killed within the year. He intimated that he had given instructions to that effect.

Ketchum's threats against the three men failed to materialize. Another newspaper account of the execution quoted Ketchum as giving this last-minute advice to others contemplating an outlaw career:

"My advice to the boys of the country is not to steal horses or sheep, but either rob a train or a bank when you have got to be an outlaw, and every man who comes in your way, kill him; spare him no mercy, for he will show you none. This is the way I feel about it, and I think I feel right about it."

Ketchum's remains, with the head sewed back on, were placed in a pine box and transported by wagon to a small cemetery on the Wootten Ranch about one mile east of town and buried without services or mourners. Here Ketchum remained buried until 1933, when it was decided to remove his remains to the Clayton cemetery in town. Witnesses said they found Ketchum's body in a remarkable state of preservation after more than three decades in the grave. They also found that he had been denied his request to be buried face down.

*   *   *

Fred Lambert, pioneer Cimarron lawman, said in a 1958 interview that a man known as "Pegleg" Sullivan, who died of influenza in Cimarron in about 1918, told him shortly before his death that he was the G.W. Franks of the Ketchum gang. The man, who was missing one leg, had been operating a small hotel in Cimarron.

Lambert said Sullivan told him that he had gone to South America following the second Folsom train robbery and the Turkey Creek Canyon battle, and that he had lost his leg in South America. Upon his return to the United States, he told Lambert, he had recovered money taken in the train robbery, buried in some cedar hills west of Clayton, and had used it to purchase an elaborate saloon in Trinidad, Colorado. Later, he moved to Cimarron, where he operated the hotel.

Lambert said that Sullivan had only one relative at the time of his death, a niece in Kansas City, and that her letters to her uncle in Cimarron were addressed to Bill Karnes, apparently his true name. Lambert said he was certain this man was G.W. Franks, as he remembered seeing him in Cimarron with Sam Ketchum twenty years before, at which time he was wearing a beard.

If Sullivan's confession was truthful, he also may have been the outlaw known as Tom Capehart, whose fate was never determined after he reportedly went to South America. The true identities of the original Black Jack and those who reportedly succeeded to the title have never been definitely established.

Index